The Good Old Days Then & Now

Days free of worries.
Everything is right with the world.

Kirby Fint, Jr.

Published By

TRAFFORD

USA ▪ Canada ▪ UK ▪ Ireland

© Copyright 2006 Kirby Fint, Jr.
All rights reserved. No part of this publication may be reproduced, stored in a retrieval system, or transmitted, in any form or by any means, electronic, mechanical, photocopying, recording, or otherwise, without the written prior permission of the author.

Note for Librarians: A cataloguing record for this book is available from Library and Archives Canada at www.collectionscanada.ca/amicus/index-e.html
ISBN 1-1-4251-0170-4

Printed in Victoria, BC, Canada. Printed on paper with minimum 30% recycled fibre. Trafford's print shop runs on "green energy" from solar, wind and other environmentally-friendly power sources.

Offices in Canada, USA, Ireland and UK

Book sales for North America and international:
Trafford Publishing, 6E–2333 Government St.,
Victoria, BC V8T 4P4 CANADA
phone 250 383 6864 (toll-free 1 888 232 4444)
fax 250 383 6804; email to orders@trafford.com

Book sales in Europe:
Trafford Publishing (UK) Limited, 9 Park End Street, 2nd Floor
Oxford, UK OX1 1HH UNITED KINGDOM
phone 44 (0)1865 722 113 (local rate 0845 230 9601)
facsimile 44 (0)1865 722 868; info.uk@trafford.com

Order online at:
trafford.com/06-1927

10 9 8 7 6 5 4 3 2 1

CONTENTS

Dedication — v.

Explanation of Front Cover pictures — vi.

Fint Clan — vii.

Camp House at Lock #5 — viii.

Chapter 1 — 1

The ferry operator's house on the Woodford County side of the Kentucky River at Tyrone, Kentucky 1930-1934

The Ferry Boat

Chapter 2 — 2

Camphouse #1 in Anderson County, Tyrone, Kentucky 1934-1936

Baby Skunk

Chapter 3 — 3

House on the point that Pop built when he bought the farm in Anderson County, Tyrone, Kentucky 1936-1938

Bugs & Other Insects – Wildcat Road – Doctors and Medicine – The Good Old Radio – The Grocery Truck – Christmas A Long Long Time Ago – Spring Water – High Water – Water (Then and Now) – Hunting Knife And Dog – The Flat Iron – Wash Day – Rocks – Movies

Chapter 4 — 19

Camp House #2. Moved here when Pop sold the farm and went to work at Ripy Brothers Distillery up on the hill above Tyrone, Kentucky 1938-1939

Sunday School And Church – Visiting Kin Or Neighbors – Baseball Tyrone Style – Christmas Trees Back When – Unofficial Olympics

Chapter 5 — 24

House on the Distillery property. Only place that we lived that was not on the river – 1939

Toys – The Drum Stove – Stripping Room – Power Plant at Tyrone – Shells – Special Kind of Trees – Snakes – Anderson County Fair – Turtle Hunting – Wild Greens – Dead-Falls, Snares and Steel Traps – What A Mom We Had – Christmas One Week A Year – The Old Camphouse Above Lock #5 – Watermelons and Cantaloupes – The Wild Grapevine – Food Then And Now – Just bushes – Wild Vines of Kentucky – Duty On The Home Front – Ash, Sugar Maple and Red Cedar Trees – More Trees – Hunting – Taking A Ride – Minnow Seine – The Party Line – Making Hay while The Sun Shines – The River – Special Dishes – I Love Valentine's Day – Safety First – Flat Bottom John Boat – Things Not Missed – Pen And Pencil – Christmas Dinner – The Horse-Tails

Chapter 6 — 60

Camphouse #3 just above Lock #5 on the Kentucky River. This put us back on the river but high enough to avoid the high water – 1939-1940

Bat Rock Camp – New Ground – Things That Drive A Mother Up The Wall – Horses And Mules – The Seed Catalog – Kerosene Lamp And Stove- Things Stored For Winter – Birds – Dogs – Things Bought At The Store – Tobacco Barns – Social Security Card – Skipping School – Hemp – Pets – Crimes In School – Things Saved For Later Use – Smoking Then And Now – The Setting Hen – Mudslide At Swimming Hole – Canned Chicken – The Fish Box – Fishing – Tobacco Beds – One-Half Of A Canoe – The Clubhouse – Flowers – Hitchhiking – The Stockyard – Time Spent As A Lock Tender – The Milk Cow – Trash Pickers – Catching Rabbits By Hand – Barrel Stave Sleds – Bugs That Would Bite – Hog Killing Time – Firewood From The River – Picnicking At Panther Rock – The Milk Truck – One Room School – My First Garden – My First Summer Away From Home – Fish Bait – Getting To Work – Rabbit Hunting With Pop – Opossum Hunting At Nights With Dogs – Fishing The Kentucky River Year Round – Groundhog Meatloaf – Barrel Of Pickles – Blackberry Picking And Why – Music – Penny Chapel – Anderson County Caves – Anderson County Creeks – Hedge Apple, Hickory and Locust Trees – Still More Trees – Trees – Pine Trees – Pros And Cons Of The Woodchuck – Schoolhouse Maintenance – Wild Fire – The Lowly "Pop" Bottle – First Girlfriend – Things That Would Explode – Visit To Lock Road – Lye Soap – The Sewing Machine – Hunting Season – Hand Me Downs – First Snow – The Rock Wall Or Fence – Toilet Paper Or Substitutes – Noon Whistle – Noodling – The Funnies – The Crowded Class Rooms – Fishing Then And Now – The Mailbox – Hillside Plow

Chapter 7　　　　　　　　　　　　　　　　　　　　　　　　　　142

Skeleton House. Pop bought the farm next to the camphouse and joined the Lock #5 property on the other side – 1940-1943

Stores In Millville – Ships Voyage – Clifton – Swamp Land At Trumbo Bottom – Rock Bar At Mount Of Glenns Creek – Train Travel – Gardner House – The Bottom – First Rifle – First Bicycle – Drive-Ins – Five And Ten Cent Stores – Before Fast Food – Catching Soft Craws – Coat For Heating And Cooking – My First Week In The Army – Cutting A Bee Tree For Honey – Moving Day Call For A Trip Down The River – Saturday Night In Town – The Grab Bag – The Concrete Mixer – Lover's Leap In Anderson County – Blue Bonnet Ice Cream – Style – The Spittoon – Power Lines – The Mud Puppy – A Typical Day On The River – Warden – Big Mistake – The Peach Tree Inn – Coffee Over The Years – The Washing Machine – Pool Table – Road Kill – The Penny – Greyhound Bus – The Service Station – Mom and Pop – The Tooth Brush – Work – Third Tour South Korea – Korea 1948 – My VW – Troop Train – My Nash Rambler – My Gas Mask – Survival – Fishing In Virginia – Fishing In Texas – Yuma Proving Ground – Nags Head NC – Yuma Arizona – Korea 1950-1951 – Poinsettias – Shoe Factory – Vietnam – The Shopping Cart – Remembering The King – Baby Things – Hair Roller – VW Camper – Germany 1953 – Blunts Creek NC – The Greeting Card – The Coat Hangar – Excess Baggage – Short Order Cook – Picture Taking – Remembering Ft. Eustis And Ft. Lee Virginia – The Cloth Water Bag – Ft. Hood Texas – Pills, Salves And Liniments – The Toothpick

Chapter 8　　　　　　　　　　　　　　　　　　　　　　　　　　217

The Gardner House at Gardners Landing in Franklin County. Moved down river to this house when Pop's job ran out at Ripy Brothers Distillery and he went to work at the Old Crow Distillery. He was only about a mile from his job.

Fast Food – The USO Clubs – Television Then And Now – Amusement Parks – The Coon Drag – Before The Big Roads – Catching A Live Raccoon – St. Clair Mall – Pluto (Dog That Chased Rocks) – 1942 Oldsmobile – The Quire House Across From Crow – Special Swimming Hole

Chapter 9　　　　　　　　　　　　　　　　　　　　　　　　　　229

The Quire House across the road from Old Crow Distillery. This was the worst place we ever lived because it was two miles to the river and there was no space for a garden and no place to cut wood to heat with. This was in Woodford County and everyone had to change school – 1948 – until family

was split up when Mom passed away in 1949. This chapter also includes time frame from 1951 until present.

Cincinnati Reds – Weekends At Beaver Lake – Kids And Catfish At Beaver Lake – Kids – The Rubber Boat – Bicycle Experience – Camping – Road Work – Progress – Cabin Fever – Hats – Ice Fishing – Christmas Shopping Then And Now – Thanksgiving And Christmas (past and present) – Cushaw Pie – Christmas Shopping – Coupons – Frog Gigging At Beaver Lake – Telephone Insulators – Digging The Dumps For Glass – School Backpacks – Paint Ball Guns – Friday Night Poker – Pen and Pencil – The Shoe String – Christmas Trees Over The Years – Pants With Pockets – Old Riverfront Stadium – Army Schools – Yount's Mill – The Grill – Hot Water – Nickel And Dime – Take With A Grain Of Salt – The Doctor – Honey, Have You Seen My Keys – High Water – The Time Piece – Interstate – Brown And White Beans – Things Missed – Switches – The Umbrella – Kites – The Parking Lot –The Nickname – Sports In School – Kids With Nothing To Do – The Grand – Things Lost And Found – The Sweet Potato – The Apron – Collectible Nails (Dated) – The Can Opener – The Landfill – March Madness – Flowering Shrubs And Trees – Copy Machine – Ed And Fred – Negative Thoughts – Mother Nature – Safe Place To Live

Biography of Author   293

*This book is dedicated to my wife, Mary E. Fint.
She has spent numerous hours typing, making
corrections on my spelling and a lot of time on the
copy machine and locating pictures. The main thing
is that she put up with me through it all.*

Front Page Pictures

Left Picture

Kirby Fint, Jr. ca 1941 or 1942

139 Bluegills

Top Right

Kirby Fint, Jr. – Cecil Everett Fint – John Thomas Fint – 1930

Kirby Fint, Jr. with pet chicken – 1941

Kirby Fint, Jr. – Korea 1951

Kirby Fint, Jr. – Germany

Kirby, Jr. and Mary E. Fint – October 1999

Left to Right – Bottom to Top
Donald Ray Fint – Irene Catherine Fint – Albert Elwood Fint Maurice Hawkins Fint
– Kirby Fint, Jr. – John Thomas Fint
Andrew Woodie Fint – Richard Franklin Fint
James Carlos Fint – Cecil Everett Fint
ca. 1939 Tyrone, Kentucky

Left to right
Front Row – John Thomas Fint – Irene Catherine Fint
James Carlos Fint – Albert Elwood Fint – Kirby Fint, Jr.
Top Row – Donald Ray Fint – Richard Franklin Fint
Maurice Hawkins Fint – Andrew Woodie Fint – Cecil Everett Fint
ca. 1958 Frankfort, Kentucky

Camp house at Lock #5 on the Kentucky River

CHAPTER ONE

THE FERRY BOAT

About three or four years ago, I was going to a Ruritan Meeting at Valley View across the river from Nicholasville. Wound up down on the river and found there was no bridge – just a Ferry Boat.

It brought back a lot of memories. Pop was running the Ferry at Tyrone in 1930 when I was born – do not remember this. I was only about five years old when the Ferry at Tyrone closed down. Not sure when the one at Clifton closed. There were a lot of them on the Kentucky River at one time or another (McCowns Ferry, Clays Ferry). Down river below Frankfort there were a number of them – Lewis Ferry, Shadrock Ferry, McDonald's Ferry – to name a few.

The last Ferry I remember well was at Hopewell, Virginia. I was stationed at Ft. Lee and lived in Williamsburg. Had to cross the Appomattox River. Closest route was to cross at Hopewell. Could go down Route 10 and over the bridge at Surry but the drive was miles out of the way.

Still some Ferries in Virginia along the coast but the one at Hopewell has been replaced by a bridge.

Do not know if the one at Valley View is still operating, or not. They say it is open during daylight hours. Not sure, for it has been a while since I was up that way.

Tried to get the wife to buy the one at Valley View. Told her she could run the Ferry and I could fish – sell a few and eat a few. Wife said it sounded too good and would not buy it at any price. She told me that if we bought it, they would build a bridge and put us out of business. Then all I would have left to do was fish – sounded good to me.

Last I heard, the Ferry at Valley View was the only one in the state that was still operating. More a tourist attraction than anything.

I miss the Ferries but the bridges are a lot faster and very few of the bridges have toll booths on them.

CHAPTER TWO

BABY SKUNK

The wife and I were on our way home from Bald Knob Eagle Ruritan Club Board of Directors' meeting the other night and stopped by brother Richard's house to see how he and Ann were doing. Well, they were doing fine. While there, he told me a story that was too good not to write down. This is the way he told it to me.

This happened before I started school, so I don't remember any of it.

Brothers Richard and Carlos were on their way home from Lawrenceburg and they had taken the railroad tracks rather than the road because it was a lot shorter.

He told me that some place between Cedar Brook Trussel and Tyrone Crossing they came upon two baby skunks. Somehow they had gotten between the rails and were too small to get over them.

He picked one of them up and stuck it in his pocket. Carlos picked the other one up and pitched it over into the woods after it sprayed him.

We had a momma cat that had kittens still nursing. When he got home, he pitched the baby skunk down with the other kittens. The baby skunk did not hesitate for one minute – dug right in, grabbed him a nipple and made himself at home. Momma cat took him in and raised him just like her own.

Now, we had dogs and they were used for hunting at night and skunks were one of the things we hunted.

Richard said of one of the dogs got too close, the skunk would just stomp his front feet on the ground as a warning and the dog would leave him alone.

A couple of our cousins were the downfall of this skunk. Uncle Willie had a little dog and when the skunk was about two years old, this dog caught him in the field between where we lived. Chased him into a rock pile and two of the girls moved the rock to where the dog could get to him. The dog killed Richard's skunk.

He said the skunk got his revenge because no one could stand to be outside for a long while.

The skunk had lived under the house for almost two years and had not smelled the place up – not even one time.

CHAPTER THREE

BUGS AND OTHER INSECTS

When I was young, one of my favorite pastimes was watching insects – which we called bugs.

My special one was the ant. I could find an anthill and watch them for hours because they were so unusual. They would pack in all kinds of things and pack out small balls of dirt. It seems they could pack some unbelievable large loads. All of this was done to get ready for winter and raise their young.

The dung bug was a good one. We called them tumbling bugs. They worked the pile of cow dung from sunup to sundown.

The June bug was easy to catch. They looked a lot like the Japanese beetle but a lot larger. You could find plenty of them in any blackberry patch. Fun with them was to use about four feet of Mom's sewing thread and tie to one leg while holding the other end and watch them fly around in circles for hours. Lightning bugs were fun at night. You could catch a jar full and use them for a light. Never did work well because I think they had to fly around to keep charged up.

I was the only one in the family that could catch a doodlebug with a broom straw – and still do this. This was not really a bug but a worm. The inch worm was fun to watch. I was always told if you saw an inch worm, you were going to get a new piece of clothing. This did not always work.

Caterpillars were very colorful. Woolly worms are the big things in today's time. Did not really like them when I was younger because they did not do anything except crawl around and curl into a ball if you touched them.

Spiders could be watched for hours as they worked their webs. The garden types were big with a lot of color. Black widows were to be avoided when possible. We knew where to locate them and just stayed clear. Trap door spiders were hard to find but I did locate a few. Jumping spiders were easy to find but not much fun to watch. Granddaddy long legs were easy to find but just wanted to hide.

Potato bugs, snails, stink bugs, crickets, katydids, bean beetles, lady bugs and worms of all kinds were always around but could not hold my attention for very long. Butterflies could take a full day. There were so many different varieties. It was fun watching moths and butterflies develop from a cocoon. This took all winter and into the summer.

I am still called by the nickname of "BUG" by family and most people I know. The nickname was earned over sixty years ago by watching bugs.

WILDCAT ROAD

The Wildcat Road in Anderson County runs along the Wildcat Creek from Tyrone to Stringtown about three miles. Walked this road a lot back in the 30's. From Stringtown for about two miles it had been blacktopped. The other mile or so had not changed in sixty years.

I remember growing up, it was all a gravel and dirt road with big rocks in places. Over the years gravel had been added. Driving down it the other day, the mile or so looked about the same except the trees are bigger. Not many dumps along it but dumps are still there.

The creek along side is still the same. The big ledge or water fall is still there. Spent many hours under this ledge just sitting around a fire until late at night. Dogs were on the trail of something and barking.

About a mile up the road from the point where we lived there was a spring where our drinking came from. The spring is still there and water still pours out but is probably polluted.

Some things along Wildcat Road have changed. Only the rock is left that Carl Beasley's cabin sat on – everything else is gone. Some of the ledges have a little more rock showing. Some dirt has washed away exposing more of them. Have not checked Wildcat Creek from up close but looks about the same except maybe a little deeper in places. Lots of rock washed out in the last sixty years. Can almost walk across the river where it empties into the Kentucky River.

Stopped at the chalk mine about a year ago. It is still there but almost covered up with dirt from above it. Really not a mine – just a hole in the cliff where we got out chalk.

The house on the point is different. The one we lived in burned a few years back and another one has replaced it. Up behind the house is a quarry where the rock for Wildcat Road was quarried out. Some of the big rock that was taken out still lies along the road. Some as big as a desk. I was told by Pop that they dug these big rocks out, rolled them down the hill and a crew broke them up and put them on the road. These were left over when the road was finished. Then the big quarry opened and rocks were hauled in already crushed.

The hill across the creek that Pop cleared for a tobacco crop has grown up again. Can still see where the edges were but the old road is still the same. No curves have been straightened out and as far as I can tell the mile that has not been reworked still has no one living along it – no houses at all. Could walk up it late at night and it would take me back sixty years until a car came along. One of the bridges on the dirt portion of the road looks the same. Timbers have been replaced but you still have to drive on the timbers there for that purpose.

DOCTORS AND MEDICINE

A friend of mine went to the doctor the other day and got put in the hospital. She was put in an oxygen tent with all kinds of medication and doctors in every three or four hours. This was something Mom could have taken care of with a little talk and a good home remedy. My friend is only four years old.

When growing up, Mom could cure almost anything. Step on a piece of glass and cut your foot and Mom would stick the foot in a pan of kerosene until bleeding stopped, wrap it in a rag of some kind and then set you down for a few hours. There were no stitches or cream – nothing.

Get a boil – a patch was put on it with a piece of fat, salty bacon. If bacon was not on hand, you could get the same results with shavings off a potato. This would bring the boil to a head. That is all there was to it.

Get a cough – if the old Smith Brothers cough drops did not do the job, nothing would. Sore chest –Mom had a polish of some kind that was applied, covered and left over night. She had another one rendered out of some kind of fat. Did not know what a vaporizer was because she used a pan of hot water and a blanket. Bad cold or the flu of some kind – a little sugar and some bourbon was the cure. Drink this, cover up with a blanket or two and then sweat it out.

Mumps, measles, chicken pox – something like this, the doctor was called to the house and everyone was treated at the same time. Broken bones called for a run to the doctor's office because Mom could not set a bone or put a cast on.

Get burnt – can of clover salve came out, smeared on the burn and left to heal.

All kids went without shoes all summer and we got a lot of thorns and splinters. When they became infected and sore to the touch, this called for an operation which was Pop's department. A good sharp knife most of the time would do the job. A stone bruise on the foot called for a new razor blade because a lot of skin had to be shaved off and with Pop working on it, you did not dare move.

Wasp, bee, and hornet stings were taken care of with a paste made out of water and soda. A bad case of heartburn or indigestion called for Mom to mix water, vinegar and soda. Drank it down while it was still foaming.

All aches and sprains were treated with horse liniment. Never got sunburned when I was young but some did. I think she took care of this with vinegar – just smeared it on. Sometimes I think she used butter. Mom could cure almost anything with one of her remedies and a good stern order for us to rest. If no one knew what was making you sick, the doctor gave you an aspirin or kidney pill (cannot remember the name of this pill).

THE GOOD OLD RADIO

I took count the other day of the electronic gadgets in my house, shop, car and truck, and to my amazement I had over seventy. These included radios, televisions, record players, tape players, and compact disc players that play music. This does not include the computer, fish and depth finders on the boat, telephones, microwave oven, clocks, music boxes and musical instruments. There are so many things now days that play music such as watches, candles on cakes, greeting cards and kids tennis shoes, just to name a few.

Back when yours truly was about seven years old, Pop brought home our first radio. It was a sight to see because it took two grown-ups to pack it in the house. I don't claim to remember what all this contraption took to operate but I do recall a few things.

It took a wire antenna about four hundred feet long. This had to be put up about thirty feet from the ground. One end was fastened to the top of the house and a pole was cut and sat in the ground for the other end. An insulator was placed on each end, so it would not ground out, with a guide wire which led to the back of the radio.

With this completed, we had to have a car battery – which we did not have. We borrowed a battery until Pop could afford to buy one.

The big day arrived when we were to try it out. Everything worked after a lot of knob turning, a little cussing and help from a few neighbors. It worked most of the time.

The battery had to be charged every Saturday. Pop was the only one allowed to turn it on. Saturday night was the big night because Renfro Valley and Grand Ole Opera were on for about two hours. There were always eight or ten of the neighbors or kin around to hear it and no one was allowed to talk while it was on.

Special events, such as a boxing match or ballgame, were always attended by a gathering of folks. The soap operas were on during the day but we could not hear them when Pop was not working.

During the week, if the battery did not run down, everyone listened to programs such as – Amos and Andy, Gang Busters, The Shadow, Lone Ranger, Fanny Brice, George Burns and Gracie Allen, Fibber McGee and Molly, Hopalong Cassidy, to name a few.

There was one fellow who had a car with a radio. He would park someplace in the neighborhood and everyone would gather around to hear some of the programs, election returns, or the news. The problem was that it would fade out a lot and sometimes the weather would block it out completely.

If everyone's battery was out of juice, we would just get together and sing.

THE GROCERY TRUCK

When the bridge at Tyrone on Route 62 opened in the 30's, Pop lost his job operating the Ferry Boat. He bought a small farm across the river in Anderson County. He put up a house on the point where Wildcat Road came out on Route 62. We lived there during my first year of school.

Memories are vague, but I can remember that once a week the grocery truck would come down Wildcat Road. He would always stop to sell or trade his goods to everyone. There were two houses on our road but always a few people from cross the river in Woodford County.

He sold everything from groceries, pots and pans, traps and of course candy. This is what the kids wanted especially me. I was too young to trade but the older kids always shared their loot with me and the younger kids.

We had very little money, so all the kids would spend the week gathering things to trade. Items for trading were: copper, aluminum and metal of any kind. A sack of dried bones was always good for a handful of penny candy or four or five all day suckers. The bark from the root of a wahoo bush (beaten off and dried) was really good if we had enough. Yellow root or blood root were not worth much but good for trading just the same.

He would trade for dried hides. Also, by request from the grocery man, the week before, we could trade a good straight dogwood tree or a nice redbud tree. He already had them sold to someone probably in town.

We had what was called a mine. He would request a sack of the white rock from the mine, which I did not understand. I learned later that this was the boys chalk mine. We would use this to draw on the road or sidewalk at school. The chalk was great for drawing hop-scotch games on any solid surface. I checked this out a few years ago and the mine was still there.

Sometimes the older group would even trade fish, chickens, ducks, eggs, butter, small pig or lamb for groceries. Most of this he would sell to someone on his route further down the road.

It was really a big day for the kids when the grocery truck stopped. We were always on hand because he was known to hand out free candy. What kid would want to miss out on free candy.

CHRISTMAS
A LONG LONG TIME AGO

November has arrived and all the stores are decked out in Christmas duds. All the shelves are stocked with Christmas goodies.

I remember back in the 30's when all Christmas shopping was done within a week of Christmas Day. No one was allowed to talk or think about it until after Thanksgiving. If you came up with a few pieces of change before then, it was okay to save it for shopping – just don't talk about Christmas shopping.

A few days before Christmas, two or three of the kids were asked to cut the tree. They would drag it home on a sled and then put a stand on the bottom. The tree was put inside in a corner and everyone got to enjoy the trimmings.

Some of the trimmings were bought to be used year after year. A new string of tinsel or a few icicles. Most were from last year's tree. A few new ones were made from the seed pod of a sycamore and wrapped in aluminum foil. We never strung popcorn on the tree because it was edible, so it would not last anyway.

All shopping was done. Packages wrapped and put under the tree except for what Santa brought. All of Santa's showed up under and around the tree on Christmas morning.

Stockings were hung on Christmas Eve. They were always one of Pop's work socks because they were the biggest. On Christmas morning the stockings had the same things in each of them. Santa had put a banana, orange, few grapes, hand full of hard candy and a few nuts. Sometimes a small toy or some kind of school supplies were included.

Mom did all the cooking and fixings without help on some things. Cakes and pies were baked, along with a ham or some chickens were cooked (whatever was on hand). Vegetables were all from the root cellar or from a jar. A large fruit salad was made. Jell-O was mixed and placed outside to chill with bananas cut up and mixed in. It made no difference what we had, it was always good.

After breakfast, we were allowed to eat what was in our stockings. We always saved the nuts for last because this was the only time of the year we got the nuts. They consisted of Brazil, English walnuts, one that looked like a peach seed and one that looked like an acorn. I know now what they are called but back then they did not have a name. Always one or more coconuts that we had to share. Did not like the milk but the meaty part was good and still is.

By mid-afternoon, when everything was ready, we all sat down to eat, and eat and eat. If you got full, you got up and walked around, then sat and ate some more. No left overs were put away. You ate until everything was gone and dishes washed and put away. By now, it was close to bedtime, most of the new toys were broken, cap guns were out of caps, new clothes had been tried on and put away. The younger kids were asleep and the older kids were ready for bed. Most had a few aches from the full day and some with a belly ache from too much cake, pie and candy.

Around two or three days later, the tree was taken down and used for firewood in the kitchen stove. Plans were made for the first day back in school, showing off the new clothes, pocket knives, balls and bats. Some of the kids had new lunch boxes, pencils, paper and maybe a book or two that everyone got to look at (mostly comic books).

Today, Christmas is too commercialized.

SPRING WATER

Spring water is bought in a bottle at Kroger. I can remember when you could get a drink of water from any spring in Anderson County. Any place where water was running out of the ground was good to drink and most times it was cool. You did not have to take water with you when hunting, day or night, because there was always a spring or creek nearby. If not, maybe a farm pond or the river – back when water was water. If you needed water you used what was at hand.

I was not allowed to drink river water in the summer months or in the winter when it was muddy.

A well could be dug any place you could find water and boy was it good.

Rain water was good – piped into a cistern or in a rain barrel – if it was fresh. Water caught in barrels was mostly used for washing and sometimes cooking.

Growing up, the water bucket was a part of living – could not survive without one. If the bucket got a hole in it, there was a patch on the market for this. A small circle of metal was bolted over the hole. Also, used for the wash tub or the metal pot for heating water on the stove.

About everything has been replaced with plastic. If something gets a hole in it now, you throw it away and purchase a new one. Growing up – things were patched. You could use a match stick or a twig if a patch was not on hand. If the handle (or the bail as we called it) got broke, it could be replaced with a piece of wire or a rope. Things had to be in real bad shape before they were thrown away.

I could never understand why we did not have two buckets because it would have meant only half as many trips to the spring.

In the winter, someone had to start a fire and thaw the bucket before you could get a drink. The water bucket would freeze during the night when all the fires went out.

People talk of the good old days to me and I say – these are the good old days. Just turn the tap on and get a drink, not as good as spring water, but will quench my thirst.

HIGH WATER

The television and radio are putting a lot out about the high water in all the river and streams, along with the ice problems we have.

Had a flash on the news showing the high water at Bill Fint's Boat Dock at Tyrone in Anderson County – they were evacuating the village of Tyrone.

I was living in Tyrone during the 1937 flood. Pop had the farm where Wildcat Road came out on Route 62 and he had built the house there on the point. River did not get in the house but did go under it and we had the john boat tied to the door on the front of the house.

All the houses on the river side of the road were under water. Most houses on the other side of the road were on the hill side and escaped the high water. Big two-storey house across the road from us had water in the upstairs of the house.

Had two grocery stores in Tyrone at that time. They took everything out of them before the water got in and spoiled it. Would fill a big pot full of everything, cook it and give it to anyone that showed up with a bucket. Road was under water, so Pop went up over the hill and brought back enough to feed us for a couple of days. They called it some kind of stew – had everything in it, even some canned meat.

People that lived on the river did not let the high water bother them. Just load everything on a truck or wagon, move to high ground and wait for the water to go down. Wash the mud out of the house and move back in. Very few of the houses even had painted walls on the inside. There was no dry wall or carpet to replace. Some had wallpaper but that could be replaced anytime. Just sit the stove up, build a fire and in a day or two of drying out, it was ready to live in.

The house we lived in at Lock #5 and the Gardener House on Glenns Creek Road had been under water a number of times, but not when we lived in them. Brother Woodie and his wife had to move out of the Gardener House a couple of times while they lived there. They just moved everything up on the railroad behind the house, covered it, then moved right back in when the water went down.

Frankfort has the river pretty well pinned in. If it ever goes over the flood wall, we will have some big problems. Have seen it within a foot of doing just that. This is not something to look forward to.

WATER (THEN AND NOW)

Everywhere I go these days, someone is walking around, or sitting, sipping on a bottle of water – which when bought by the case, cost x number of dollars. Growing up, I was taught that water, like the air you breathe, was free.

Well, now we still have the same water and same air that we had back in the 30's and 40's – it has just been recycled a number of times. Problem is they have both been polluted rather badly due to the number of people we have on the planet.

Between the age of one and about sixteen, when we were awake, wherever we were, we drank the water that was handy – be it the river, creek, farm pond, rain, spring or a mud hole.

Lived on the Kentucky River most of my life to a point. River water was used for drinking, cooking, bathing and laundry. If the river was muddy, the water was put in a bucket to let the mud settle to the bottom, and then used. Have swallowed a barrel of pond water just while swimming in them over the years and it tasted better than the water in pools today.

Only water I could not drink was the water that ran out of the sulfa springs and a few wells around that were the same way.

When in school we drank water from the cistern – rain water that was collected from the roof of the school. I never knew what was in it – varmints, insects and about a foot of dirt that had settled to the bottom.

First time I ran into water purification was when the Army issued me a bottle of pills and ordered me to put one in each canteen of water that was used. Don't know what the pills were made of but they made the water taste bad.

Won't get into the air but they put it in bottles of cylinders also. Just don't know how the oxygen machine works.

Don't drink water anymore except in coffee, tea, or some other sources where water is used. Just don't believe there is any such thing as pure water anymore.

HUNTING KNIFE AND DOG

I remember the day well that Pop came home bruised and scratched all over. The story that came out later went this way.

Pop went up the river to Tyrone to get something at the store. Did his shopping and went across the road to have a couple of beers.

When he did not get home when he should have, Mom decided to walk to Tyrone to see what was holding him up. No big thing and not the first time this had happened.

This day she passed a big walnut tree where some kids had been playing and she found about a 10 or 12 inch hunting knife. She stuck it up her sleeve and went on to Tyrone.

Walked in the place where Pop was. Pop and another fellow were sitting in a booth with two of the women that worked there. Nothing would shake Pop too bad but when Mom walked up to the booth, the knife slipped out of her sleeve and stuck in the floor. Now, everyone in the booth knew who Mom was and when that knife hit the floor everyone in the booth took off for some place far away. All three of them ran over Pop in their effort to get away. After Pop got back to his feet, he and Mom got in the boat, with the knife and came home.

Nothing was said about this for a month or so but everyone knew something had happened because Mom walked around for weeks with a smile she could not get rid of and Pop was on his best behavior.

Another story told around Tyrone about the fellow who went out one morning to look for his dog and found him spread out on the sidewalk about 2" thick. Looked like someone had put him on a hide board and spread him out to dry. Now, this was a small dog but a mean one. He had bitten Pop three or four times.

The night before, Pop had been to a meeting at the Odd Fellows Hall down at the end of bit bridge. Had probably taken a pint with him to drink at the meeting. To get home after the meeting, Pop had to pass the house where this dog lived.

True to form, when the dog saw Pop coming up the sidewalk, he took after Pop but this time Pop was ready for him. He had a big flat rock with him (all he could pack). When the dog got close enough, Pop just turned around and dropped the rock on him, then picked the rock up and rolled it over the hill into the creek and went on home.

Fellow never did find out what hit his dog and it was years before Pop let it out that he had taught the dog not to bite him.

THE FLAT IRON

The flat iron is out of style now for ironing. Today, the only thing I can see it is used for is a door stopper or paperweight. Have thought about putting one on a rope as a boat anchor but they are not quite heavy enough.

Time was when the flat iron was used for lots of things. Having them around all week and used only one day for ironing clothes. It would have been a big waste if not used for other things.

Always took the place of a hammer for hanging a picture, driving a nail to hang a coat on, and just about any small job that called for driving a nail.

Sitting around at night, they were great for cracking walnut or hickory nuts on the fireplace hearths (made out of rock).

They could be used for door stops when not being used for something more important.

Many a time the kids used them for toys – truck, car, boat, airplane and they made great dozers for pushing dirt and rock. All you needed was a good imagination and a couple of flat irons and you could make it about anything.

Playing with them was okay but when done they had to be cleaned and put back where they were kept. Never put one away wet or damp, as they would rust fast.

Putting two sticks together for a kite. They worked great as a weight to hold them down until the glue dried.

A ball of string and a flat iron could be used for making a crane – throw the string over a limb or anything and use the iron as a counter balance, you could move about anything.

Flat irons made a great weapon in about any situation. So much so that this is one thing we were not allowed to use them for – no matter what.

Could use them for breaking up firewood, if it was small. Crushed rock - we could make little rock out of big ones. This was frowned on because it would scratch the ironing surface sometimes.

We lost the irons when we moved down river and got electricity. I think Pop used them for weights on a trotline and lost them that way.

WASH DAY

Today, the wife was making comments on the large amount of laundry that had to be done as she had gone a few days over on getting it started.

Now doing the laundry is a big job as she has to separate the clothes, then a load is put in the machine, turn the machine on, and watch television until the washer goes off. That load comes out of the washer and put in the dryer and another load is put in the washer and watch more television until the bell on the dryer rings. Then all the clothes have to be folded and put away or hung on hangers.

I can remember when things went a little different. Mom would start out by getting the kids to cut wood to heat the water with, then pack the water in to be heated. The lye soap had been made months before and put away until needed.

Took two tubs as the clothes were washed in one on a washboard and rinsed in another tub of clear water. This had to be a lot of work as the clothes had to be scrubbed on the board until they were clean.

Ten kids and two adults used a lot of clothes in a week. Throw in the bedclothes, sometimes the curtains, tablecloths, spreads on all the furniture, throw rugs and others.

After everything was washed and rinsed, it had to be hung on the outside clothesline to dry. In good weather, this only took a short time. In winter it could take days. During rainy weather you could only wait till it stopped.

After everything was dried, it was taken down and brought inside. Shirts and blouses had been dipped in starch, along with the tablecloth and spreads. All these items had to be sprinkled and rolled into a tight ball.

Then the big job – everything had to be ironed. Three or four irons were put on top of the cook stove in the kitchen. When hot, the ironing board was set up and the irons on the stove were used in rotation until the ironing was done. Irons did not stay hot long and they had to be changed often. Things were folded as they were ironed and put away or hung up as required. You could listen to the soap operas in the radio as you did this, if you had a radio and the battery had a charge on it that would last.

The only good thing about wash day was we did not have a lot of clothes back then. About the only thing we wore in summer was swimming trunks or a pair of short pants. Did not wear any shoes, so needed no socks. Wore a shirt only when in school and underwear was a waste even to own any.

Back before wash and wear, wash day could turn into two or three days a week, if the weather was bad enough.

Have been in places where it was all done with a bar of soap and two rocks. A big rock to put the clothes on and a small rock to pound them with. This was all done in the creek without a tub.

ROCKS

Today, rocks are mostly in everyone's way. A few people around take some rocks and polish them to make things and some are used to build houses.

When growing up rocks were used for everything – needed a fence, build it out of rocks (any kind of rock). They had to be cleared from the land before you could plow it for putting in crops, so build a fence.

There are places in Anderson County today where all the rocks in a field were picked up, put on a sled or wagon, hauled to the middle of the field and stacked in a pile. This did not serve any other purpose except to get them out of the way. Fields had to be cleared every three of four years. For some reason they would work their way to the top of the ground. (Winter freeze and spring thaws were the big reasons for this).

When building a house, the foundation was made out of rock. Concrete blocks were around but there was no point buying them and hauling them in, when you had plenty of rock to do the job with. Outside grills were made of rock. Whatever you had was what you built things out of.

Lots of different kinds of rocks in Anderson County and surrounding counties. Fieldstone for fences. Creek stone was big in some areas. Lots of stone was quarried out of the ground to build roads with (still is today – only they mix it with tar and make blacktop).

Growing up, most roads were made from ground rock and then graded every month or so. Traffic had thrown it off to the side. When the road got rough and full of holes, county would just grade it back up on the road, level it out, and drive on it some more. (This also cleaned the ditches out and took care of any drainage problems).

Did not get into fossils until years later but know the location of a lot of different kinds. The old round rock, wrong color (brown), did not look like any other rock. I believe the proper name for them was jode or something like that. We had another name we called them but I don't think I should put it down here.

Polished rock from the river or the creek were rare and prized when they were found. Don't know of any flint rock in Anderson County but do know of a couple of places in Franklin County where they can be found.

There are rocks everywhere. Have been around the world a couple of times and saw rocks everywhere I went. Got a story about a farmer in the Bald Knob area who raised rock for a living. Must be over a hundred kinds of rock right in this county. Next time you are out, look around and see how many you can identify and think of all the things you can use rocks for – besides bending the blade on your lawnmower.

MOVIES

Want to watch a movie today, go to the Video Warehouse, rent one, go home and watch it. Not so in the 40's.

My first movie about scared me to death but got to like it by the time it ended. Was at the theater in Lawrenceburg on Main Street where the bank is now. At that time the theater had a ticket booth with two windows – one for white and one for colored. Could buy my ticket and go in the front door. The colored folks had to get their tickets from the other side of the booth, go up a set of steps to the balcony. The balcony was on one side of the theater and they had to look down at the movie. Don't know if this made a difference or not – was never in the balcony.

First movie was a western as it was on Saturday and that was the only type of movie shown on Saturday. I believe it was a Hoot Gibson movie. On Saturdays, it was Hoot, Roy, or Gene and always in black and white.

Wanted to see a musical or a good movie with lots of romance, you had to go back on Sunday. This was the best time for taking your date to the movies.

Did not bother me that I had to walk seven miles to get to the movie and seven miles home if I could not get a ride.

Only one theater in Lawrenceburg and one in Versailles within walking distance. Types of movies were limited. Saturday and Sunday were the only time we could go, so it was something to look forward to each week.

Had it made after we moved to Franklin County. Frankfort had three movie theaters and on Saturday they showed a double feature. Two movies for the price of one. Still had westerns most every Saturday.

Lots of Saturdays I would make the two movies at the Grand Theater on St. Clair Street and then rush to the Capitol Theater on Main Street and with a little luck could catch the late move at the State. All this before 10:00 p.m. when it was time to start home.

On Saturdays I had to live on popcorn and candy with a coke. But if there was a new movie in town on Saturday, I had to see it or go home unhappy.

Still go to the theater once or twice a year. Still like movies but they are not as much fun as they were back in the 40's.

Movies are not the same. Have made a few where the good guy does not come out the hero. Some do not have a good guy in them. All of the actors are bad guys

Big difference in movies now is the cost. Can remember when you could make all three theaters in Frankfort, eat and drink at all of them, for about two or three dollars. Now a trip for two to see one movie, have popcorn and a drink, costs over twenty dollars.

The house that Pop (Kirby Bowen Fint, Sr.) built when he bought the farm at Tyrone, Kentucky, ca. 1935.

CHAPTER FOUR

SUNDAY SCHOOL AND CHURCH

I was at a Halloween Party at Church in October, where due to a contest the preacher and a couple of other people for a pie/cake in the fact. This brought back memories from about age seven when I got a big interest in going to Church.

We lived across the street from a Church – not sure but I believe it was a Baptist Church built out of logs. When it was built, someone had made a mistake and did not brace it right. The roof had begun to settle and was pushing the walls out. To solve the problem, a hole had been drilled in each side. A large round metal rod placed all the way through to where it stuck out on both sides. Threads were cut on the rod after a metal plate was put on each end. A nut was screwed on and in this manner the walls were drawn back together until the walls were straight up and down.

This worked good for the walls but it was about eye level for the grownups and went all the way across the middle. Walking down the aisle, they had to duck under this bar which was a hazard for most. The preacher used it to his advantage. Every night when he got to preaching, get all torn up and loud, he would run down the aisle, grab the bar and do a maneuver – we called it skinning a cat. Folks would walk as far as ten miles to see this. As for me, I would not miss it for the world. All the kids that were big enough liked to imitate him on this rod after Church.

Oldest brother was a preacher. Do not remember anything he did like this to get me to go to Church but he would reward me with something each Sunday that I went with him.

The store at Tyrone was owned and operated by Mr. and Mrs. Thompson. Their son was my Sunday School teacher at age seven and he kept me coming back by teaching me something new each Sunday after Sunday School was over. An example was one Sunday he taught me to make a necklace out of clover blooms. Took him a couple of Sundays to teach me how to find a four-leaf clover. Took about a month to teach me to tie a cherry stem in a knot with my tongue. During the summer he taught me to take stiff grass stems and put leaves together to make a hat or a skirt.

None of this cost anything. Took his pocket knife and showed me how to take the stem of a touch-me-knot, cut it in sections, place the small end inside the large end. Put one end in the spring, lay it downhill and water would run through it. How long it was made depended on how much time you had to work.

The object of this, then, as it would be now, was to give the kids something to do and learn. All the class was in on this, not just me.

VISITING KIN OR NEIGHBORS

I remember in the mid to late 30's, there was no television, very few radios around and church only once a week. Families and neighbors did a lot of visiting.

The little community of Tyrone was cut off from about everyone with the opening of the new bridge on Route 62.

After work (during the week and on weekends) about the only thing around to do was visit. Nowadays people do a lot of visiting but not the way they did back then.

About everyone in Tyrone and Fintville were a little kin and all were good neighbors.

The young, unmarried adults had their thing while the older folks sat inside, or on the porch, and talked. The group I remember best were the young ones (5 to 10 or 11 year olds). During the day, games were played one way and after dark the rules changed.

Daytime tag was a good one. No one even ran into anything and the safe base was easy to find. At night (no street lights and the kerosene lamp gave very little light through the window) a lot of things were hit at full speed but that is what made it so much fun. Not much damage was ever done except for a bloody nose, cut lip or a little skin knocked off. If you were the one to get hurt, you got a lot of attention. If the game was at your house, you knew where all the trees, fences, ditches, etc., were.

Hide and seek was good in daytime but after dark you could forget it. You could look all night and never find anyone. My favorite hiding place was a new plowed garden because I could lie down in it and the only way to find me was to step on me.

Don't know what game it was, but our front yard was about 400 feet from the front porch to the sidewalk. Half the crew would hide in the middle of the yard and the other half had to get from the sidewalk to the porch without getting caught. Whoever you caught had to give you a kiss – of course one team was the boys while the other team was girls. We had to be quiet at this game because if the grownups caught us then we all had to go inside.

Hopscotch was a good one but I could never get my rock in the square I wanted it in.

Follow the leader was okay but a lot of the girls had a hard time if the leader was one of the older boys.

One of the good inside games was storytelling (kind of like acting) or reciting a poem you knew. This took place during bad weather or we got run inside.

Now days, kids can have a lot of fun but it cannot possibly be as much fun as we had during a visit from kin or neighbors because our games did not cost anything.

BASEBALL TYRONE STYLE
(Hardball prior to 1940)

My first experience with baseball was at a very young age of six or seven. We only had one school in Tyrone and the closest one to us was too far away to get together with us to have a game. All the guys would get together and chose teams. I was too young for playing but did get to a game most weekends (Saturday or Sunday).

Normally, the players only had one ball and one bat. Sometimes the bat was homemade out of a hickory sapling about the size of a bat with the bark taken off. This was trimmed down on one end for a handhold. The ball diamond was a bottom owned by the Distillery or Rock quarry. It was always moved by whoever came by with horses and a cycle mower. Bases and pitcher mound were probably a piece of cardboard and there was not a backstop. Spectators sat on the ground.

Games were always a lot of fun to watch and I am sure the players had a good time. The players did not really know how to play but games were always finished. That is, unless someone hit a home run and the ball went too far out in the river and could not be retrieved. One or two people were posted on the bank to recover balls hit in the shallow water, up to about ten feet deep.

Umpires were another problem. Someone, too old to play, was picked for this job. Most times he knew less about the game than the players.

Games always took all afternoon. Back in the 30's, there was not better way to spend a Saturday afternoon.

I went to the games most of the time with Pop. Two or three of my older brothers were on one team and sometimes both teams. All the other players were first or second cousins. Just about everyone living in Tyrone were kin.

Later, one of the property owners let the players use a field where they could not hit the ball hard enough to knock it in the river. This also meant we did not have to cross the bridge in order to get to the game.

CHRISTMAS TREES
BACK WHEN

The time of year is coming up again. Time to get the old artificial tree out of the attic. Also, lights to string outside.

Not as much fun as it was when we went out and cut the Christmas tree and packed it home. A fresh one every year.

Always a cedar and much too big. Was trimmed down and a wooden stand nailed to the bottom. This had to be done only a few days before Christmas, so it did not dry out too bad.

Ornaments were unpacked from a bushel basket. Each one had been wrapped in newspaper and put away very gently after last Christmas.

The ornament I remember most was a glass teapot which hung on the front of the tree every year. The rest of the collection was a collection of different color round balls, and a star for the top which was made from cardboard and covered with aluminum wrap.

Always circled the tree a couple of times with tensile – silver in color and always the same each year.

Icicles were made of aluminum wrap were added. A new package was bought every year or two because they were hard to keep.

Did not have any lights to put on the tree because we had no electricity to plug them into. Sometimes we would string popcorn on it but we would eat popcorn, so this was not done often.

Took the seed balls off a sycamore tree, aluminum foil from a cigarette pack and wrapped them. The seed pods from a gum tree would work but they had to be painted. Just dip them in paint, hang them up to dry and they worked good.

Made a lot of chains out of paper. Could not get colored construction paper, so we used the colored funnies out of the Sunday paper. We also used these to wrap packages.

The old fashioned Christmas tree was not very pretty by today's standards, but to me it was the most beautiful thing on earth and I loved everyone of them.

UNOFFICIAL OLYMPICS

While watching the Winter Olympics and all the people that got disqualified (for one thing or another) brought a flood of memories back. Especially when I was about seven or eight and the competition they put me in at the Anderson County Fair in Lawrenceburg.

I was a second grader at Tyrone School and the teacher entered me in the foot race at the fair. She stated that she was sure I could win because I could out run any girl in my room.

Now, as for me, I was not too sure of this. As everyone in 1937 knew, the boys could run faster that the girls. In this race they were putting me up against other boys and some were older than me.

The school had a lot of projects entered in the fair, so it would not be too bad if I did not win the Blue Ribbon. If I ran in the race, it meant a ride in an automobile all the way to the Fairgrounds and back to Tyrone.

Everything was great. They got about twenty of us lined up on the track, someone yelled GO, and we were off in a cloud of dust. I cross the finish line and was yards in front of everyone. Man, I was one proud fellow when we gathered to get our ribbons.

Well, I hit rock bottom when the judge disqualified me because I did not have any shoes on. There was no way to explain to him that it was summer time and I did not even own a pair of shoes.

He gave all three ribbons to the other boys and sent me home with nothing.

That was the last time I entered in anything at the Anderson County Fair. Still went to the fair each year but only to watch people.

All of that was bad enough but then a couple of days after the race, a stone bruise developed on one of my heels. Pop whittled on my foot for about thirty minutes with his pocketknife to open it. Had to walk on my toes for about a week until it healed.

This was not in the league of today's games, such as bob sledding, cross country skiing, figure skating etc., but it made me give up all sports for years – except chasing the girls at school.

CHAPTER FIVE

TOYS

I don't remember having many toys that were bought. Each Christmas I could get a cap gun and caps and sometimes a holster to put it in.

Most toys were made. Come up with a couple of wheels of any kind and would spend days making something out of it. A wagon could last for a long while. When it was worn out or wrecked, the wheels were used to make something else.

A piece of string or bailing wire could be turned into a bow in minutes with a small elm sapling. Arrows could be made out of any kind of a weed or wooden stick that was fairly straight. A little dangerous but that was the price that had to be paid. Don't remember anyone who was hurt very bad.

Have spent days on the riverbank building roads. Cars and trucks were made out of mud and when dried they worked fine. Whole towns were made out of mud. Houses were made complete with mud furniture. All this worked fine until a hard rain and then it all turned to mud again. They have it down to an art now days which they call sand art.

If you had a hammer and a few nails it only took a few pieces of wood to make a great airplane. All types of sleds were made for winter fun. With two small cans and a couple of pieces of wire, you could make a great set of walkers. Made you about six or seven inches taller for a short time. Also, if you could come up with two cream cans (carnation milk cans), with both ends still in the can, and step on them just right with the heel of your shoe, the ends would lock on and this made it very hard to walk for most of the day.

Two poles (six or eight feet long), two 4 inch blocks, a piece of wire and a couple of nails made a great pair of stilts. And old iron rim off a buggy wheel and a piece of stiff wire were good for hours of fun. Better if there were three or four others, so you could have a race.

Never had a tire swing. That came along later. But did use a lot of rubber inner tubes – mostly for making sling shots (forked stick, two short rubber bands, leather tongue out of a shoe) and bingo, you had a great toy. It was practical because you could kill a squirrel or rabbit if you got real good. Anything could be used for ammo (rock, good green plum, walnut, hickory nut) as long as it was hard.

A large button and a piece of thread or fishing line was good for making a humming sound and lasted for hours. Metal bottle caps made great pins. Take the cork out, put it on the inside of your shirt with the cap on the outside, press the cork back into the cap. This would not fall off but had to be pulled off.

These are just a few of the simple things that were so much fun.

THE DRUM STOVE

I can remember when the old drum stove was the prime heat source in winter. Most homes had one even though they were not a pretty stove but a very practical one.

About as big round as a barrel and almost as long with four short legs on the bottom, large door on the front big enough to take a large piece of wood and opening on the top for stove pipe to fit. Pipe had different types of dampers on them. If the stove got too hot, damper had to be closed some to cool it down. Also had a damper on the bottom of the door that could be opened to make the fire burn better.

Each morning, before the fire was started, ashes had to be removed. Later the ashes were put on the garden.

All the stores, school and most stripping rooms had a pot belly stove that would burn coal. No coal was ever burnt in the drum stove because the side was too thin. Coal would about melt it and was made for wood only.

Only lasted one winter. Each year a new one had to be bought. Take it down in spring and throw it away. Tried polishing them and save for the next winter but they would rust out from the inside.

The old drum stove was only meant to heat one room so the bedrooms were never heated. Some heat would get into them but not much.

No one wanted to cut wood for more than one. Cooking stove in the kitchen kept the kitchen warm most of the day but when supper was done, that fire was left to burn out and everyone went to the room with the drum stove or went to bed and covered up to keep warm.

I would stay up as late as I could, hoping a couple had gone to bed before me so the bed would be warm.

The drum stove was round on top like an oil drum and a pot of beans could not be cooked on it unless you had a pot with three legs on it that would sit on top.

Not the best stove on the market at the time but it was the cheapest. Served the winter months to keep the house warm and did burn about any kind of wood.

The old drum stove may not have been very pretty but it was a life saver in cold weather.

STRIPPING ROOM

Stripping rooms have not changed much in the last 50 years and most still look the same. Some of them that were in use 50 years ago are still being used.

Heating may have changed. Gone from a wood stove to a gas stove and some still heat with coal. Stripping bench may have changed a little (maybe rebuilt and maybe not as big).

The last time I worked in one, I think there were the bottom leaves (spots), then the lugs, or good leaves in the middle of the stalk. Then the red and the tips. Each grade was tied in a hand (all that you could hold) wrapped with a leaf, tied, and put on a stick. When the stick was full, it was put in a press on the wall and clamped down. The stick that was in the press was taken out and put on the book out in the barn and covered. This was all separate at the warehouse where it was sold and all grades were sold separate. All would bring a different price.

Back to the stripping room – was a lot of cooking took place. Take a pot of beans, set it on the stove and cook them while you were working.

When young I was the extra hand most of the time. My job was to keep the fire going, carry the tobacco from the barn to the stripping room, sweep the trash under the bench and take the tobacco back out when it came out of the press. Also had to pack the stalks out of the room and stack them. Later they had to be scattered on the field where the tobacco grew. Pretty good job if the wood for the stove was already cut.

Weather was involved here also. Had to wait for rain to bring the tobacco in case before it could be booked down and covered. This was just pitching it down, taking it off the sticks and stacking it in a pile. Now days they just steam it to bring it in case.

The stripping room today has a compressor, hydraulic cylinder and a box for a press. Most just strip it off, pitch it in the box, press it down, tie a couple of strings around the bundle and it is ready for market.

That about covered the changes. Most everything is done about the same. The bundles weigh a lot more than the hands on a stick. I think they try to hold the bundles to about 50 pounds. That makes it easier and faster to stack, load and unload.

Wish I could remember some of the stories I heard in the stripping room 50 odd years ago. A 65 year old could tell them that went back 115 years. Can only remember parts of some of them. Should have listened to them more and thought less of the weekend that was coming up in a few days.

POWER PLANT AT TYRONE

I remember when this power plant did not exist. All that property was one big farm owned by the Hogg Family. Crops were raised by 3 share-croppers who had houses, barns, outhouses, and controlled certain areas of the farm. Each family raised a portion of the crops.

The farm covered all the land from Route 62 down to Lock #5 property. Bordered on one side by Route 62, one side by the Kentucky River, one side was a creek, and one side was bordered by two other farms. Several hundred acres of land. Pop's 13 acres was across the river on the Anderson County side. The Hogg Farm was all in Woodford County.

The railroad from Lawrenceburg to Versailles ran across this farm and split the top acres off from the lower portion.

This lower portion is what the Power Company bought or leased – I don't know which. It was about two-thirds of the farm and took in all the bottom land.

That is when the area began to change. They started by building a spur off the railroad – all the way around it to the river where the plant was to be built.

All the share-croppers, but one, were moved and all buildings were torn down. Mr. Lloyd was allowed to remain in the house on the river and was hired by the company to maintain all the property. He had to keep it mowed, keep the line fences in good repair, raise no cattle, but he was allowed to raise what crops he wanted to grow.

When they got around to putting the channel in from above the plant to down river where it came back into the river, the house was in the way, so Mr. Lloyd and family had to move.

By the time the plant was built we had moved down river.

Did get back up that way a few times and did some hunting and fishing with the Lloyd boys.

No one is allowed to hunt or fish on this land anymore. They have guards that roam it to keep people off and signs all around the fence and on the riverbank. Most of it has grown up now. They still keep parts of it mowed. I don't know what shape the ponds are in but would love to fish them once more.

The big spring house is still there and can see it from the other side of the river.

SHELLS

Growing up, I did not see many sea shells but there were lots of local shells. The following had shells: mussels, turtles, water tarpons, snails of all sizes, penny winkles and dry land tarpons. All of these shells had a value.

In a youngster's make believe mind, anything was possible. We used shells for money and each one had a value by type and size. This is how I was taught to count money.

In our make believe world, we had a store stocked with the following: everything that came in a box, a can that had a label on it, some jars with labels, and bottles. One of the older kids was the storekeeper and the rest of the kids had to have the shell money of they wanted to buy anything.

Shells were found in different locations. Snail shells were about any place. Small ones were used for dimes. The next size was a penny, etc. (nickel, quarter and half dollar). Prices were as follows: half a mussel shell was one dollar. tarpon shells were five dollars, and turtle shells were ten dollars.

Sea shells were like gold because each one had a different value according to size.

When I got old enough to be storekeeper, I would take one of the tin boxes, get it full of shells and bury it under a rock or stump. I never did dig it up and guess the box is still buried.

Sometimes during the summer we used tree leaves for money but they did not last long.

We set up a clothing store, once, with pictures out of the Sears and Roebuck catalogue. This was good for selling and collected a lot of shells with it.

At school, the kids used marbles for money. You could buy really good things with them including fish hooks or line. Once I bought a kite with a handful of marbles. You could always buy someone's lunch if you had enough marbles.

All this really came down to trading. The grown-ups would trade two dozen chickens for a pig or a goat, or a pig and goat for a horse or mule.

Guess what it all boils down to is real money was in short supply back then and a good rabbit dog or coon hound was worth a lot in some circles.

SPECIAL KIND OF TREES

I can remember when growing up on the farm in Anderson County, each kind of tree was used for a purpose. All the trees were special but only a few could be used for some things. The first and only house Pop ever built had shingles split out of an oak tree (I believe it was a white oak). This was cut into, about, a 3-foot section, split with a special tool and wooden mallet. They were split off and nailed on the roof. This is also what tobacco sticks were made out of. They would split straight if no knots were in the way.

Sycamore – we used the seed pods to make Christmas ornaments. We had one that was special because it was hollow at the bottom. A very big tree and four or five of us could stand up in it at the same time. Always amazed me how it would grow new bark each year and the old bark would fall off.

Hedge-apple – was special, not for the fruit (only cows and squirrels would eat it) but the wood was hard and tough. Went looking for one of these when we needed a new single or double tree for plowing. These were also good for wagon tongs and a new pitman arm for the horse-drawn mower.

Locust – nice flowers in spring. Every farm had these and were used for fence post, post that had to be replaced in the barn, or one of the outbuildings, chicken house and smokehouse. Split easy and could be used for fence rails. Now many of these were around in the 30's.

Persimmon – guarded and taken care of. Fruit was good when ripe and made a fine pudding. You could always catch opossum in one at night with no dog.

Sassafras – not used for anything I know of except for walking sticks. The root made good tea. This was the only kind of tea I knew of until I was about grown.

Hickory-Nut – very tough wood and used in place of the hedge apple lot of times. On small trees the bark was stripped off to line the bottom of chairs. This was a full-time job for a few people.

Slick-Elm – this is what we called then because they were a very strange tree. Peel the bark off this tree, take the white inner part, and use it for chewing gum. Bark also made string – used for a lot of things.

Pa-Paw – fruit, like a banana was great when ripe but you had to get to it ahead of the raccoon.

All trees were used for firewood once they were dead. Sometimes in the winter, live trees were cut for wood but only if we had to. Only one cedar was cut a year and that was for a Christmas tree. Trees were special to Pop and only cut when needed.

SNAKES

Most people don't like to read about snakes, but they are out there. They were a big part of growing up. We were taught that all snakes were bad news. We made them live a hard life and did not care what kind it was – it was a snake.

The old cow sucker was harmless. He got to be the biggest around and that alone made him an endangered species. The biggest one I can remember I got one day when reaching into a nest for eggs and got the snake. Did not dare turn him loose with no damage. I had to keep him moving but he did not bite me. I believe he was as scared as I was.

Was not too scared of a black racer. They would chase you during the mating season. You could not out run them, so you had to stop and fight. If one did bite you, it would not so much as get sore and no more than a scratch.

Green snake laid around in the bushes. Garden snakes were harmless. If we happen to dig up a small ground snake, we kept it and took it to school to scare the girls with.

Most water snakes were harmless but we did have the cotton mouth water moccasin around and had to keep a sharp eye out for him. They were very poisonous and had to be avoided when cooning for fish or turtle hunting.

Copper heads were the most feared and most times were found on old rotten logs, rock piles and ledges on the cliffs. Could tell when one was close by smelling him and then just vacate the area. They gave off an odor that smelled a lot like cucumber.

There was one Pop said was deadly – called a spreading viper. Found mostly in a road or path, lying in the sun. Walk upon him and he would spread out almost paper thin. I can remember walking up on one of these and taking three or four steps backwards without moving an inch.

All snakes were to be killed when possible, any kind. There was an old saying back then – if you left them lying on their back, it would either keep it from raining, or make it rain. I can't remember which it was.

Heard lots of storied about the rattle snake and the hoop snake. Never in my life saw a hoop snake and the only rattle snakes I ever saw were in Arizona and Texas. Know they are in a lot of places I have been but never did run across any of them.

Most snakes were good for something. Lots of farmers would keep then in the corn crib to keep the rats and mice under control. The black snake and cow sucker would kill a copper head – saw this happen twice. Do not bother any of them anymore – just try to avoid them.

ANDERSON COUNTY FAIR

It only happened once a year in Anderson County and from about age 8 through 16 it was almost as good as Christmas.

I would work at anything for a couple of weeks and save all my money for the fair. Would even skip a Saturday night or two in town so I would not spend any money.

Don't know what it was that drew me back year after year. I could never win anything on the Midway but would always try.

The rides were great and I would always ride the swings a lot. They were nothing like we have today.

My big interest was the contests between the kids. I was a good runner but never the best. Never got a blue ribbon but did get second or third place a few times. Came in first once but got disqualified because I had taken my shoes off and ran it barefooted. Got a blue ribbon a few times on projects I made at school which the teacher had entered.

Always enjoyed the cattle shows. All kinds of animals – hogs, cows, goats, sheep, different types of chickens, horses, mules and some blue ribbon bulls.

Had horse and mule pulls before tractor pulls. There were all kinds of races but I sat in the stands for these.

All kinds of crops were on display – corn, tobacco, soy beans, and vegetables of all kinds. There were also potted and cut flowers.

Rode the ferris wheel a few times but for me the big draw was the people. I have always been a people watcher and still am. People came in from all over the county and this was the only time I got to see some of them.

It was 10 miles from our house to the fairgrounds. Always walked to the fair (Pop, several brothers, and me). A full day at the fair was tiring and 10 miles home was a long walk. It was up to everyone to make arrangements for a ride home. Had to leave before we wanted to especially if our ride home had to be up early the next morning. If they were farmers with cattle at the fair, we would have to help with loading and unloading. Went to the fair a few times after we moved to Franklin County but gave it up after a few years because of the distance.

The fairgrounds is still there and lot of things still take place on the grounds. The grandstand has been taken down but the race track is still there and I believe the fair is still held there. I am not real sure because it has been 45 years since I have been to a fair.

TURTLE HUNTING

Today, if you want a nice big snapping turtle to cook or make soup out of, you take a fishing pole and find a farm pond or lake and catch one.

Turtle hooks are still used and I have one with my fishing gear. It is a five foot steel rod with a hook made on one end and a loop on the other end for a handle.

This story is about one summer I spent with my older brother at Sinai KY in Anderson County. His father-in-law was also living with him. Mr. Allen talked me into going turtle hunting. We did not have a turtle hook, so Mr. Allen made two rigs he said we could get turtles with. He took two broom handles and drove a nail into one end (leaving it sticking out about two inches). This was used to poke into the pond until you found a turtle. You then reached down and got the turtle by the tail and put him in the sack. Sounded easy – but I could never determine where his tail and head were. A small problem, since snapping turtles are mean and they bite. Mr. Allen was from the mountains (around Hazard) and said this was the only way to do it.

Well, we hunted a number of times that summer and caught a lot of turtles. I could find them with the stick but it was Mr. Allen's job to put them in the sack.

All summer did not get one bite from a turtle, although sometimes it took more than one try to get the tail.

We ate a lot of snapping turtles that summer. Now days we have the soft shell turtle. This one has a longer neck and bites. It is not as mean as the snapper.

Every time I am on the river or lake and catch a turtle, I think of Mr. Allen and the summer he taught me how to catch one by hand.

WILD GREENS

Springtime is best for wild greens, when they first come up, because they are young and tender. Almost anything is edible if cooked and seasoned just right. The more different kinds of greens used – the better.

The types most common in this area are: polk, flat greens, watercress, narrow dock, dandelions, violets, shinny and wild mustard.

Polk was easiest to find because you just had to look for the big dead stalks from the summer before. It had to be picked while small. After it got large it could be fried as polk salad.

Flat greens were only found on open ground where crops had been raised the year before. Watercress grew around the fresh water springs and creek banks. Narrow dock was found in damp areas and the young leaves were best. The wide dock was not good for greens.

Dandelions were good but not too many because they would make the greens bitter. These were best picked before they bloomed. The blooms were used for making wine. Wild violets were good cooked in greens or eaten as a salad. Pop called these "Johnny-Jump-Ups".

Shinny (real name - "Last Rose of Summer") was picked young. Not much of this was used but cooked with polk is good. This was chopped up and wilted with hot bacon grease or used like lettuce (before it was ready in the garden).

Wild mustard had to be picked after it bloomed. This was the only way I could locate it. Used a little because it would make the greens bitter.

Pick a bushel basket full of all the above and do the following for a delicious meal: wash good, remove large stems, place in iron kettle, fat bacon, salt, pepper and cook. Boil a few eggs to chop up and top off a plate full of greens.

The polk had to be parboiled and drained before adding to the pot. This was a must but I don't know why.

Still cook my greens – only now when everything is ready for the pot, I just put it in my crock pot, set on low, cook for about eight hours, add the eggs, and eat.

Bit of a problem now days is finding them. Also, keeping wife out of the pot until they are completely done.

Great with a skillet of baked cornbread and buttermilk.

DEAD-FALLS, SNARES AND STEEL TRAPS

There were a couple of ways to set a dead-fall. We always used a large flat rock which had to be set on something solid (preferably another rock). The rock was lifted up and sat on a wooden trigger with about a twelve-inch stick, which was used to hold the bait. The back of the rock was lying on the ground while the front was about six or seven inches off the ground. Normally, a piece of apple was used for bait. If something took hold of the apple, the trigger was tripped and rock would fall. Most of the time it worked but sometimes it failed. We mostly caught rabbits but sometimes we did catch an opossum. These could also be set with a wooden box and a large rock on the top. It worked good if you wanted to catch the game alive. If you caught a raccoon or skunk, it required a lot of skill to get them out.

Snares worked really good but were tricky to set. They called for a small sapling, six or seven feet tall with all limbs removed. Setting up a snare consisted of the following: (a) sixteen inch piece of twine with a small twig about one-half inch long, tied in the middle of the string; (b) small fork cut from a limb and driven in the ground; (c) small trigger or bait stick about three inches long; and (d) six sticks (about three inches) were stuck in the ground in a circle. With the forked peg, the twine was tied to top of sapling and a loop made on the other end. The sapling was pulled over and the bait stick was placed inside the loop. The short stick, on the string, was poked through the fork. The bait stick was laid along side the fork with pressure put on the bait stick and fork with short stick as the sapling was released. This put the bait in the center of the loop. If a rabbit took the bait, he was as good as in the pot for supper.

Steel traps were used for catching fur, coons, muskrats, opossum, fox and skunk. We would take a rabbit if he happened along. Traps were set along game trails for most game. They were set under water (river or creek), baited with fish for muskrats or minks. The bank had to be made straight up in order for the game to get into the water and take the bait.

All traps had to be checked every afternoon and baited. Then checked again in the morning. Game was skinned and cleaned before leaving for school. A lot of this took place after dark and before daylight and always took place in cold weather.

The hides had to be stretched on boards with fur side in. These were hung in the smokehouse or barn to dry. The hides were shipped to Sears and Roebuck. A check was mailed back to us and used for Christmas shopping and new clothing for school.

WHAT A MOM WE HAD

Back when there were ten children at home, everything was different. Nothing worked the way it does today. I don't ever remember living in a house with more than three bedrooms until the time I went into the Army in the late 1940's.

All cooking was done on a wood burning stove in the kitchen. In the wintertime, all entertaining took place in the kitchen or living room (which had a bed). In the summer time, it all took place outside.

Most of the time when breakfast was over, lunch and supper were started. It took all day to cook for twelve people.

Smaller children went to bed first and in the winter their job was to get the bed warm for whoever came to bed later. The advantage of this was that the first ones got the head of the bed while the latecomers slept at the foot (two children lying in opposite directions). On cold nights there could be six or seven in one bed. The only room heated was the one with the stove for fireplace. This room got cold later because the fire was never kept burning all night.

Every morning a new fire was set in the heating stove and one in the kitchen stove. Water buckets had to be thawed before coffee could be made.

After fires were started, everyone jumped out of bed at the same time and raced to the stove to get dressed.

Everyone washed up in the kitchen, a couple at a time, using water that was heated on a tank that was part of the kitchen stove. This was heated as the following was cooked for breakfast – coffee, biscuits, gravy and sometimes bacon/eggs or hot cakes.

Sounds like a hard way to live when I think back on it but everyone living in the country lived the same way.

Today we call it primitive when we go camping for a weekend and use only a campfire for cooking and heating. In the 1930's and 40's, it was a way of life for most folks I knew.

CHRISTMAS
ONE WEEK A YEAR

Well, it is August and Christmas is right around the corner. Another month and signs will go up and Santa Claus will be on television each night until up in January.

I can remember when Mom started cooking around December 20 (5 days before the big day) and now we could talk about Christmas. If you had any shopping to do, now was the time to do it.

The first Christmas shopping I did I was taken to the Dime Store in Lawrenceburg and had $1.50 to spend on whatever I wanted to get everyone. It had to be spread thin because there was Mom, Dad, 8 brothers, and 1 sister to buy for. After four hours of shopping I was down to fifteen cents. It was time to go home that night with a few newspapers and Mom's ball of string (to tie school lunches with). Everything was wrapped, tied, marked and put under the tree.

The rest of the week was spent helping Mom with the following: packing water in, cracking walnuts, cutting wood for cooking, and licking pans/bowls before they were washed.

Mom baked 5 or 6 cakes and a few pies (chocolate, mince meat, and custard). The meat was what she had on hand, usually a ham from the smokehouse. Sometimes it was a turkey but most of the time a few chickens were dressed and baked. Jello was a big item because with cold weather it could be chilled sitting on top of the back porch. A couple of bananas were cut up and put in the jello on December 24. A large bowl of fruit salad was chopped up and put together. The rest of the meal came out of the cellar, which consisted of: mashed potatoes, chicken gravy (just as good as giblet gravy), stewed tomatoes out of a jar, green beans and a blackberry cobbler.

Christmas morning everyone had a stocking full of goodies (candy, orange, banana, few grapes and sometimes nuts). Breakfast was coffee, biscuits and jelly or jam. Afterwards, you could eat what was in your stocking and open gifts.

In my excitement of shopping I had gotten everyone something except for myself. Someone got me a cap gun and a couple of boxes of caps and that was all I wanted anyway.

Between 12:30 and 1:00p.m. everything was put on the table and everyone ate until it was gone. Sometimes it took the rest of the day. Nothing was taken off the table until all dishes were emptied. By bedtime all the food was gone and most of the toys were broken, so we sat around and talked about what we were going to do next Christmas.

By December 27 or 28, Christmas was behind us for a full year and everyone was getting ready to go back to school and show off the new clothes they had gotten for Christmas.

THE OLD CAMPHOUSE ABOVE LOCK #5

The old camphouse above Lock #5 no longer is standing. It fell over the hill in the 50's. The only sign of where it was is part of the fireplace and the foundation the fireplace sat on.

We moved into the old camphouse about 1939. We only lived there about two years, then Pop bought the farm next door.

The camphouse was on about ten acres of land. It was the only place I ever lived that did not have enough flat ground for Pop to put out a garden. All ten acres were a river cliff. The back of the camphouse sat on the ground with four cedar posts (about twenty feet tall) under the front porch, which ran all the way across the front and one end.

The camphouse was two stories with three rooms upstairs and three rooms downstairs. When we moved in there were no windows in it, just the holes there they were to go. These were covered in some type of material - not plastic. It let the light in but you could not see out. Built like a barn (and about as air tight). The boards on the side went up and down with a strip of wood nailed over each crack. There was no electricity or running water. It was hard to heat in the winter but cool and dry in the summer. One good thing – a good roof.

This was considered real hard living by a lot of standards but we were never down sick (any more than anyone else).

As far as I know there was never any paint put on it (inside or out). Some of the walls inside were covered with paper or cardboard for keeping the heat in.

Summers were great. We could go out the upstairs window and lie on the roof of the porch at night, tell stories and plan what we were going to do the next day. What we talked about were: which group was going in what direction; what we were looking for; and how many in each group. Groups consisted of the following: (a) four were needed to go over to a creek and seine bait for the lines (two to operate the seine and two to carry the bait buckets – one for crayfish and one for minnows; (b) three were needed to go to a farm to work in hay and tobacco; and (c) one was need to stay to help sis and Mom.

To us kids this was living at its best. Guess we did not know any better. We had fun at whatever we did.

I don't believe anyone ever moved into the camphouse after we moved to the farm. All that is left are memories and a picture to get out and reminisce.

WATERMELONS AND CANTALOUPES

In today's time if you want a watermelon or cantaloupe, you go to a grocery store or market and buy one. There are so many kinds of melons that you never know which one to get.

In the 30's if you wanted a watermelon all you had to do was go and pick it. The only thing you had to know was where they were located.

All the farmers along the river and on the higher ground raised watermelons along with everything else. Anything that would grow was raised.

Times when we were a long way from home and wanted a melon, we gathered one from the nearest patch and ate it. Sometimes the owner of the patch would join us.

There were a lot of rules for picking a melon from someone's patch. The following rules applied: (1) you never picked the largest one in the patch – the owner could be raising this one for a special purpose to show at the fair or just for bragging; (2) you took special care not to damage the rest of the patch; (3) you made sure of getting a ripe one – picking one that was still green was a no no; (4) you did not pick from the same patch every time; (5) you picked only what you could eat and did not take any home or waste any; and (6) you used your patch when possible. These rules applied to everything, not just melons.

Choices in melons were limited to watermelons, cantaloupes, and mush melons. There was another one, about the size of a baseball, but I cannot remember what it was called.

Everyone always raised more melons than could be used. When the first frost hit, there were melons left that the frost killed. This was a sad time of the year because it meant we had a long wait for the next melon patch to get ripe.

Another use for melons was food for hogs and chickens. The green hard outside of the rind could be peeled off and the white portion (about one inch thick) was used to make pickles.

Until I was about twenty years of age, I never heard of anyone buying a watermelon – trading for one maybe, but never buying.

THE WILD GRAPEVINE

I drove past a house the other day that had a big wreath hanging on the front door made out of grapevines. It made me remember back when we used the wild grapevine in the woods and on the river cliffs for all sorts of entertainment.

Sometimes a large search would take place along the river for a vine big enough and in the right location. After it was cut in the right place, everyone would gather on the bank and use it in place of a rope to swing out over the water and drop off into the river. This was used most of the summer, unless it broke, or pulled loose from the tree limbs. When this happened, we just had to change locations of the swimming hole.

This could be done anywhere there was a good vine to use for a swing on the steep cliffs. You could get a long way up sometimes.

We had a couple of places close to the house where there was a thick stand of elm trees about twelve to fifteen feet tall with a lot of vines growing on them.

About six or seven of us would get together and starting at the same tree, we would see who could go the longest distance without touching the ground. You climbed the same tree and went in the same direction. Usually three or four hundred yards was a record. This is how I broke my collarbone. Accidents were rare but a lot of skin was knocked off plus a lot of scratches. This was very normal for us.

We used vines to put our log rafts together. They did not last too long but we had lots of time to replace them.

Vines were used for ropes in lots of places. Rope was hard to come by but the vines were plentiful.

I should not mention this since we were at a very young age but you could take a dead grapevine and smoke it. Use any vine with a diameter of approximately one-half inch, cut it in sections about three to four inches long. You did not get high but got a sore tongue.

Grapevines still make nice walking sticks. They bend easy when still green.

The only bad accident I remember from using the grapevines is that an older brother came across one on the way home one day. It had been cut the year before and when he swung out on it, the vine broke and when he hit the ground he broke his left arm.

FOOD – THEN & NOW

As a young man in Anderson County – when food was fixed and put on the table – that is when you sat down and ate it. No one said – I don't like this or that, or so and so took too much corn bread and you didn't get any, just wait until the next meal and be on time and get to the corn bread first.

I can remember going to bed hungry but it was because of staying somewhere too long and getting home late and had to eat what was left – if there was anything.

Don't know how Mom did it because there is more food brought into my house for two of us than Mom had to feed twelve with. Could this be why a few of us are a little overweight?

Pop would buy flour, sugar, corn meal, coffee, salt, pepper, brown beans, white beans and sometimes potatoes. Everything beyond that was raised, hunted or gathered from the wild.

Pop raised the hogs and goats while Mom raised the chickens. Everyone spent time fishing or hunting. Picking wild berries or greens was everybody's job. We did not know what beef was. Thought cows were raised for milk and butter only. Only hamburger was ground at home - mostly from groundhogs or a goat. At Christmas, a few oranges, bananas and grapes were bought. Rest of the year, all fruit was gathered from where ever you could find it.

Pop did come home with a little lard sometimes if we were out. I can remember a can of Crisco Oil for baking now and then and the one-pound blocks of margarine, if he had the money. One of my jobs was to mix the yellow powder to make it look like butter.

Mom cooked the best brown beans that I have ever eaten but sometimes she would cook dumplings in them to make them go farther. I could eat around the dumplings and do just fine but never did develop a taste for dumplings.

No way anyone could have bacon and eggs for breakfast. Sometimes it was eggs and biscuits, bacon and biscuits, or sausage and biscuits, but never all three at the same time. Most times it was biscuit and gravy or a couple of biscuits sopped in a cup of good strong coffee – now that was good eating.

So many preservatives in the food today that you cannot cook it and make it taste like it did 65 years ago. This is why my catfish are so good – catch them, take care of them my way and cook them my way. YUM-YUM-YUM.

JUST BUSHES
(Elderberry, Leather, Buck, Staghorn Sumac)

I am going to get off trees and write some of the bushes that I remember – really just small trees.

The buck bush was not good for much that I can think of – except a good shelter in the winter for rabbits – because it only got about knee high. They were everywhere and all had to be removed, put in a pile and burnt when clearing new ground for next years crop. Had lots of small berries on them but don't know if anything ate them.

The elderberry was another one that did not get very big – about 10 feet tall. This one had a cluster of berries on top of the stock or limb about 10 inches across with about 500 to 1000 small berries in each cluster. The wife and I still pick them each year to make elderberry jelly. They are not good to just pick and eat because they taste bad. They also make pretty good wine. These can be seen in the spring each year, mostly along the road right-of-way and in fence rows. This is when they have a large cluster of white flowers.

The old staghorn sumac is another one that only gets about 10 to 12 feet tall. It doesn't have many things to use it for, maybe temporarily for a walking stick or could be used for bean poles – but only for one year. The sumac has a cluster of seed that grows in the top of it – very pretty but not good to eat. They turn red and can be used in dried bouquets. Good for the winter before they turn black.

The one that I have heard about all my life is really a tree but does not get very big. It is called the leather tree. Pop said this was the only one that you could tie in a knot, go back after a while, and it had untied the knot.

The first one that I ran across was only a few years ago. I was home on leave and brother Woodie took me ginseng hunting up on the hills along Clear Creek, in Woodford County. Started down the creek at a point along the road and went all the way to the river just below Lock #6, then back up the other side. We only found one patch of ginseng that day but did find two thickets of leather trees – only ones I have ever seen. We did not get back to check and see if they were still tied in knots. That was about 33 years ago and I probably could not find them anyway.

WILD VINES OF KENTUCKY

Growing up in Anderson County, one of the things that had a big influence were the vines. Most vines were unnoticed by most people and were good for nothing.

The wild grape vine was not one of them. Besides growing a tasty grape (good to eat only after the frost had got it at least once), a lot of wild animals, birds, and kids (including me) ate them. This vine was great for making swings – just cut it at the ground and if it was big enough, it could be used all summer. Don't try to use them the second year because they die, season out and break very easily.

Take a thicket of small elm trees with a lot of vines growing in them – could get up in the top of them and go for hundreds of yards without touching the ground. This was much more fun than watching television these days.

One of the things we used the grape vine for was smoking them. You had to find a dead one about the size of a cigarette – cut it the right length, light it and puff away. The dead vines had a lot of small holes in them and that allowed it to be smoked. Smokers beware – it had a real bite to it and too much of it made the tongue very sore. Now days they are used to make wreaths for the doors.

Another one that got a lot of attention from me was the green brier. This is one you tried to stay away from. Charging into a bunch of these was like running into a patch of barbed wire. Learn where these are and avoid them when possible.

The poison oak and poison ivy were a couple more that you tried to stay away from. They did not have any thorns like the green brier. Run through a patch of it and in a couple of hours it would show up big time.

A few more vines that were well known were the blackberry, raspberry and dewberry vines. All had delicious fruit on them that was used in a lot of ways.

Another vine to avoid was the wild rose. Some of the farmers in Anderson County used these as fences. You could crawl under a barbed wire fence and a woven-wire fence you could climb, but a wild rose fence you went around it because there was no way possible to go through one of them.

Other types of wild vines are out there but don't know the names of them. Most just get in the way when you are trying to do something – like hunting or just roaming the countryside, as we did a lot of when growing up.

DUTY ON THE HOME FRONT

I can remember the war years very well, 1941 – 1945. I was too young to go into the service and do my share, so it was up to me to do my share here on the home front.

Had three brothers in the service – two Army and one Navy. Two of them were in Europe and one was on a carrier someplace.

One of the brothers was married and one was going steady with a girl in Lawrenceburg, the other was in the Navy and true to from – he had a girl in every port.

Now brother's girlfriend and my girlfriend both lived on the same street, so on Saturday, when picking my girl up, it was my duty to pick his girl up at the same tine when we were going to the movie (if there was enough change in my pocket) or just for a walk through town a few times. Maybe just get in someone's car and watch the people go by.

Back in the 40's, everyone in Anderson County went to Lawrenceburg on Saturday night.

The ones that drove a car or truck to town, parked on Main street, went and did their thing – be it Dime Store, movie, pool hall, etc.

None of the cars were locked and if some of the kids wanted to sit in them for a spell, that was okay. Did not have to know whose car it was because most had the keys still in them. If it was winter, it was okay to start them and warm them up.

About 9:00 p.m., it was time to walk the girls home and then rush back to the pool hall (Sim's) to see who was still around we could get a ride home with. Drink and orange crush or a grapette, and eat a hamburger if there was nay money left.

That was a normal Saturday night back then, when we had a good week at work. We also walked to town on Sunday for the movie – as Sunday was a good musical or a drama. Saturday was always a western.

Guess I did my job okay, as brother married his girl when he got back from the war.

Still spent a lot of weekends with them but by now my girl was dating another fellow. Brother did reward me by giving me a German unifrom he had brought back with him.

ASH, SUGAR MAPLE AND RED CEDAR TREES

I can still remember the ash tree was one that I liked for firewood because it was so easy to split. Have a block of it in the shop about twenty-four inches across that my anvil is sitting on. Don't do much work on it but everyone should have one of them because with a good hammer you can make about anything straight – lawn mower blades. This wood is so easy to split that my block has a few slabs nailed back on that have fallen off while pounding on the anvil. Makes good lumber but a lot of this wood is used for making baseball bats. I believe the Louisville Sluggers are still making them.

There are lots of sugar maples in Kentucky and are noted for some of the brightest colors in the fall when the leaves turn. The lumber from this tree is great for making furniture, shelving and lot of other things. Have heard that the sap of this tree makes fine pancake syrup. Have used a lot of syrup from New Hampshire but never tried to make any from the tees around here. Don't know if the trees in New Hampshire that they make syrup from are the same as they are in Kentucky.

The red cedar is my favorite kind of wood to work with. Growing up, the cedar lumber was hard to come by as back in the 20's and 30's most of the large ones were cut and used. The ones that were left were used for fence posts, posts for the framework of barns, or other places where posts were needed. The old camp house we lived in at Lock #5 was built on five or six of them. The back of the camp house sat on the ground (really a rock ledge) and the front of it sat on a row of cedar posts about twenty feet tall.

The good thing about cedar wood is the white outside of this wood will rot away but the red center will last for ages – and the termites will not eat it.

Bought all my cedar lumber at the sawmill on Lebanon Road before they went out of business. There are still not many big cedar trees around. Most of the sawmills were just squaring the posts and shipping them south for mailboxes and fence posts. Some they were planeing down, grooving and making thin lumber to line closets with.

All the cedar lumber can be used – saw dust, shaving, small blocks for the dresser drawers (keeps moths out and makes the whole room smell good). I used some of the small pieces to make hangars for the closet. Keeps everything fresh and no other wood smells as good as fresh sawed cedar.

MORE TREES

Growing up on the two small farms that Pop owned for a while was an adventure. Pop had rules for each and every tree that was on the land and he had his own rules about each type of tree.

Had lots of dogwood trees and he was very strict about them. We were not allowed to just break a limb off when they were in bloom. At the right time of the year, he would allow some of the older kids to dig up some of the small ones to trade to the fellow in the grocery truck for candy. When he cleared the side of one hill to raise tobacco, there was one large dogwood tree about twenty feet tall and the only one that I ever saw that had a straight trunk on it. This one was dug up and transplanted in my uncle's yard. When it did not live, Pop about cried.

Another one that is very pretty is the red bud. This was not as prized as the dogwood, but these were not cut. We could break the limbs off for Mom when they were in bloom. There was a market for the small ones because they could be sold or traded.

The buckeye tree was fair game for whatever we wanted to do with them except for firewood to cook with. If this wood was brought into the Kitchen, Mom would throw it out. The one that had cut it was handed the chopping axe and told not to come back until he had better firewood. Buckeye wood would not burn – soft and easy to cut. By the time it had seasoned out and dried, it was rotten and would just fall apart when picked up.

The large buckeye trees that survived were another good location for squirrel hunting when they got to the right stage. The buckeyes were also carried in everyone's pocket – saying was they were good for arthritis. Also, always heard that each pod had two buckeyes – one was poison and the other was not and the squirrel was the only one that could tell which was which.

The lowly old linden tree was not good for anything that I know of. Maybe a shade tree – not a good shade tree – but they did have a seed (small seed pod, but don't know of anything that would eat them – not even birds or animals). If Pop found one of them he would send a couple of the kids out to chop it down. He said they just took up space where some other kind of tree could grow. The linden was also a soft wood and easy to cut with an axe. It was hard to saw down because it did not make saw dust like regular wood and the saw would bind in it. This is another one that could not be used for firewood.

HUNTING

My, my, how hunting has changed. Growing up, the family had the following three guns: twelve gauge pump shotgun for rabbits and birds (about a $15 gun); four hundred ten gauge shotgun mostly for squirrels and Pop only paid fifty cents for it in a trade with a fellow who needed to get his car across the river on the ferry; and most times we had a twenty-two caliber rifle for other uses – groundhogs – and it was carried on the night hunting trips in case we got a coon or opossum up a tree that no one could climb. These three guns were used by everyone in the family that was old enough to hunt.

Same clothes were worn for hunting that were worn for everything we did and we walked everywhere when we were hunting.

The guns were only used when we had the money to buy shells for them. If shells were not available, we used other methods for hunting but that is another story in itself.

Today, you have to have a gun for rabbits and birds, another for deer, one for turkey and a couple of other things – targets, clay pigeons, etc.

Boots, pants, shirt, jacks, hat socks and mask for deer and turkey. This can run from three to four hundred dollars.

When hunting deer, you must have a rifle and scope costing around four hundred dollars. A three hundred dollar bow for bow season and about three hundred dollars for a black powder rifle for the black powder season.

It runs into thousands of dollars for a four-wheeler to haul and two hundred dollars for a deer stand, one and about twenty thousand dollars for a 4x4 pick-up to haul the four-wheeler to the site of the hunt.

I don't hunt anymore because my legs won't let me but I do have a couple of memories of hunting years ago. This was when it was affordable and you could hunt anywhere. Property owners did not mind and you could find rabbit or a cove of birds almost any place.

TAKING A RIDE

Pop's car was a 'jim dandy". I believe it was a 1929 Model A Ford and had only two doors but could seat six easily.

Pop could only drive the car to the top of the hill and park it. The road down the hill to the house on the river was a mile or better. Most of the road was okay but he had a few spots where the ledges were too much for the car to get up and down – could only be traveled by foot or with a horse and sled.

The car could not be locked and just a toggle switch to start it. Some nights we would take a ride in it just for fun. One of the older brothers would drive and the rest of us would just sit back and enjoy.

The road from Route 62 to Lock #5 was bout four or five miles with no other traffic, so it was safe to drive without lights at about ten miles per hour.

Never could get away with it though. Someone would hear us and tell Pop about it and he knew it was us as we had the dogs out hunting that night.

For some reason, Pop drove the car down to the house one day and on the way back up the hill, at a bad spot in the road, he got one side of the car off the road. In the process of trying to get it back on the road, the next day, things got out of hand and the car rolled all the way down to the creek.

No one was hurt but no attempt was ever made to get it out. It was cheaper to just buy another car.

We (kids) used it for a playground for a while. Each time the river came up over it, the mud settled on it and was soon buried with only the top of it above the ground.

MINNOW SEINE

The other day I was in my workshop goofing off and noticed the two minnow seines hanging on pegs overhead (one six foot and one ten foot).

This really brought back a lot of memories of growing up and what we used the seine for as kids and some of the material we made them out of.

Just a square of mesh with sinkers on the bottom and floats on the top with a broom handle on each side laced on with twine. A willow pole or a bush of any kind could be used for the sides. We used this to catch minnows anywhere if the water was less than four foot deep.

We made them out of everything such as screen wire, burlap bags, onion sacks and even curtains – anything that water would filter through. The store bought ones cost money and sometimes Pop would buy one. These did not last long as a rock or snag of any kind was hard on them.

We used them for catching minnows, but we also used them to get other types of fish bait – could fill a bucket full of crayfish in no time. Had to have one for catching go-devils – just put it down at the bottom of a ripple in the creek and have two or three people on the ripple turning over rocks and kicking things around. In Elkhorn Creek you could get a bucket full in no time. You could also catch leaches the same way.

A seine was a must if you were fishing trotlines or jingle lines.

Could take a ten foot seine and with one dip in a small farm pond, you could get a big mess of bluegill and save half a day fishing for them.

This did not hurt the environment as the bass or larger fish would jump the back of the seine and escape.

Caught some things in them that you did not want – mostly snakes, sometimes a snapping turtle would really make them mad and they were hard on the seine.

Really don't need them anymore because every kind of bait can be bought at the Bait and Tackle Shop or Wal-Mart. There is even a machine, now, you can get it out of anytime.

THE PARTY LINE

People with phones are everywhere – at home, in the car, walking around, even mowing the lawn. Everyone has a phone in their car, pocket, purse, etc.

I can remember back when everyone was on a party line. That was one line down a lane with up to five parties on it. You picked up on your ring (one to five rings), told who the call was for and most times everyone would listen in.

We never lived in a house that had a phone in it but ran into this a lot when visiting with relatives for friends.

It was hard to get a call out because someone was always on the line. You could ask them to let you have the line but they did not have to give it up. This kept a lot of people upset and mad at their neighbors.

This was back when all the calls went through the switchboard with live operators. Before the time when machines answer most calls. It has gone so far as to the point that machines will call me and they have to talk to my machine.

At present time, there are six phones in my house, one answering machine and one caller identification. Therefore, I do not have to answer when it rings. I just wait and if I want to talk to the person calling I just pick up or call back later.

The old party line was great for keeping up with what was going on with everyone. A great way to know what the gossip was. One short phone call and everyone in the neighborhood knew what you knew.

It would be good to go back to the party line and do away with cell phones, beepers, e-mail, two-way radios, fax machines and a few other things. Maybe we could get people back talking to each other on a one on one basis and you would know within five or six people who you are talking to.

MAKING HAY WHILE THE SUN SHINES

Cutting and storing hay today is a snap – mow it, let dry, rake and bale in large rolls, and store out of the way until needed. All done by one man on a tractor.

Not so easy back in the 40's. Started it off by running the horses down and getting the gear on them. Then the farmer or one of the grown-ups mowed for days, very slow, and after it dried, it was sometimes baled in the small square bales and hauled to the barn on a wagon and stored. This took a big crew and was not all that hard – just hot work.

The way I remember –it was all done with pitchforks

After a few days of drying, horse was hitched to a rake. This put the hay in small piles and took only one man for this. Then the crew came in – two men on the ground to pitch hay onto the wagon; one man to control the horse (usually a team of two) and one or two men on the wagon to place the hay so you could get a big load on. Was a little skill needed for this because the load had to be placed so it was locked together and would not fall off before you got to the location where you were stacking it.

Start the stack out on the ground and build it up as high as could be pitched with the fork. Had to be one man stay on the stack until it was finished because if he got down it was hard to get back up the side.

Stack had to be locked in just like the wagonload. Also had to be tapered at the top so the water would run off when it rained.

Sometimes loose hay was put in a barn. People who had a diary barn sometimes stored loose hay in the loft. Also was used for small square bales. Loose hay stored on the ground in a tobacco barn was hard to get out once it settled.

Haystacks would have a fence put around them if cattle were grazing in the same field. Then a saw was used to saw blocks out of the stack and pitched over the fence for them to feed on. A hay saw was not like any other saw. You would have to see one to know why I am saying this. Still a few of them around in antique shops.

Storing hay in a stack was a hot, dirty and hard job. It really got bad when you got tangled in some blackberry briars or a small thorn tree that got mowed down and raked up with the hay. Also, locust bushes, wild rose bushes, and some type weeds. Most hay fields had one or more of these in them. Also had a few run ins with the old devil ear cactus. Still a few of them around.

Fun part of putting up hay was when being mowed. You could walk on the opposite side of the field from the mower and catch a few rabbits as they came out. They could not run on the loose hay that had been mowed. Very easy to catch them.

THE RIVER

Now they are talking about closing all the locks on the river again. Guess they are going to put in more boat ramps. This could be a good thing or bad thing.

Don't have the sand barges running any more. River is only used for sports and as a water supply.

Pop worked on the oil barges for a short time. Only time he was at home was when they went up or down the river. He would have them tie up some place close to the house so he could have a short visit at home.

They had a tug that pushed a couple of barges. One had a crane on it. They kept the channel cleared of places where the banks had caved in and the trees slid out into the river. They would remove them and put them back onto the bank. Also, where two creeks came out on opposite banks they would dredge them out. Also dredged out when the lock gates got clogged with rock and sand.

There were a number of sand dredges on the river. The one in the pool between Lock #4 and Lock #5 would park just above Glenns Creek and for two or three days it would sit there – pulling everything up, sifting it, loading the sand on barges and the rock went back into the river.

This did not hurt the fishing and it helped keep the channel clear. The rock bar at the mouth of Glenns Creek is about half way across the river now. It makes for a great fishing hole but a few of the speed boats have bottomed out on it over the years.

Back when all 14 of the locks were open, some of the cruise boats and yachts that came through were from as far away as New Orleans, LA. I helped lock some of them through Lock #5 when I was a helper there for a while during WWII.

Had the whiskey spill at Tyrone a while back that killed a lot of fish. Could never understand why they did not open a couple of the gates at Herrington Lake and flush it out and mix it with the water in the Ohio. This should have taken care of the problem. I would rather the lake be a little low than all the fish dead.

SPECIAL DISHES

I can remember growing up and you went to the table to eat, the meat was on a platter, beans, tater and gravy were all in bowls. In front of you was a plate, spoon, fork and sometimes a knife, sup/saucer if you were having coffee, and glass for cold liquid. The glasses could be small jars that cheese spread had come in or just a pint fruit jar. Tablecloth - if you had one – was used for a napkin or your shirt sleeve if you were wearing one.

Now days there is a special dish for everything. There are gravy bowls, relish dishes, butter dish, soup bowls, salad bowls, glass for water, glass for tea, wine glass and a beer glass. The place mat consists of the following items: plate, napkin (ring around it), silverware – spoon for eating, spoon for coffee, spoon for soup, fork for eating salad, knife for cutting meat, and a butt knife. There are special spoons if you are having ice tea, pickles or olives. A dessert spoon and a dish of some kind to put the dessert on – if ice cream, it is a special bowl. The cabinet holds glasses of different sizes and shapes – from a 6 oz juice glass to a 16 oz glass and larger.

Had a run in with a few of these special dishes when growing up. We were working for a fellow over around the Switzer area one time while housing tobacco. Would go to the house each day for lunch – always plenty of food on the table. The man's wife would take the butter (home-made butter), pat it into a round ball and heat the plate before placing the butter on it. Stick the knife to it and it would spin around. She discontinued that procedure after Pop stuck his fork in it, took his knife and cut it in half. He then said – "Help yourselves, boys".

I don't believe that my mother could have handled it with all the extra types of dishes, glassware and silverware while feeding 10 kids. Her dishwasher consisted of washing all of them in a pan with water that had been heated on the stove.

No way she could have kept them all in the kitchen. Only cabinet she ever had was of the old style kitchen cabinets with a flour sifter in it. In fact, the wife and I have one of the old kitchen cabinets in our kitchen.

Mom never had the leisure of running water – hot or cold, sink or dishwasher. In fact, she only had a washing machine for a few years before her passing.

I LOVE VALENTINE'S DAY

Well, Groundhog Day has passed, so it is time to look ahead to Valentine's Day again. Now, this is a holiday I can really get into.

The wife always gets a box of candy, flowers, fluffy stuffed animal and a small piece of jewelry – what could be simpler. It will definitely keep peace at the old homestead until next month (March) when her birthday arrives. It was not like this back when I was in school and later when dating started.

In school, it was a big day for most of the kids. There was no way we could buy cards but the teacher would allow us a couple of hours to make valentines for the ones we wanted to give them to. Also had to make the envelope to put them in.

Ever tried to make a pretty card out of white tablet paper with lines on it? Could draw a heart just fine but never seemed to have a red crayon to color it with. Could write "Be My Valentine" on it. This was done so it could be folded just right and some girl's name on it. It was not very pretty and did not get me many valentines in return. One on my desk was good, but two would make my day. Carry them around for weeks.

Later, after I was out of school working a little, had a bit of change to jingle in my pocket, could go to the dime store and get a pack of valentines (10 or 15) complete with envelopes. Just write the girl's name on them and deliver them.

Now back in my younger days, we lived in Anderson County at Lock #5 on the river. We spent our off time in Lawrenceburg and Versailles (Woodford County). All travel was done by walking and dating girls in both places. The delivering of the cards took some time and doing.

A lot of the girls between these towns were on my list of girls (in my mind). Who got one, whether they wanted one or not. This got rid of all my cards and sometimes they would give me one. (Young love can be a lot of fun).

Got older, went into the Army, and all valentines were sent by mail. Transportation was better (did not have to walk) but by now the girls were in other states besides Kentucky. Some were in other countries, so mail was the only option.

For the wife, it is a trip – of love – to Kroger for flowers, jewelry store for earrings and Wal-Mart for everything left on my list.

SAFETY FIRST

As a kid you expected to catch the following (or have it happen to you): whooping cough, measles, chicken pox, mumps, bad cold, ear infections, sore throat, boils, stone bruises, numerous cuts, scratches and bruises. At least once a year, someone came home with head lice and bed bugs. During the summer there were lots of sunburns, poison ivy, chiggers and ticks. A lot of run-ins with bumble bees, honeybees, wasps, yellow jackets, and hornets. A few bites from one of the dogs or a wild animal we were trying to raise. Then there were the snakes to look out for, turtles and dry land tarpon gave a good bite if you gave them the chance. Lots of burns from fires, hot water, or hot grease. Domestic animals had to be watched. The mule or horse could deliver a good solid hit with the back hooves. Stay out of the field where the bull was. The goat was good at hitting you a good lick if he got the chance.

Always lived on the river and swam there. Also swam in farm ponds, creeks and lakes when we could. Had to watch the water in the winter, as we would skate on anything that was frozen over. Lots of times a fire had to be built to dry someone out.

Someone was always falling out of a tree while gathering fruit, walnuts, hickory nuts, hunting at night or just horsing around. Only bones that I can remember ever being broken were by bother John when he broke his arm, and when a limb broke with me on it and my collar bone was broken. Brother had to wear a cast for a while but we just let mine heal itself.

Some the of the things that had to be watched were the chopping axe, pitch fork, all knives, fishing hooks and barbwire fences. Being bare footed most of the summer, you had to watch out for the thorn tree, green briars, locust trees, blackberry briars and splinters of any kind. Get one of these in the foot and Pop had to take it out when it got infected.

Had to know what eat, what not to eat and how much you could eat. Too many green apples would set the teeth on edge and also make the stomach ache. Pears were okay but too many and they caused all kinds of problems. Too many blackberries, strawberries, hackberries, paw paws, black haws, wild grapes etc., would cause stomach problems. It was easy to eat too much of anything that grew wild and some of them did not mix too good if you ate them at the same time.

The one thing we did not have to worry about was water because there was always a spring, creek, river, pond, cistern, well or pump close by. Wherever you were, all with good drinking water most of the time.

FLAT BOTTOM JOHN BOAT

The flat bottom john boat was the work horse of the boats back in the 30's and 40's. There were other boats on the river, but not many, and some even had motors. Everyone that lived on the river had a john boat with a set of oars.

This boat was used for many things. A lot of our firewood was gathered with the boat. Anything that came down the river during high water, that was floating, was there for the taking. All river fishing was done with the boat. It was used for hunting at times and transportation if work was on the other side of the river. The one we had (sometimes two) never stopped during the day, sometimes all night. Only time the boat was not used was in winter when the river was frozen from side to side, then we walked.

When one of the oil barges went up or down the river, no matter where we were, and if there was a boat nearby, we would ride the waves behind them. (They were all paddle wheelers and made nice big waves, good for about a five-minute ride).

Everyone kept them tied to something with a chain or rope and they were never locked. It was okay to use them if they were put back and tied up so they would not float away.

The john boat did rot out after a year or two and a new one had to be built. You took two large boards for the gunnels, some small boards for the bottom, two ends and the three seats (back, front and one in the middle for the operator. The oars and locks could be reused. Then it took one long 1 x 4 inch down the middle on the inside to stabilize it all. Ends of the boat had to be 2 x 10's in case someone wanted to put a motor on it. A new one had to be put in the river for a few days to swell the lumber before it could be used and you had to have something to keep the water bailed out. Never saw one that did not leak.

Never saw one on a trailer. They were too heavy to move to a lake. Once they were put in the river – they stayed there.

Most people that lived on the river on shanty boats had a john boat that was used when they moved up river. It would just float if they were going down river. Had to have the john boat for landing.

With the boats now a day – they have taken a lot of fun out of fishing and all of the work.

THINGS NOT MISSED

Things have changed a little in the last 60 plus years.

Definitely do not miss the three-mile walk to school and back. It was barefoot on a gravel road in summer and through a foot of snow in winter. I loved going to school but did not like that walk.

The chores in the afternoon such as cutting wood for the stove/fireplace, milking the cow, feeding the horse or mule, packing water from the spring, feeding the chickens, gathering eggs, and feeding the hogs (if we had any).

Fishing lines had to be checked and baited each evening and run each morning. In the winter, all traplines had to be checked each day. Everything caught had to be skinned and hides stretched on a board to dry.

When not in school, it was a one-mile walk each day to get the mail. Up hill one way and on Friday night everyone had to be at the top of the hill to help with the groceries.

Going to bed in the winter in a room with no heat – well remembered but not missed. Taking a bath in a washtub after three or four others not missed. The second setting at Sunday dinner with only the chicken wings to eat when we had company.

Reading and playing games by the light from a kerosene lamp. The maintenance on them was a chore – filling them with oil and cleaning the glass chimney was tricky along with keeping the wick trimmed.

Now the varmints – bed bugs, chiggers, ticks, head lice, roaches, red ants, old corn worms, flies, wasps etc – are still around but easier to control. None are missed.

The outside plumbing. The little house out behind the big house. Bad in the summer with the wasps and all, but really murder in the winter.

Could never miss the one pair of shoes a year that never lasted more than 6 months. The hand me downs were good but do not miss them. The seven-mile walk to Lawrenceburg or the ten miles to Versailles jus to see a movie or girl. Not missed at all because now I can drive.

The shortage of fish hooks. Lots of large hooks around for the trotlines but good bluegill hooks were hard to come by. If fishing with one and hung it on something, you got in the water and got it loose because it was the only one you had. Do not miss this and keep lots of them on hand now.

PEN AND PENCIL

Looking around the house the other day I noticed a number of writing tools that were in the house and the shop. Growing up they were called school supplies (pencils, pens, magic markers, crayons, high lighters) and a number of different kinds of paper. When I was growing up, children got one pencil at a time. When it got too short to use you might have gotten another one. In my shop, there are two (3lb.) coffee cans with all the pencils they will hold. Also, there are plenty of writing tools by the computer.

When in school, we sometimes had a fountain pen (before ball point pens) and a bottle of ink that we shared. Have got two cigar boxes full of ballpoint pens, ink pens and mechanical pencils.

Crayola crayons were the only things that we had to color with. Most of the time they were borrowed from one of the other kids. In the house we have a box of crayons, box of magic markers, some high lighters and a set of water colors (kept on hand for the grandkids, great grandkids and other kids that visit).

When the school year started, we got a tablet of paper with lines and when it ran out we got another one. Now we have a stack of letter size pads, legal pads, typing paper (by the box) for the printer and copy machine. A lot of this is also used by the kids. Also keep coloring books on hand.

The list of things that a kid must have when they start the school year would have been enough to supply all eight grades when we were in school. Cannot believe some of the supplies the kids need for school today. We had books that were used for years. Most of the books today are work books which are used only one year or one month and then you get a new one.

I was not the brightest kid that finished the eighth grade at Lock Road School in 1943. Did not go on to high school because I went to work. I could read pretty goo d and if I bought something at the store for forty cents and gave the clerk a dollar bill, I knew that my change was sixty cents.

Back in the 30's and 40's, if I had had all the pencils, paper, pens and crayons that I have right now, I could have sold them and retired at the age of ten. Don't think they would have made me any smarter though because only the teacher could have done that.

CHRISTMAS DINNER

It's that time of the year again when everyone is putting together food baskets and gathering toys to pass out at Christmas. I don't ever remembering this happening at our house and don't know of anyone that was poorer than we were. Most people were about the same as we were. With no money to buy what we needed, we had to fall back on what we had on hand. If we did not have a ham in the smokehouse, or turkey, a couple of chickens would do. If all the chickens had been eaten, it called for a trip to the woods to kill something (rabbits, squirrel, raccoon, couple of opossums). This was the time of year for trapping and muskrats were easy to catch and rather tasty if you were hungry. Always had flour handy, so gravy was easy. Fruit salad was sometimes a problem. Potatoes and green beans came from the root cellar – don't really know where it all came from. There were always cakes and pies on the table. Fruit, nuts and hard candy always appeared from some place and all ten kids had their stockings hung somewhere. All candy, nuts and fruit were consumed by noon when the food was put on the table, then everyone ate until all bowls and platters were empty – sometimes it took all afternoon, the meat could also be a meat loaf from a goat we had killed or a couple of groundhogs that we had dug out while they were sleeping. Made no difference what was put on the table – no one ever said they did not like it. We ate it because that was what we had to eat. We would have settled for a pot of beans.

Always had coffee but if we wanted tea we would find a sassafras tree, dig a few roots and bingo – we had tea. Kool-aid was cheap and a little sugar made it drinkable. Sweet potatoes were always on hand.

Our Christmas tree was cut from somewhere on the farm – brought in and trimmed with decorations we had used for years.

Pop worked most of the time but we were far from being rich. Most of what we ate for Christmas was gathered during the summer and put away. It all came from the garden or from the wild. Cannot find a nut of any kind today that was as good as the black walnut or the hickory nut that was gathered in the fall and used all winter. Nothing as good as a bowl of jell-o with a banana or two – mix it and sit it on the porch roof until gelled.

Some say we lived a hard life but I can only remember it as a happy time. Family was all together, all were in good health. We made do with what we had. There was nothing wrong with frying up a big platter of buffalo fish for Christmas Dinner, if that was what we had.

THE HORSE-TAILS

I came across the horse-tail plant when we moved from the camp house to the Skelton Farm, just above Lock #5. Did not know what it was or what it could be used for but as kids we found lots of things to use it for.

It grew about twelve or fourteen inches tall and was in sections that could be pulled apart – kind of like pop beads. Used them mostly for make believe logs. Could haul then on a truck, lay them down to make a road and could build a log cabin out of them. Most were about the size of a cigarette – don't think we ever dried them to smoke. This was one thing we did not smoke.

This is the only place that I ever saw these growing. Been all over the world but that was the only patch that I ever came across – about two acres of them and they stayed green all winter.

I was about forty years old when I came across another patch of them while on a picnic at Carter Cave State Park.

Went back up the river, one time, and pulled some of them. Placed them in a flower vase and took them around to show to a lot of people but could never find anyone that had ever seen one.

At the age of about seventy, I did a little research on them. Found a picture and the name that went with it. I found nothing else beyond the following: "pen-size rough-stemmed horsetails are living descendants of tree-size plants that grew 300 million years ago. Pioneers used them to scour pots".

The one that were potted did not live for long – don't think I had enough roots with it. If we ever get into that pool for another fishing trip, am going to get me some more and try my luck once more. Will have to watch my step though because they may be an endangered species.

I don't know of anything that would eat them – horses, cows, and goats would not eat them. I never tried feeding then to the hogs.

CHAPTER SIX

BAT ROCK CAMP

Growing up on the river, our range was from about Clifton up river to above Camp Offutt above Fintville. Had an aunt and uncle that lived about a mile up river.

The camphouse where we lived had a name, I am sure, but don't think I ever heard what it was. The camphouses on the river were not put there to live in. They were mostly for weekends and only in summer. All were closed in the winter.

The Sims Camp, just below Lock #5, had two camphouses on the river and one up on the hill. Spent some time around there with the Sims boys (big coon hunters). Always had a kennel full of coon hounds.

Ripy's Camp, about a mile up river from where we lived, is the one I remember most. This one was owned by the Ripy's that owned the distillery where Pop worked. This was a big two-story rock house. Don't know how many rooms it had but it was big. They had a big party about every weekend. Had a dock on the river and people came by boat. I was never at one of these partied but passed by a lot while they were in progress.

Monday was out day. Party was over and everyone had gone home. The doors had no locks on them and we would go in and kind of clean up the leftovers. Always plenty of chow left and I think we were expected to go in and eat it. No one ever said for us not to and no one ever complained when we did. Well, maybe one time when we made a big mess and did not clean it up and we got word not to do that anymore.

Spent a lot of rainy days in this camphouse. Had a wind-up victrola and records to play and could take a nap. The fellow who took care of it came by but he never said anything about us being there.

Only thing left the last time I was there was the foundation, a few walls, cistern where they caught rainwater and some of the timbers from the dock. There never was a road put in – just a walking path.

Camp Offutt was a scout camp. Never was up there much except in summer when the scouts were in. This camp is across the river from Panther Rock.

Have run across a couple more camps in my readings but for the life of me I cannot remember the. Once was called Camp Lone Star. Ran across one called Buckner Camp but I believe it was in the Frankfort area.

NEW GROUND

Many many years ago when I was into farming no one used fertilizer on the tobacco and corn crops. The crops were not as big as now. Guess we just put more out.

The family always lived on the river and most times there was new land to plow each year. Good thing about bottom land was that each winter between crops, the river came up and the mud that settled on most of the bottom land was washed down from up river. This meant new land after each high water.

At times when the water got high we had to leave the house and move everything up to higher ground. Then clean the house out before you could move back in as the mud settled everywhere.

This was easy compared to what the farmers on top of the high ground had to go through. If they cleared new land, they could raise crops on it for about three years without moving to a new section of land.

What they did was if they raised 9 acres of tobacco and corn – each year they would clear about three acres of new land. Lay aside about three acres each year that had been planted for three years. This was set aside and let grow up again.

Clearing the new land in winter meant all trees had to be cut and the stumps and as many roots as possible removed. Blackberry briars, buck bushes and all small bushes had to be dug up, stacked in a pile and burnt.

After new land had been cleared and all exposed rocks had been removed, the ground was plowed and more rock hauled off. The new ground sat until spring when it was plowed again along with the rest of the land to be planted.

Clearing new ground for crops was not a big job but it did take a lot of time and work. Worst part was if it had a cane brake on it, could never get all the sprouts out. Would spend the summer keeping them chopped out with a hoe.

Just as bad was where locust trees had been growing. They would come up from every little root that was left in the ground and the thorns would give up a fit when setting tobacco plants by hand and doing it with bare feet, the thorns were everywhere.

Farmers keep the land cleared these days. No place to hide or live, so all the rabbits and squirrels have moved to town where no crops or cattle are raised. The land is so grown up that the only thing that can get around on it are deer and turkeys. Some of them have moved to town also and they are hard on windows and automobiles.

THINGS THAT DROVE A MOTHER UP THE WALL

Was not on hand for this but have had the story told to me many times. We were living on the old Skelton Farm just above Lock #5. Baby brother Donnie and sis (who was only two years older) were helping Mom with the wash. They were both small. Sis was operating the handle to draw the bucket of water up the wire from the river. Should explain how we had it set up, a wire from a post on top of the hill and anchored to a post in the river. A pulley on the wire, snap on the bottom for the bucket, small rope to let the bucket down to the water, then pull the bucket back up full of water. Everything used up was pitched over the bank (broken dishes and such). This was the dump where everything was thrown.

Sis was turning the handle and Donnie was helping her dump the water in the tub. They had pulled a bucket full up and for some reason sis let go of the handle without locking it. Brother was holding the bucket of water. Bucket started back down the hill with brother holding on. About halfway down he turned loose of the bucket. Hit in the middle of the dump and rolled all the way to the river. Brother was cut, scratched and bruised all over. This could have been worse, because brother could not swim and could have drowned if he had not let go of the bucket.

Only memory of when we lived on he Gregory Farm just up the road from Fintville. There were four of us up on the hill behind the house playing under some cedar trees. There had been some people talking about a black bear that was in the area. An older brother was telling the story about the bear. Don't remember if it was Pop or one of the older brothers hiding behind a tree. Right in the middle of the story he let out a big roar and believe me everyone vacated the spot in a hurry and headed for the house. Problem: between us and the house was a barb wire fence. The two oldest brothers jumped the fence. I was small enough to go under the fence. Big problem was brother John was just tall enough and moving too fast to see it. Fence caught him right on the bridge of his nose. He survived but it was a mess for a while.

Brother John left us at age 68 and still carried the scar across the bridge of his nose from that wire fence.

HORSES AND MULES

I can remember working a mule for plowing, pulling a sled, dragging logs out of the woods, and pulling the brush out to burn the tobacco beds. Also used a plow horse for this. Only one mule or horse, as Pop's operation was not big enough to support a team.

I am sure that the horses or mules understood verbal commands but getting them to do something with only a verbal command was something that did not take place often.

We used what we called a plow line. This was a small rope tied to the bit in the horse's mouth, brought back and looped over the shoulder of the man behind the plow, then tied to the bit on the other side of the horse's mouth. There were round loops on the harness to run the plow line through to keep it from getting tangled in anything.

Wanted the horse to go left, pull on the left side; go right, pull on the right side; and stop, say whoa and pull on both sides at once.

To make him back up pull a little harder, and to get him started again, just say get-a-up, flip the plow line up and bring it down on his hind end a little hard. That would make him move most of the time. If he did not move, bust him with a big clod of dirt. That would do the job every time.

Don't believe I ever saw a stagecoach, wagon, sled or buggy being pulled by mule, horse or oxen that did not have a set of reins in the hands of someone to steer the team, unless someone was walking in front to lead the team by hand. Just riding a horse, you need a bridle for control.

The one exception I know of is a team of dogs pulling a sled because they do work on verbal commands.

Elephants are controlled with a stick that has a hook in it. Camels have to be steered with a bridle and bit in the mouth.

Animals can be trained to do about anything but horses or mules on the farm must have a method of control besides verbal commands if they are to be worked – be it plow, wagon, sled, mower, hay rake, or just pulling anything from one location to another.

Single trees were used with one horse. Fro a team, you had to use a double tree and two single trees.

The elephants in Vietnam that we worked were very gentle and could move some very heavy logs.

Never worked any of the animals in Korea that they plowed the rice paddies with. They were called water buffalo and they used a big wooden yoke for a team of them. They were also very gentle and easy to work with unless they were spooked someway.

THE SEED CATALOG

Everyday when the mail comes there are from one to seven catalogs in the mailbox. Really need to get a bigger mailbox.

Growing up, catalogs were free but they were limited. Sears put one a year out. Now they put what seems like one a week out. Montgomery Ward put one a year out. One or two companies put out a seed catalog once a year.

Come spring we will get catalogs from eight to ten companies selling seeds, plants, bulbs, trees, and shrubs of all kinds. Complete with pots, tools, how-to books, clothes to wear when working in the garden, with colored pictures of everything on the market.

The early seed catalogs mostly had words – very few pictures and these were hand drawn. Had to order the seeds, plant them and watch them grow to see what they looked like when they were fully grown.

Can remember when we would order a box with x number of packages of seed in it. Sell the seed and mail the money back in for so many points. Collect enough points and earn all kinds of good things – from a small pin to a bicycle.

Sell one box of 50 packages at 10 cents a package. Send the $5.00 back to the company and could get a gift worth up to 50 cents. Sell about a hundred boxes and could get a rather nice gift.

I could never sell even one box. Tomatoes and some others were easy to sell. Carrots, beets, cabbage, and onions were rather hard to sell, so Pop would pay for them and plant them. He was never real good with carrots and some of the other seeds.

Mom bought most of the flower seeds but mostly she saved her seed from year to year.

I always wound up with a 50 cent gift that I broke the first time I used it. This cost Pop about $2.00 for seed that he did not want and he grew a lot of things that no one would eat.

Only one of the 10 kids was allowed to order see each year because it was all Pop could afford.

The reason for this was each family with kids did the same thing and that did not leave many people to sell seed to - as about everyone had kids. A lot of the seeds were sent back to the company.

About a month from now will get my catalogs, look at them and then throw them away. This spring when the weather breaks will go to Wal-Mart or K-Mart, get what plants I need, bring them home, put them out and hope they are what I want. Sometimes they get mixed up and are not what the name says they are.

KEROSENE LAMP AND STOVE

I was 15 before got around to living in a house that had electricity. Never went to a school that had electricity or the bathroom inside. Visited a few places where they had all these good things.

Did all my studying by kerosene lamp. A few times we had a gas lamp but the mantle and globe for them cost too much.

One of the things that was bad about the lamps we used was they had to have the kerosene. This oil came from the store and it was about a 5-mile walk each way. Can for the oil only took one gallon, which was enough for about two days.

They smoked a lot so you had to keep the wick trimmed just right or the glass globe had to be cleaned every day.

The kerosene stove Mom cooked on had a glass jug that would hold about one and a half gallons. This had a handle on it and could be packed to the store and filled. Wicks also had to be trimmed to keep it from smoking. The stove was also a big fire hazard and had to be watched when it was lit. Had an oven on top of it to keep things warm but did not have a water tank on it to keep water warm like the old wood stove.

Pop kept us in kerosene most of the time. Picked it up at work and brought it home.

Candles were kept around in case we did run out of oil.

Always had one or more lanterns around that used kerosene. These were used for hunting and anything that had to be done outside after dark.

The lamp and lantern were very dim and did not give off much light but I don't think any of us suffered any ill effects from it. Very few people back then wore glasses.

Back in the 30's you could buy enough kerosene to last a year for what one light fixture costs today.

The old lamp did not give off much light but they did the job they were made for and we appreciated them. Still have one of them I keep around for when the power goes off.

The old kerosene stove Mom cooked on for a while worked good for some things and did not have to cut wood for it. This biscuits baked in it were not as good as the ones cooked in the old wood stove.

THINGS STORED FOR WINTER

With eight brothers and one sister a lot of things had to be put away for winter. If this did not take place during the summer, a lot of people could et hungry before spring.

The following were canned in fruit jars: green beans, tomatoes, berries of all kinds, corn, pickles (all kinds), pumpkin, apples, peaches, pears, plums, some greens, and beets. Mom must have had over a thousand jars (one-half gallon, quarts and pints) and all were filled with something.

Beans were also dried and stored. A lot of butter beans and pole beans (grown on poles and in the corn in the cornfield). Corn was also dried, shucked and stored in the corn crib. This was used for feeding the hogs, chickens and we roasted a lot of it to eat. Popcorn was dried, stored and used as needed.

Onions were pulled out of the ground, strung up on a string or tied together with the tops and hung up in a dry place. These had to be put inside before the weather got too cold.

Bell peppers were used in the relish along with the hot peppers. Most hot peppers were hung up to dry and then used for cooking.

Potatoes and turnips were buried in a hole below the frost line and then dug up as needed. If a cellar was handy, they could be stored there for months.

Peanuts were pulled, tied in bunches and thrown across a rail to dry. As soon as they were mature (dried real good), they were picked off the vines, bagged and put inside. They kept good all winter and could be boiled in salt water or baked in the oven. Very few people grew these. They did real good in the sandy soil along the river. Gathered the black walnuts, hickory nuts and a few butter nuts. After hulling and drying them, we put them in a bag and they would keep any place.

Cushaws were gathered after frost had hit them a couple of times and stored most any place. We kept them in the barn under a big stack of straw or hay.

All green tomatoes were picked before frost and made into tomato relish.

Honey and sorghum could be stored in metal buckets or lard cans – all we could come up with. Meat was cured and stored in the smokehouse. Most meat we ate during the winter was wild game, fish or chicken.

Herbs were dried and used as needed and most were used in the canning. Sassafras root, for tea, could be gathered, as it was needed. Great when sweetened with honey or sugar.

During the winter, if we ran short of something, we would take the excess of something we had and trade it to a neighbor for what we needed. Sometimes we just borrowed it and paid it back later.

Guess a lot of it was catching. Still like to store for the winter but a lot of the hard work has been eliminated with the coming of the freezer.

BIRDS

I can remember the black crow the best. This is the one we used for pets the most. We were allowed to shoot them if we had more shotgun shells than we needed for hunting. The crow was hard to hit and was a lot smarter than most people gave them credit for. Could have one sitting someplace close, open the door and stick the broom handle out, and he would just sit there, but stick the barrel of a shotgun out the door and the crow was gone in a flash of black feathers.

The blue jay was very entertaining but never knew what they were going to do next. They would attack if you messed with their nest or the young. You could watch them but don't mess with them and they are still that way.

Loved the hummingbirds but did not see many of them. They only came around when certain kinds of flowers were in bloom. Lots of them now as I feed them. Have a hummingbird vine growing on my back deck. They go south for the winter.

Everyone should already know about the buzzard because a brother has already written about the one we tried to use for a kite.

Have felt bad about it the last few years, but the cardinal (or as we called it the red bird) was one that we were allowed to shoot when we were young. Pop did not like red birds.

The blue bird and yellow bird were good ones to watch. They are small but lots of them around. Have a few of them come around now when you put out a certain seed.

One I can remember very well was what we called a mud hen. Always some of them on the river. It is hard to say how many boxes of 22 shells I have shot at them. Never killed one, never even wounded one of them, because when the gun went off, the mud hen would dive. Could hit where he was at, but he always came back up about 10 feet from where he went down.

Always a lot of pigeons around. They nested on all the old railroad trusses and bridges. The young could be caught by hand if you had the nerve to climb the bridge supports. They were a food source so we caught a lot of them.

The old shike-polk was a river bird and a good fisherman. I loved to watch him. He had a long neck and a straight gut, so he ate a lot. The old hooting owl only came out at night but could scare the life out of you if you were close by when he hooted. The small screech owl was worse.

One bird we mistreated was the redheaded woodpecker. He would make all that noise and spend all that time building him a house in a dead tree and we would cut it down for firewood.

DOGS

Growing up we had three kinds of dogs, not breeds, kinds. We had big dogs, little dogs, and middle size dogs. Some had long hair and some had short hair. Some had short tails and some had long tails. Some had long ears and some had short ears. Some had long legs and some had short legs. Some had big feet and some had small feet. But they were all small, medium, or large dogs.

If you had a big dog that had 4 pups, you would give one to us and it was mutt, give one to the Sims family and it was a coon dog, give one to the Hopper family and it was a foxhound give one to the Hunter family and it was a watch dog.

Dogs in the middle size category were mostly beagle hounds. They were all rabbit hounds. They may never chase a rabbit but they were still rabbit dogs.

Some of the large dogs were collies. They were used mostly on the farms for control of the cows or sheep. They had the long hair so were not much good for hunting. Could not get into the briar patches and the burrs and stick tights got so matted in their hair they had to be cut out.

Small dogs were not good for much of anything except to lie around the house and sleep, chase chickens and create problems.

Some of the large dogs were called bird dogs. They cost too much as some could be traded for a good work horse or a good milk cow.

The dogs we had were what we wanted them to be. They were taken along when we went hunting at night, went rabbit or squirrel hunting, went to dig a couple of groundhogs out, or went fishing. Same dogs for everything. They were also used for guard dogs. Kept the foxes out of the hen house and coons or opossums out of the smokehouse.

Can only remember one dog we had that was allowed in the house. A small one that we called Wren. He was I believe, inherited from Grandmother Herrold. He lived to be about 15 years old.

Had a big yellow hound with short hair that would catch him a groundhog about once a week. He would go find him a groundhog hole that was being used. Then he would lay down close by, wait for the groundhog to come out and get far enough from the hole to where he could get between him and the hole. Then it was bad news for the groundhog. Don't believe that hound ever lost a fight with one but came home a lot of times bleeding real bad from the battle – but he would have the groundhog with him.

Always had two or three dogs around. Most were good for something, even if it was just keeping us company when we were out roaming around the country.

THINGS BOUGHT AT THE STORE

I can remember Pop went to the store only once a week. Traded at the Kroger store in Lawrenceburg on Main Street, just up from the Courthouse.

This was about the same thing each week – took the list in, got the order filled, put in the car, and then went to the pool hall for a few beers (sometimes it was a lot of beers).

When he got ready, he got in the car and drove home. Had to park about a mile from the house. Most times someone would meet him with the horse and sled. If they were not available, everyone had to meet him and pack the groceries in.

The groceries consisted of the following: (a) 2-24 pound bags of flour (for biscuits and other cooking – pies, cakes and gravy). Also used for paste to hang wallpaper; (b) 2 pounds of coffee in bags (ground and bagged at the store); (c) 10 to 15 pounds of sugar (except during the war when we had to use a substitute); (d) black pepper and salt as we needed it; (e) 50 to 100 pounds of potatoes (if we did not have any stored from what we had raised); and (e) can of lard if we were running low.

Sometimes a couple of pounds of butter (most time margarine). This was white (looked like lard) but had a package of yellow coloring with it. When mixed would make it look like butter but did not make it taste like butter.

Sometimes Pop would bring home a roll of bologna (about 5 pounds). This was a treat for everyone. Always had some kind of candy (enough so that everyone could have some). Never knew what kind until he got home because it was always a surprise.

Can goods were very rare because they cost a lot and did not go very far.

In summer, if Pop had any money left, he would pick up a 100 pound block of ice when he left town. About 50 pounds left by the time we got it to the icebox.

Jello was a big item to me. Boil the water, mix it in, set it on the back porch until meal time. This was great. Sometimes we had rice pudding with pineapple which was very good.

A few sacks of golden grain smoking tobacco for Pop.

There were times when the following were bought: dried beans, bacon, and maybe a roast. If times were good and Pop was working every day, we got a few bananas or oranges. This was not often and guess that is what made them so good.

The following school supplies were picked up by Mom: pencils, paper and crayons. Sometimes a ruler or colored paper.

All clothes and shoes were ordered from Sears or Montgomery Ward.

Kerosene for lamps, cooking stove (if we had one), and for starting fires each morning, was picked up as we needed it. I can remember packing it 4 or 5 miles.

TOBACCO BARNS

Tobacco barns are still around. A lot of the old one had been replaced by new barns. But if you go out and look, a lot of them that I played in as a kid are still there.

Can drive down the road going into Lock #5 and point out the ones that were there back in the 30's and 40's. Each one of them brings back a flood of memories,

Going in the one just past the old school house is where we spent a lot of time inside during bad weather. Half the boys in school would gather there in rainy weather. Most time we just sat around and talked. We would climb around the rails, see who could find and catch the most mice, and anything to keep us busy for a few hours.

This is also the barn where I got my first experience at breeding a milk cow. Bull was a mean one and I got run down a couple of times. Finally got the job done and took the cow back home.

Just down the road, the farmer used one of his barns to store hay in after the tobacco was stripped. Spent a lot of time there just keeping warm in cold weather.

On down the road, just above where we lived, was the barn where the farmer kept chickens. This was our egg-gathering barn when we wanted eggs to boil. Owner did not mind us getting the eggs but we had to take them some place in the woods to cook them. No fire was allowed in or near the barn.

On down the road was a barn where sacks of walnuts and hickory nuts were stored. Something was put there by the farmer to crack them with and you could eat all you wanted but don't pack any of them off. This farm also had a barn with a basement like under it and was used for milking cows. Tobacco was dried in one end of it and the other end had a hay loft. There were kids that lived here, so we all spent a lot of time in this one.

Most tobacco barns looked about the same on the outside but on the inside most were different. All were tall in the middle and the rails were made out of everything. Most were round poles with end flat where they were chopped out. Some barns had square 4x4's for rails while others had 2x6's or 1x6's. Anything that would support about 20 sticks of green tobacco and a 200 pound man, all at the same time.

All barns had doors on each side that could be opened for ventilation. Closed in damp weather or when stoves were being used.

Some barns had the stripping room inside or built on the side of the barn. This way tobacco could be moved in and out of the stripping room without going outside. Tobacco had to be booked down on a wagon and hauled to the stripping room if the barn did not have a stripping room.

SOCIAL SECURITY CARD

The Social Security Card has a story behind it, just like everything. I can remember coming to Frankfort in 1943 to get mine – 54 years ago. World War II was at its peak. People to work were in short supply. They would not let me work until I got my card. Mine is hard to read but it is the same one typed up for me in the lock tender's office at Lock #4. This was the closest place to get it done at that time.

Everyone has one and if they would think about it, I am sure that each one has a different story to tell.

Did not mean much to me at the age of only 13. Just meant they were going to take some of my pay and send it to the Government. In my case at that time, the Government was just going to keep part of it as I was going to work for the Government.

My card is not like most cards in the area. Got to looking at them a few years back and thought I had the wrong number on it. I discovered that cards issued in Kentucky started with the numbers four-zero-something. Mine started with two-seven-three. Thought about it for a while, then checked around and found out that my number was one in a group of numbers that the Government was going to keep a check on for some reason. Never did find out why and have never been asked about it by the Government. Could be a big Government secret.

Did not use my card between 1947 and 1957. Was in the service and they did not take any social security tax out of military pay until sometime in 1957.

Guess that when all this started it was a good plan and was a move in the right direction. But it has had so many changes made to it you could take all the lawyers in the state and they could not put it straight.

Seems like the people that pay into it for years are supposed to get the benefits out of it. From where I stand this is not the case.

Have known people drawing out of it that in no way have ever paid a dime into it at any period in this life. Some people I know have been getting checks all their loves. All this does not bother me a lot, but it seems like they have to go broke sooner or later.

Can remember when I had a Social Security Number, Army Serial Number, Driver's License Number, Fishing and Hunting License Number – all different numbers. Now all my numbers are the same as my Social Security Number.

This is good as I am not real good with numbers. Only have one number to remember.

SKIPPING SCHOOL

Skipping school at age 12 took a lot of nerve in the early 40's. I still don't know why we did it because it was not very smart. It did not make anyone like me any better. As it turned out, it made a lot of people dislike me for a long while.

Will not talk about the actions that Mom took when she found out about it, but will say it was not very pleasant.

This took place in hot weather. I was the oldest kid in the bunch and was made the leader. Therefore, I got all the punishment.

It all started on the way to school on Monday. My two younger brothers and I decided to go swimming instead of school, for a little while. The school could be seen from the pond.

We swam for a while and then we discovered there were catfish in the pond (yellow-belly pond cats). With the mud bottom we could catch them with our hands. As it turned out, we spent the entire day at the pond. When school turned out, we just fell in behind the other kids and went home complete with a bucket full of catfish. This worked so well we did it again on Tuesday.

Worked out so well on Tuesday, that we did it again on Wednesday. This day we stayed at the pond too long and some of the kids, going across country to get home, joined us for a little while.

Thursday morning, 4 or 5 other kids joined us for the day and we all had a big time. We thought nobody was the wiser.

On Friday, when about 10 other kids showed up, we were going to really make a big day of it. As it turned out this was not going to happen.

So many kids were missing from school that day that the teacher asked if anyone knew why the number of kids were staying home. By now, about half of the school was missing. As always all good things come to an end if too many people know about it. One of the girls, that had been with us the day before, told the teacher we were down at the pond swimming. About noon the teacher climbed the fence and before we knew it she was standing on the bank asking what was going on.

Too late to run, so we all got dressed and spent the afternoon in school getting dressed down by the teacher, while the other kids looked on. All the parents were notified and we paid for it for weeks.

This was the one and only time I skipped school. We had a fellow that was a truant officer and after he talked to us, most would not miss school even if we were sick. He convinced us that we could go to jail for missing too many days of school.

Took us all year to get back on the good side of the teacher.

HEMP

Hemp, as I remember it, was a crop just like corn or tobacco. Sometime, back years ago, it was outlawed for a good reason.

Back in the early 40's the people I worked for part-time were ordered by the Government to raise hemp in place of tobacco for the war effort. The funny part of it was we did not raise it for the stalk to use in rope. All we harvested were the seeds.

In the spring, ground was plowed and made ready just like we were going to plant corn. Instead we were planting hemp.

It was really strange to watch it grow. It came up, was plowed and chopped out just like corn. Got about 10 to 14 feet high and bloomed.

When the seeds matured, it was cut and stacked just like corn.

This is where things changed. The government sent in a machine to thrash it with. The machine was cranked by hand and had a big roller in the middle with wire on it that beat the seeds off the stalk. They fell down into a hopper and there was a fan blade that blew the husk out the other end of the machine.

Seeds were stacked in 50-pound bags and shipped to market.

I never did hear if the farmer made any money on this. Can only remember helping with it for 2 years and then they went back to corn and tobacco.

The thing I remember most was these stalks were just thrown down and it was a river bottom. Before the following spring, there was a rise in the river (after rains) and all these stalks floated off and went down river.

In this way, the riverbanks from Anderson County down to the Ohio River and all the way into the Mississippi were seeded from the seeds we missed.

I don't know how it did on the Ohio and Mississippi Rivers but for the last 53 years I have seen it growing along the Kentucky River banks. It grown just like horseweeds along a lot of banks, seeds itself and grows year after year.

River bottoms are a good place to grow crops but there is always about 30 feet along the bank (usually a tree line) where no crops are put in (always a lot of weeds). While on fishing or hunting trips, I have seen hemp growing there. This is not put there by anyone but just growing wild.

This is not the type of hemp they grow for other purposes. To me this is just a weed that grows wild.

Never did know why the Government had us grow it. Someone said it was for the oil they got out of the seed.

PETS
(LATE 30's and EARLY 40'S)

While watching a kid the other day playing with a hamster it really brought back memories of some of the pets we had a few years back. We would try to raise anything.

Young squirrels were the best but far from the easiest to catch. After they grew up, they did not stay around long especially when they met a lady squirrel. It was more fun for them to live in the wild, therefore most of them would leave home before summer was over. I can only remember one that lived in a big water maple in the front yard for a couple of years. Flying squirrels were nice pets but hard to find.

Tried raising a lot of young rabbits but never got one to live long enough to really tame them. Groundhogs made good pets until they grew up and became hard to handle. Raccoons were good but always into something. Never did try a skunk because Mom would not hear of it.

The big problem was we were never allowed to put one in a pen or cage. So when they got ready to leave – they left.

I think my favorite was the crow because they could be trained and were easy to feed. Sometimes they would leave for a few days but would come back and stay for a couple of years. They would leave for months at a time, then one day you would look up and there he sat hollering to be fed. This was the only bird we were ever able to raise and we tried them all.

We brought a few snakes home but Mom really put her foot down and we had to get rid of them.

There were always dogs and cats. Also, had some goats, ducks and chickens. One time, tried geese until we fed them some leftover cornmeal where Mom had fried some fish. The salt was not good for them and they only survived a couple of days after the feeding.

Pets were never allowed to stay in the house. Most of them lived under the house (crawl space) or in the barn. Sometimes, even the dog or cat would leave home if they found someone to feed them better.

Now days you go out and buy the pet you want. In my days of growing up, you went out and caught one while they were young. The kind of pet you had was what you found.

CRIMES IN SCHOOL
CRITERIA 1938 – 1943

The big crime when I was in school was playing hooky – now called skipping schools. Do this too often and parents were hauled into court and fined.

The one I helped with most was destroying the boys' outhouse. On average about once a year – sometimes it took longer. Each time they built a new one. All the boys were to whittle a few shavings off with the pocket knife each time they went to the outhouse. All boys had to pack a pocket knife or borrow one for this purpose,

Did not show much as it was done very slowly. By the end of the school year you could stand on one side and see anyone standing on the other side. When it got so bad that it was in danger of falling down, they would build a new one.

In winter, the teacher would bring a large onion with her each morning and as soon as the fire was started, she would lay it on top of the stove. It would lie there all day and it was really something to look forward to – sitting there all day and smelling it. Was a feather in your hat if you could get this onion, take it outside, and throw it away. Teacher said this would keep us from catching a cold.

My big crime was spending as much time on the girls' side of the school as they would let me. The games they played were more fun that the ones they boys played and I did not have to get in the boxing ring the boys had set up   - just to prove how tough I was.

Climbing the fence and getting over on the farm property behind the school was a no-no. The road ran in front of the school and no one got in the road before school was out. Sometimes three or four cars would pass each day. Lower side of the school property had a rock fence. Cross this and you were on the property of the colored school. No one ever went over this fence unless we had a ballgame with them.

Bother someone's lunch and the kids would put you out of the school for a few days.

Teacher hit brother John across the head with a ruler one day and he took it away from her. She expelled him on the spot and I think he was ready to quit anyway.

Cistern house was off limits unless it was your day to carry the water.

Benches or desks seated two people. You had a seat and this is where you sat. Only the teacher could tell you to change seats. Boys and girls were not allowed to sit together.

This is just a few of the things about a one-room school with all eight grades together. It worked for me and a lot of other people. We went to school to get our education and nothing beyond that.

THINGS SAVED FOR LATER USE

Growing up I can remember Mom taught us to save everything. Most people who know me real well say I am still that way. This is not so because I don't save string like I did as a kid. I still have a pair of wool pants that I had issued to me in 1947.

Got a box with 32 wrist watches in it. When they stop running I put them in the box and get a new one. Oldest one I have had since the early 60's.

Back to the 30's and 40's – everything was of value. String of any kind was saved until needed. Got a chance at old worn out clothes and they were taken home. Any kinds of rags, Mom could make a quilt top out of anything. Buttons were saved in case one was lost from a shirt or coat. Never saw anything wrong with wearing something with seven or eight different kinds of buttons on it as long as they were close to the same size but did not have to be the same color.

Nails of any kind or size were saved, as were nuts, bolts, washers and any kind of screws.

Old shoes were saved. Worn out and falling apart but were still good for repair on the harness for the horse. Soles were for hinges on the barn, out building and any gate we had to put up.

All cans, jars or boxes were used for something so we saved them. Have lived where the only insulation we had was the cardboard boxes tacked to the wall.

Any scrap wire was saved and used for mending fences, clothes lines, hanging things up (such as a ham or shoulder) so the mice could not get to it. Also for tying logs that were caught from the river. Could tie the boat with it or mend a broken oar. Good for all kinds of things.

Sears or Montgomery Ward catalogues were saved for the outside john. Newspapers were saved to wrap lunches, start fires or paper the walls with them.

Bottle caps were saved by all the kids for trading. All bottles were saved mostly to play with but some of them could be returned for a deposit.

Any potato peelings, overripe fruit or vegetables were fed to the hogs. If there were no hogs or chickens to eat it then it was put on the garden for fertilizer.

The small tobacco sacks were saved. Mom dyed them different colors and made a quilt top out of them.

About everything was saved. If something broke and could not be fixed, it was stored in the attic, barn, or one of the sheds. Sooner or later someone would use it for something.

SMOKING THEN AND NOW

Growing up, smoking was not a big deal. Smokes were hard to come by. When you were lucky enough to get a sack of tobacco or a pack of cigarettes, you kept it hidden because everyone was looking for a cigarette. Could use a full pack in short order and only smoke 5 or 6 of them.

Pop smoked Golden Grain tobacco. Came in a small sack with a package of papers. Rolled his own and that was not an easy job. There were other kinds of tobacco - Bull Durham and Dukes Mixture. Each bag came with about 20 papers. I started out smoking Dukes Mixture because the label on the sack was yellow and looked better than the others – only reason I can come up with. Took about fifty bags of tobacco before I could roll one like Pop. He could roll one with the wind blowing hard. I still cannot do this.

Really started out smoking other things – not tobacco. Had a weed that grew wild in the area we called Rabbit Tobacco. Once it grew up the leaves on the bottom dried out. This is when it was gathered to smoke. Sometimes we used corn silk – rolled in the corn shucks. This had to be in the fall after they had dried.

Grapevines could be smoked year round but you had to find dead ones. This was very hard on the tongue as they had a bite to them. Too many and the tongue was sore for days.

Could always get tobacco out of the stripping room – really the trash that was not sold – newspaper or brown bag to roll it in. If you could come up with a few good leaves, could roll a cigar out of this.

Got around to trying all of it. We would roll cigarettes out of pipe tobacco. Bugler came out with a machine that you could roll a good one with – tried them all. Have tried smoking chewing tobacco but that does not work at all.

Then we discovered ready made cigarettes – they cost a lot. To be cool, you had to have a pack of Lucky Strikes – still rolled your own. The pack of Lucky Strikes was packed in the sleeve of your T-shirt. Run out of tobacco, it was okay to smoke these. Mostly they were for show.

Tried a pipe and spent a lot on pipes but never found one that I liked. Cigars are okay. Still smoke them – only a few brands. Most I don't care for.

Have walked ten miles as a kid picking up cigarette butts along the road. Take the tobacco out of them, dry it good and then smoke it. Sometimes would get enough for a full bag of tobacco. Then they started to put filters on them. This did away with recycling the cigarette butts.

Back then you could smoke about anyplace, except church or the movie house. Today it is hard to find a place where you can light up without someone complaining about it. That's okay though because sometimes I light a cigar just to hear them holler. Most times I try to be nice though and not light one where I'm not supposed to.

THE SETTING HEN

I can remember the setting hen very well, not because they were fun but because they were mean. She could be your pet all year, eat out of your hand and follow you like a good dog but come setting time – stay clear of her. She would flog you in the bat of an eye. I don't know about ducks, turkeys, geese or gennys but setting hens I know about.

Most hens took to one of the nests in the chicken house and they would let me know when they were ready. When I went to gather eggs, Mom would put a big X on about a dozen or more eggs and put them under the hen and leave her alone until they started to hatch. They were the biggest and best looking eggs we got from all the chickens we had.

Our flock consisted of domineckers, rhode island reds and sometimes white leggings. Most of them would hatch if Mom picked them.

Being kids we would dream of having a few fighting chickens. We would gather a few eggs from the neighbor's barn (who had game chickens) and sneak them under the old hen. If they happened to hatch and got frying size, they would wind up in the skillet as fried chicken.

My grandmother gave me some goose eggs once and I was allowed to put them under one of the hens and four of them hatched.

We tried duck eggs a few times but never had any luck with them.

Some of the hens would not lay eggs in the chicken house but would pick a spot, lay her eggs and sit on them until they hatched. If the weather was right and some varmint did not find the nest, she would show up with a flock of baby chickens.

They were great at hiding a nest. If we knew she was sitting some place we would follow her after she came in to eat. Most of the time she would out fox us.

To get the hens to lay eggs in the nest Pop had built, we had to keep a nest egg in each one. A nest egg was carved out of marble and cost a lot. We would use a doorknob or rock shaped something like an egg.

The setting hen was very protective of her eggs and baby chicks. She could draw a little blood on the hand or arm if you bothered her or her chicks. It was a treat to watch her feed and teach them what they had to know. She could whip three or four other chickens if they got close. A dog or cat did not have a chance at all and it did not take them long to learn to stay clear of the setting hen.

MUDSLIDE AT SWIMMING HOLE

All big swimming pools today have a slide of some kind in them. I believe many were copies off the old mud slides we had at all good swimming holes.

Pick a place with a steep bank, add a little water, get your clothes wet and after sliding down the bank a few times, the mud would smooth out and get slick as ice. After a couple of hours the slide was worn down to where everyone would fit into it just right. The more it was used the faster it got.

Once a slide was established it could be used all summer. If it sat for a few days without being used, it just took a couple of trips down and you were back in business.

Mud could be added at the bottom to make a jump and this could be as high as you wanted.

It was an extra thrill if a swinging rope could also be put up. This could not be done if there were no trees close to the slide.

All the homes along the river, where there were children, had at least one slide and rope swing – sometimes more.

The slide was a great source of fun as long as no one got mad and booby trapped one of them. A small rock buried in a slide made for all kinds or problems. This could take the seat right out of your pants and sometimes a little hide. Rocks were the only things allowed for this. If glass or tin had been used it could have hurt someone real bad. A scratch was okay, but a cut was a no-no.

The slides were hard on clothes and a lot of jeans were worn out on them. A good patch on the seat took care of the hole and made them ready for the rest of the summer.

CANNED CHICKEN

I remember back in the late 30's we did not have a freezer or refrigerator, just an ice box. Mom would can about 100 chickens twice a year. I don't know what all she did to them but I helped pick the feathers off and clean them.

It all started in the spring when the baby chicks were ordered from Sears and Roebuck. Arrival day was a guessing game so we would meet the mailman every day until they arrived. They would die if left out in the weather too long.

They were kept inside a shed where they were fed and watered until the feathers started to develop. Then, every morning, they were turned out to scratch and feed themselves, or food could be put outside for them. Keeping up with them was assigned to the kids because they had to be kept out of the garden and away from the old setting hens that had their own chicks. Around sunset they were returned to the shed and closed up for the night.

Mom was the only one who knew when the time was right. An older brother had the job of chopping the heads off while the rest of the crew were put to dipping them into a tub of boiling water so the feathers could be picked off. Big feathers were thrown away while suitable feathers were dried and used for a new feather tick for the bed.

They were scorched with a burning newspaper or any paper to burn the hairs off, dressed, cut up, packed in jars and cooked. I believe salt was added to the jars along with water. This was called cold packing. After jars were cooled they were stored with the beans, tomatoes and blackberries.

Chicken livers, hearts and gizzards were cooked and eaten. Sometimes the neck and other parts were used to make chicken soup with a few homemade noodles. I could eat it for days with biscuits or cornbread.

This happened twice a year, as there were another 100 chicks ready in the shed.

When they were frying size, it was another day for canning. Enough was put away to last all winter and no one ever put up a fuss when they were put on the table.

During the summer, we ate a lot of fried chicken. When the ones that had hatched at home reached frying size, the roosters were taken out and cooked. Pullets were allowed to mature for egg production.

THE FISH BOX

Today, the summer is spent on lakes and on the river catching fish, cleaning them and freezing them for the winter. As for me, I like catfish and try to freeze about 100 pounds of fillets each summer. This way, there are enough of them to give a few pounds away, now and then, to my friends.

Back in the 30's and 40's things worked a little different. If you wanted a mess of fish in the winter, you braved the elements by going out and trying ways to catch them. The big secret of keeping them for later was the fish box.

The fish box was constructed out of chicken wire and a few pieces of wood about 2 inches square. This was about 3 foot square and could be made out of slats if chicken wire was not available. I have seen them made out of small twigs or bamboo.

Box had to have a small door on top, which was put on with two pieces of leather (usually cut out of an old pair of shoes). Sometimes the sole was used and the door was fastened down with a staple used for putting up fences and a piece of wire. Put a four-foot chain on it to tie to something and put the box in the river. This way you had fresh fish whenever you needed them.

The fish had to be caught but with the help of hoop nets and trotlines the box had fish in it most of the winter.

I have heard that some people along the river still use the fish box. With the boat's live well we can keep then alive until we get home. Then they have to be cleaned and frozen. Not as fresh as they are out of the box but almost as good if they are frozen, thawed and cooked correctly.

The only fish you could not keep in the box was the white perch. They would not live in the box and had to be cleaned and cooked right away because they are not good frozen and I don't know why.

Never tried the spoonbill catfish in the box because they never lasted that long. With no bones, they went from the river to the kitchen right away. If we got a big one (40 to 50 pounder), the neighbors were invited to help eat it. Today, they call it a fish fry but back then I don't think we ever had a name for it.

FISHING

Catching fish today is a lot easier than it used to be, with all the technology. There are different types of tackle, bait, fish finders, depth finders, fish callers and styles of boats. It is a matter of spending lots of money catching the fish you want, putting them in the freezer and using them as you need them.

When growing up we had to do a lot of planning to go fishing. In the fall we went to Woodford County where all the cane brakes were and cut all the cane poles we could carry back home. These were stacked by a tree and tied with a string so they would not blow down. They were left there all winter to season out. Poles from this stack were used all summer. Bait was found and gathered in all kinds of locations. It all depended on what kind we were going to use and the kind of fish we were going after.

Bluegills called for the following: red worms (dug), bagworms (in season), horseweed worms (most of summer), young wasps, crickets and grasshoppers. Plenty of bluegills in the river, large creeks and most farm ponds.

White perch called for small crayfish or green worms. Crayfish were caught in the creeks. Soft craws were the best but had to be caught by hand at night and only after the water got warm. Green worms were dug along the river bank by the bucket full, almost any place. You just took a hoe along and dug them whenever you needed to.

Buffalo and carp called for red worms, nightcrawlers or dough balls.

Catfish were hard to catch. They called for soft craws or shad gizzards (if you could locate them). Sometimes you might get lucky and catch one with red worms or nightcrawlers. Yellow belly or pond cats were easy to catch and we caught a lot of them. I believe there were five ponds in our range that had them and they would bite on anything. Chicken livers were fried and eaten – not used for fish bait. Peddle fish or spoonbill cats would not bite on anything (never caught one). Pop would get one in a net every so often.

Crappie and bass called for live minnows. Did not fish for them a lot because of special laws (size limit, time of year, and how many you could keep). Laws back then were enforced.

Suckers were easy to catch but not much of a demand for them. Alligator gars called for a piece of red cloth, rod and reel. There were caught for sport only.

There were not many times that I could enjoy anything more than a lazy afternoon on the bank of a pond, river or creek, poles sat out and laid back in the warm sun. Times were that I did not care if the fish were hungry to bite or not – just Pure Enjoyment and still is.

TOBACCO BEDS

I remember when gas and plastic were not around and float beds had not been thought of. Growing tobacco plants was quite different from today.

Plants were sowed in beds from 100 to 500 feet, depending on the amount of tobacco you were going to raise. It was not so much by the pound but by the acre.

The beds were plowed early. They were always the same width but as long as you wanted. All brush left from cutting firewood or from clearing new land was saved for burning. In fact, anything that would burn was saved.

This was dragged, packed or hauled to the site of the soon to be tobacco bed and piled on the plowed ground. How high it was piled depended o the amount of material you had on hand.

When this was dried real good, and the weather was right, it was set ablaze so the wind would ignite it all the way to the opposite end.

Three or four people were on hand with pitchforks, rakes, or poles to keep the fire going until everything was burnt to ashes. After a short cooling period the bed was raked and worked over until it was smooth and all large clods were raked to the side.

There were a couple of reasons for this but the main reason was to burn the seed from weeds, grass and trees. Wire was cut and loops placed in the center to hold the canvas up. (Sometimes the beds were lined on both sides and ends with poles to fasten the canvas to).

Pop would mix the tobacco seeds with the ashes from the stove and sow them on the bed. (Seed had been saved from last year's crop. The seed head from the biggest plants were bagged and dried all winter).

Now, the canvas was put on the bed and watered. While we waited for them to come up, Pop took a twelve foot 2x12, put legs on it and used it across the bed for weeding and for pulling plants when they were ready to set in the field. (The burning did not get all the seed. Weeding the bed took place a number of times).

About ten to twenty feet of one bed was saved for lettuce, radishes, tomato plants, cabbage plants, and any other plants that were needed for the garden.

After all fields had been set and reset, beds were disked up and some type of crop was raised in it (tomatoes, beans etc.).

ONE-HALF OF A CANOE

The summer I spent with my cousins taught me a lot. One thing was not to take things at face value unless you saw it and never buy a pig in the pole. They also taught me that if you bought something from them, first thing to do was to look at it – anything they sold you.

They told me that for fifty cents I could buy half of their canoe. This was a lot of money so I had to think about it for a few days. With a lot of talk and promises, I finally agreed to the deal. Did a lot of dreaming about using it a couple of months each summer and thought maybe for another fifty cents, later on, I could buy the other half.

The deal did not turn out the way I had pictured it. After I paid them the money, we went to the barn where it was stored. I got just what I had bought – one-half of a canoe. They had caught half of a canoe going down the river. The other half they did not have. Right off I knew they had flimflammed me. Knowing this I did not let on that I was mad. They were both bigger than I was, so whipping them was out of the question. I had tried this before and lost.

So, in a business-like way, I went to work on it. By placing a small board across the broken end, caulking it with some river mud, and a few practice runs, I could get around fairly well by sitting in the good point (pointed end). The other end had to be kept up and out of the water. Anyway, I could out run them in a john boat.

The boy scouts at camp up river talked about cutting one of their canoes in half and using it for racing. However, the camp counselors would not allow it. They did try mine out a few times. I even got to know some of the scouts.

This was used for the rest of the summer and when I went home, I paddled it all the way down river. Sure got a lot of hard stares and several comments were made.

When summer was over I had gotten more than my money's worth out of what, at first thought, was a bad buy. Also, a valuable lesson remembered to this day.

THE CLUBHOUSE

When we decided to build a clubhouse, the nearest kids lived about a mile away so they were not going to be much help. We started off big with really too much help. Everyone wanted to do things a different way. Along the middle of summer, with only the floor and foundation done, most of the help quit showing up. That is when my four brothers and I decided we had had it and changed the plans.

About halfway up the cliff there was a rock ledge that stuck out about ten feet (used a lot in rainy weather to stay dry). This spot was well hidden in summer when the trees had leafed out. The five of us went to work in this area for our clubhouse and hideout. Packing in a lot of rock we put up a wall around the outside of the ledge, leaving a hole big enough to get in. Working with whatever tools we could get, the inside was quarried out to make the bottom level and room to stand up. The back was worked into shelves where we kept our valuable things. Our valuables consisted of the following: cans, jars, shells we had picked up, empty boxes (don't remember why), glass stoppers used with the cork ring on most bottles (real prize and could be traded for lots of things), fish hooks, ball of string and all kinds of bottles. All of these were kept out of sight.

The rock wall was hard to see but we placed some cedar trees in front of the hole. These had to be replaced quite often because the needles would dry and fall off. We did not want to make a path, so we did not always go in the same way. Had to be especially careful when we had a fire going (not too much smoke). Cracks between the rocks were plugged with mud or dried leaves in order to keep the wind out and the light in at night.

Food could be kept there for a short time but had to be watched close or a varmint would get it. Items kept were: walnuts, hickory nuts, fruit, potatoes, dried corn and wild grapes. A sack full would last for a week. These were items that were mostly picked in the wild.

This was more like a cave than a clubhouse. There were only six people (someone told sis) who knew about it up until the time me moved.

As far as I know, it is probably still there. I have not been back but can remember a lot of hours spent in it. This was definitely quality time.

The clubhouse we had all started never did get finished because when the weather turned cold – it was turned into firewood.

FLOWERS

When growing up I remember Mom grew a lot of flowers. She always grew them in the garden. Marigolds to keep the insects out, lots of zinnias because they were pretty and sunflowers for the seeds.

There was always a lilac bush around someplace. Tried roses a few times but never had much luck. A few petunias each spring and always a lot of cockscombs. Sometimes there were bachelor buttons. Mom even tried the straw flowers a few times, which made nice winter flowers. Rose of Sharon was a good one.

Loved all the flowers but the real pleasure came in the spring when the wild flowers began to bloom.

The first to bloom was what we called a cliff flower (probably had another name). It grew on the face of a rock ledge. Usually a damp one with water seeping out the cracks. This was very pretty only because it was the first to bloom. Then came the very pretty blood root. It was all white and yellow but only lasted for a few days. Then the crows foot and bumble bee flowers came and would last a couple of months.

By this time, the cliffs were a carpet of blooms.

The bluebells grew in patches and you had to know where to find them. The jingle bell was a loner because it grew by itself but was everywhere.

Wild corn was not the prettiest but was different from all the rest. Pinks and reds were small but lots of them around. All cliffs had redbuds and dogwoods. Sometimes you would find a wild plum tree mixed in with them. They bloomed along with the apple, cherry, pear and peach trees in the orchard.

While hunting or just walking in the woods, something new was always showing up. Always got a big kick out of finding a jack-in-the-pulpit.

It was a bonus to find a patch of ginseng or yellow root because you could sell the root.

Along the river banks, the hardichokes would bloom and looked a lot like a black-eyed susan. The moss that grew on the rocks, in damp places, was a different kind of flower all together. The Dutchman britches and lady slippers were all around.

There was the golden rod, which grew mostly along the highway and in fence rows. Now there are whole fields of it.

There are hundreds of flowers out there and some I don't have a name for. The names I do have are mostly made up but this is what we called them. One example is the May Apple which grew a fruit that looked like an apple but each bush only grew once.

I still go out each year just to look at them and get a real treat out of it. There may not be as many of them as there used to be but they are out there if you only look for them.

HITCHHIKING

I discovered the art of hitchhiking at about the early age of fourteen. While living in the country and on my way to town with four dollars in my pocket, I was picked up by a truck driver. He was a cross-country driver who took me to town. He was hauling tomato juice from St. Louis to Kingsport, Tennessee.

He said he would be coming through town the next Saturday morning and if I would meet him I could ride to Tennessee and be back in town by Sunday afternoon. It sounded like a good deal to me and all I needed was a couple of dollars for food.

I told everyone that I was going home for the weekend and told everyone at home that I was going to work all weekend. This way all ends were covered and no one would miss me.

That was quite a ride because I had never been to the mountains and at that time Route 127 went over some big ones. The driver's name I cannot remember.

He would always stop before starting up the mountain and put a big rock on the running board. It was my job to ride on the running board and if the truck stalled out, I would jump off and put the rock behind the back wheel. This was to keep the truck from rolling backwards while he was starting it again and moving. Lots of times we were moving so slow that I could walk along side the truck.

Also had to help unload when we got to Kingsport. It was always easy going back because we were empty. Always got back to town just in time to catch a ride back to work.

Made the trip three times that summer and no one ever missed me. Thought about being a truck driver after school but they did not get much sleep (couple of hours now and then).

Later in life, I crossed the country a number of times this way. I could put on my Army unifrom in Texas or New Mexico and leave the same time as the bus and be home before the bus arrived. A lot of times I would do the driving while the fellow giving me a lift got some sleep in the back.

I don' think it would be much fun today because of the danger, and would not be as fast and easy. Still see hitchhikers out there and it brings back memories.

THE STOCKYARD

The stockyard at Tyrone was not really a stockyard. It was a pen where about two or three hundred head of stock were kept for feeding only. We kids called it a stockyard.

If we were on good behavior, the guys working there would let us help feed the cattle.

Everything left over from making whiskey at the Distillery (Ripley Brothers) was pumped to tanks at the stockyard – called slop. Some went to the drying house, where Pop worked, and was dried, bagged, and shipped out for cattle feed.

Twice a day the slop was drained into troughs around the pen, and what the workers called the husk off cotton seed was mixed with it. The cattle would eat this to put on weight until they were shipped out and a new herd was shipped in. The husk of the cotton seed was shipped in by box car just like the grain for the distillery. The husk was shoveled into the troughs which was what we got to do. This was a little work but afterwards we were allowed to play in the husk that was left in the box cars. Almost as much fun as swimming – only dry.

Sometimes there would be eight or ten children there and it would make for a real fun day.

Spent a lot of days doing this, both summer and winter. It only lasted a few years and they started drying all the feed and shipping it out. This took some fun out of our days but I still remember the day we did spend there.

We could always find something to do to take the place of the days at the stockyard.

Thinking back, the place really smelled for about a mile away and that could be why it was closed down and moved.

TIME SPENT AS A LOCK TENDER

Summer of 1943 I was asked to work for the government as an assistant lock tender at Lock #5. The fellow who had the job was drafted into the Army.

Working for the Government had a lot of drawbacks, especially at the young age of 13 but I was looking for a summer job with school out.

First problem – I had to have a social security number and card. The only place to get one was at Lock #4 in Frankfort. The lock tender, at the time, had a car so off we went. The procedure took all day but I signed up and got my card. Today, I believe you almost have to have a social security card before leaving the hospital after birth.

Working for the Government was not much of a change from the way things have been all along. The property that went with the lock went so far up river and so far down river. Lock #5 property joined our farm and had a few acres of bottom land that was used for crops each year and was raised by the lock tenders. There were not many boats to lock through, so most of the day was spent in the tobacco or corn crops (about half on each east side of the river). I spent most of the summer in the crops. A bell was rung if I was needed at the lock and I would drop whatever I was doing and report to the lock.

This was a summer I will never forget because I had spending money all summer. I don't remember what I was paid an hour but every two weeks the Government sent me a check for around $80 after taxes. Half of the money went to Mom but there was still more left than I knew what to do with.

The summer went much too fast for me and I was soon back in school. I had a lot of good stories to tell. Some of them were true and there was a lot of truth in all of them.

About all the young men were in the service at the time, which made a 13 year old popular on weekends because of having a steady job and money in the pocket.

THE MILK COW

Today, I don't know of anyone who owns a milk cow for the sole purpose of giving milk for the family. If you need milk, you go to the store and buy it.

Growing up, I can remember that most of the time we had a cow (never two or three – just one). If we did not have one of our own, a neighbor would give us what milk we needed. When we had a cow, Mom would give milk to the neighbors that needed it.

The cow was milked twice a day and milk was cooked in the spring house. If there was not a spring house, the milk bucket just sat in the spring. Sometimes there was ice for the icebox but not all the time.

Cream was skimmed off the top after it had sat for a while. This was poured into the old wooden churn. After churning for a short time, the butter was removed, shaped and cooled.

Buttermilk, that was left, was drunk at meal time. It was delicious with biscuits or cornbread.

I cannot remember at what stage the milk would clabber, but the water would settle to the bottom and the top of it would get hard. It was about like jell and could be eaten with a spoon. I always thought this was when milk was the best. Have not seen any clabbered milk since the early 40's.

Milk was used to make cottage cheese but I was never taught this process. It was always around to drink along with coffee or water.

The milk was also used to make milk gravy. Now days, I just open a can of condensed milk for this.

There were a few drawbacks to having a milk cow. We lived on about fifteen or twenty acres of land (2.3 of which was a river cliff with the exception of 4 or 5 acres). It was all grown over with bushes and weeds. Twice a day that cow had to be looked for and driven to the barn. Most times from the cover farthest from the barn. Never had one that liked to be milked.

Sometimes the gate was left open or she would just jump the fence. Checking to find where she got out and tracking her down would take most of the day or night, sometimes.

Going to the store to pick up milk brings back a lot of memories that I cherish very dearly. I don't think my neighbors would let me keep a milking cow in the backyard, so I will just have to live with things the way they are today.

TRASH PICKERS

There are so many things thrown away these days that trash pickers go around in trucks (even new trucks). I suppose they sell most of what they pick up.

I can remember back when there were not many people, no trash pickup and no landfills. Everyone hauled their own trash. All factories and distilleries had their own dumps. This definitely would not work today, but fifty or sixty years ago some of these dumps were real gold mines.

The distillery was the first place to check. They always threw something away that could be used. Such things as: old barrels that were damaged were a real find, lumber from repairs could always be used, bottles, boxes, packing crates and feed sacks. If the feed sacks had a little dried feed in them, it was great for baiting a fishing hole.

Back in the 30's, the dump for the old dye factory in Lawrenceburg was where we got all of our fishing line, string and thread. When a spool of something did not come out the right color – they threw it away. In one day, you could get enough to last a year.

The pencil factory, not long ago, in Georgetown, had a dump where in a few minutes you could pick up enough pencils to last for months. There were enough to give to everyone you knew that used pencils.

Wildcat Road in Anderson County was used for a lot of dumping – years ago. It is still a good location to hunt for antique glass.

Anderson County farms had their own dumps. These consisted of a sinkhole, holler, ditch or just over the cliff on the bank of the farm.

All bottles, jars or anything that was thrown out along the road was picked up by someone and used. Soft drinks and beer came in bottles, therefore, could be turned in at any store for cash or merchandise. There was no such thing as a trashy highway in the 30's, 40's or 50's. Bottle caps were used as a from of money by all kids (kind of like marbles).

I don't ever remember finding a large piece of furniture or appliance (refrigerator, washer, stove etc.). It these items wore out or broke, they were fixed or used for something else, but never thrown away.

A few years ago, my aunt cleared out her cellar and took the items (fruit jars and things she had not used in years) to the flea market and made more than her tobacco crop brought in.

Everything today is thrown away and not to be re-used.

CATCHING RABBITS BY HAND

Back during the big war, all shells were hard to come by. We used 12 gauge and 410 gauge for the shotgun shells and 22 rim fire for the rifle.

Anytime the hunting season was open and we were not working, a-hunting we would go. Mostly for rabbits and squirrels.

Everyone leaving the house with a gun was given five to ten shells. When they returned home, there had to be a rabbit or squirrel for every shell that was shot. If you shot and missed then it called for catching a rabbit or squirrel by hand.

I missed a lot, so I became an expert at catching by hand.

Rabbits got to be a snap because they will not go in a den with only one opening. All we had to do was take the dogs and let them run one in a hole of under a back rock. After checking the area around the hole and stopping all but one outlet, one of us would sit in front of the outlet. The other one would take a long stick and work it in the hole where the rabbit went in. You worked the stick around until you poked the rabbit and then things started happening. When the rabbit was touched, he would come out the open end at full speed. The one sitting at the opening had the job of catching the rabbit. Most times it worked. If he got away, the dogs would put him in another hole and the process was started all over again.

Rabbits did not bite, but squirrels were different. These had to be gotten out of a knothole in a tree. First, you had to climb the tree and find the hole. Then with a long piece of wire (mostly barb wire), put down or up the hole, was twisted until it became tangled in the squirrels hair (mostly the tail). The squirrel was then pulled out and it was tricky to handle a mad squirrel without getting bitten, at least once. If you could get him out of the hole and thrown to the ground, the dogs took care of him.

Squirrels could be smoked out but a lot harder to catch than rabbits. Hard to get sometimes but mighty good when fried in a skillet of gravy – meal in itself.

BARREL STAVE SLEDS

A sled made with staves for runners required four barrel staves about the same width. The following is the way to make a sled: (a) cut four or five inches off the end of each stave; (b) four 2x4 blocks about six inches long – fastened to the cut-off end or flat end; (c) two 1x4 (oak) about as long as the sled is wide covered with one inch boards (any width); and (d) one 2x4 block (with hole in middle) placed between back section and front section with bolt in middle so it could pivot and be steered by a handle placed on top of front section and bottom of back section. Steering was accomplished by hand if lying flat on sled or by foot if sitting upright on sled. A six-foot length of rope was tied to handle for pulling sled back up the hill. Put together this way, the front of the staves would run sticking up about four inches while the back would run on the snow. The sled could haul three people with lots of room.

Sleds had to be made very winter. They could not survive all summer because most were used for firewood in kitchen stoves.

The road close to school had a hill almost a mile long. Therefore, the sled went to school every day when the ground had snow on it.

For morning recess (30 minutes) we could make one run down the hill and get back before the bell rang. At noon, if we gave up eating (one hour) we could make two runs. Afternoon recess we could make another run.

It was three miles from the house to the schoolhouse with a lot of down hill for the sled. The kids going our direction, on the way home, numbered about twenty and everyone got at least one ride every afternoon. There were other types of sleds brought to school, do everyone got a few rides.

At home the sled was used in all the following chores: hauling firewood, water, hay, fodder or whatever needed to be hauled.

Most of the time, there would be a heavy snow before Christmas which stayed on the ground well into February. It meant a lot of time for fun in the snow.

When the river was frozen, good and solid, we had a hill where we could go down and run most of the way across the river before we stopped. Sometimes a few bushes had to be cut and a few rocks removed. This was also fun if we were making a run for sled riding.

BUGS THAT WOULD BITE

A long time ago we had a lot of problems that you don't hear much about today.

The chiggers I have just about figured out how to avoid, so they are no big problem.

The mosquito still bites just like he always did. Now we have sprays and lotions to put on to keep them away.

Deer flies are still around and they are tough. These are found mostly around water and cattle. Usually deal with them about once or twice a year.

However, this story is mainly about bed bugs. The meanest and hardest bug to get rid of on this planet. In the late 30's they were easy to get. Seems like when someone spent the night away from home, within a few days the bed bugs would make themselves known. If something was not done to get rid of them by week's end there would be thousands of them.

There were several ways to get rid of bed bugs but I believe Mom had the best method known. Feather ticks had to be emptied and covers washed with lye soap. Bed frames (all metal) along with the springs were pitched in the river for twenty-four hours. All clothes had to be washed the same as the feather tick cover. Just about everything inside the house had to be washed down.

A lot of work and we had to sleep on the floor for a couple of days. If you ever had to try and sleep with a bed bug, you knew it was all worth while to get rid of them.

I have not encountered a bed bug for over fifty years and have not missed them one little bit.

HOG KILLING TIME

Hog killing always took place in the fall after weather had turned cold and it did not all take place at the same time. Most of the time, two or three families would get together for this, which would take most of the week.

First, the scalding trough had to be put in place, filled with water and heated to the right temperature. Then the hog was shot and throat cut to get rid of most of the blood. It was dipped in the trough to remove the hair and then hung on the butchering pole. All internal organs were removed. The liver and all fat was saved. The following had to be cooked within a couple of days to prevent spoiling: liver, heart, ribs, tenderloins and tongue. These parts were divided among the workers. The feet were either cooked and eaten right away or pickled for later.

All hams, shoulder and bellies were trimmed, placed in smokehouse and covered with salt for curing. The head had the jowls removed for curing while someone took the rest of the heads and processed them into souse meat. All trimmed fat was put in a kettle and the lard was cooked out. Lard was put in a can and stored in the smokehouse for later use in cooking.

Cracklings left over from rendering out the lard were a treat enjoyed by young and old alike.

All of the lean meat that was trimmed off and some of the fat were ground up, mixed with seasonings and spices and made into sausage.

After the meat in the smokehouse had cured for a period of time, it was hung on wires and used until the next hog killing time.

The crew for this had to include experts at shooting the hog, cutting his throat just right, butchering and getting the water temperature just right. If the water was not hot enough, it was no good at all. If it was too hot, it could set the hair and then it would have to be scraped off.

FIREWOOD FROM THE RIVER

When I was born in 1930, Pop was running the Ferry Boat at Tyrone on Route 62 between Lawrenceburg and Versailles. From that day, until I was seventeen years old, I can only remember one or two years we did not live close enough to the river where we could throw a rock from the porch into it.

This meant that during high water, most of the day was spent drifting for firewood and anything else floating down the river that was useful.

Drifting for wood took a lot of special equipment, such as: (a) good flat john boat (skiffs were too easy to turn over); (b) good set of oars and a strong body to operate them (took two people in the boat); (c) good single bit chopping axe; (d) bailing wire; (e) rope; (f) large nails; (h) about two dozen sets of chaindogs (nice to have but not necessarily a requirement).

Needed lots of open space at the house for landing large logs and some way to secure them. The big logs were mostly out of the mountains, where they were cutting timber.

This required us to go up the river, about half-mile or so, working our way up the bank (little or no current). Once accomplished, we would get out in the line of drift going down the river (mostly in the middle) with one rowing and one in the back of the boat.

The wood that was small enough was picked up out of the water and placed in the boat. This process continued until one of the following happened: (a) boat got full of wood; (b) lost too much ground and had to stop and unload; or (c) large log came by that really looked good. If the third happened, the axe was sunk into the log while the man in the back held onto the axe handle and the rower would row for the bank, where the log was secured. The boat was unloaded and the process started all over again. This lasted all day, as long as there was daylight.

Another crew was on the bank, and if the river was still rising, it was their job to keep everything secured and pulled as close to the bank as possible.

Small wood was moved up the bank ahead of the rising water. When the water started to fall, everything was left on the bank and easy to cut into firewood. Any lumber, or such, that was caught was put to good use by repairing the barns and other things.

If you happened to land another john boat, you tied it to the bank and kept it in the water as it went down. If the owner called for it, he paid you twenty-five cents and took his boat home. This was the law of the river.

PICNICKING AT PANTHER ROCK

Back in the early 40's, my younger brothers and I decided one summer to have a picnic. We were just out on our own for the day.

First, we had to earn enough money to buy what we wanted to eat. For about three weeks we pooled everything we could get our hands on. Pop did our shopping and I guess paid the balance.

It took some time to come up with a location because all the good spots were eliminated except one – Panther Rock.

So, Panther Rock it was. An out of the way place with no one around for miles. Located about four miles up the river in a rowboat and then a two-mile hike up the holler. This was just a wedge shaped rock ledge, from the top of the cliff to the bottom. There was a cave at the bottom where the creek put forth a lot of water in wet weather. Another cave, about halfway up, which you could get into by crawling out on a ledge. (This is where the panther was supposed to have lived). A real scary place.

Our menu consisted of: crackers, bread, peanut butter, soft drinks, franks, some fruit, small cake, mustard, jar of Mom's peaches and jar of jam.

A neighbor's son, (one we did not like) about my age, found out about it and invited himself along. We told him to be there at 8:00 a.m. or we would leave him. Instead of leaving at 8:00 a.m. we got up early and left at 7:00 a.m. When we got to the location we hid the boat. This was an extra effort that was useless. After our picnic, we headed back to the river and to our surprise – boat was gone.

The boy had walked up the river bank until he found the boat. Then he proceeded to row it across the river. In order to get our boat back, we had to feed him.

Thinking about it now, the picnic was not bad. The rest of the day was spent going back down the river with stops for short swims whenever we came across some swimming hole. Also, checked out a couple of swinging ropes and a few fish boxes to see what everyone was catching. (Fish boxes were built out of 2x4's and chicken wire with door on top. This was put in the water and used to keep fish alive until needed. In today's time, the freezer takes its place).

When we got home everyone parted friends and had plans made for another picnic.

Panther Rock still exists. I have visited it a few times in the last forty years, but not to picnic. You can walk to it from Anderson County but to get to it from Woodford County someone must get you across the river.

THE MILK TRUCK

When I worked for my older brother, it was ten-miles to town and the only way to get there was to get a ride on the milk truck. My brother lived in the southern corner of Anderson County where he was a sharecropper and raised the tobacco. Most of the week I worked for the farm owner.

You left for town about 6:00 a.m., riding the milk truck. During the route, you helped to load, unload and return all empty milk cans to where they were picked up. This would pay for the ride to and from town and give us a couple of hours in town.

Milk cans were five and ten gallon sizes. All cans had a number on them. This called for stacking ten gallon on the floor and five gallon stacked on top and tied down. You were not allowed to spill any of the milk. By noon, when we got to town, we had a truckload. This was taken to the cheese factory and unloaded. The cans were sat on a rack with rollers and taken inside where they were emptied. They were turned upside down on the rack, ran through the washer and delivered back to the truck where the tops were replaced. Placing them back on the truck had to be done in reverse order. The last cans taken off were the first ones put back on. This way, the first can picked up that morning had to be the first one on the truck and it would be the last one off on the way home.

The numbers on the cans also served a way for the factory to keep records because the milk was weighed in before it was dumped. I believe it sold by the pound.

When we reloaded, the driver would drive downtown, park and tell us what time we were to start back. We usually left about 4:00 p.m. and that would put us home around dark. This trip was a lot faster than the morning trip with the full cans.

All in all, to get the ten miles and back, the route was about thirty miles each way because all the farms in the area had to be covered.

This was a lot of work (eight to ten hours) just to go to town. A lot of times we would do it for the ride and not stop in town. Also, a good way to kill a day when you had nothing to do around the farm.

The truck driver always appreciated the help. Sometimes I got invited to a real home-cooked supper and maybe a couple of fishing trips to one of the farm ponds at a later date.

ONE ROOM SCHOOL

I don't think I could have been happy in any other kind of school. There was one room for all eight grades with thirty to forty children and one teacher.

Summer was great even if it did get a little hot at times. It was not too bad, with the windows opened, if you did not stir around too much.

We had a cistern house for drinking water. All water that ran off the roof of the school went into the cistern. I don't ever remember us running out of water. There was a string of metal cups on a chain, which was on a round pulley type wheel. All that was needed to get water was turn the handle and the cups dumped the water into the bucket. This did not have to be primed like a pump.

There were two outhouses (boys and girls). These were placed on opposite sides of the school ground. They were off limits to the opposite sex for about thirty paces. This was understood and respected by all.

The boys always played marbles, mumble peg (if anyone had a knife), or maybe a ballgame. Down in the corner of the school ground, in the tree, there was a boxing ring set up. This was where all arguments were settled. Sometime sit was just used for practice. Across the road was a colored school and we got together for some good ballgames.

The girls spent most of their outside time with the teacher (always a female). Boys could join them, if they liked, but had to be quiet.

A lot of the teaching took place in the woods, across the road, learning about plants and animals. The afternoon trips included the entire school and teacher. Being in one of the lower grades you could learn a lot while the teacher was with the older kids. This could be stored away to use the next school term.

Any socializing had to be done on the way to and from school. In the winter, the boys and girls would play together. It was hard to tell which was which because of the way everyone was bundled up.

In the one room school we learned the basics of school including respect. Teachers had control of the classroom. Also, the students had to store everything in their brain memory bank and not a computer.

I have always felt this was a great way of learning. The larger schools of today may be better, but who knows. I am just glad to have been educated as I was. Never will I forget the fun we had, things we were taught, and only one teacher to know.

MY FIRST GARDEN

At the age of nine, I was allowed to raise my own garden from start to finish. A plot about twelve-foot square was laid out and staked off by Pop. He then told me "this is yours to plant what you want". I made big plans, which were diminished a little when Pop handed me a hoe and shovel and told me to go to it. Three days later, after borrowing Pop's rake, it was worked up like an onion bed (not very deep) and looked good.

Pop gave me a few seeds as he planted. My garden consisted of a short row of peas, few hills of potatoes, row of string beans, row of carrots, beets, few onion sets, three hills of corn, hand full of pole beans to grow on the corn, and four or five tomato plants.

This was when Mom came into the picture. She told me that a garden was not much unless it had flowers in it. I took her advice and put in zinnias, marigolds, sunflowers and cockscombs.

Pumpkins, cushaws, cucumbers, watermelons and cantaloupes were not allowed because of the size of the vines. They would have covered everything and smothered it out.

During the summer, I gathered a few peas and put them in with Pop's to make a mess. Potatoes were about the size of golf balls but the onions did real good. Beans might have made a mess if they had all been picked at the same time. Carrots and beets never did mature. Corn was ruined because a groundhog or raccoon got in it before it was big enough to pick. Tomatoes were real good.

The flowers were another thing. They were great to look at all summer. The sunflowers could be a story all by themselves. I planted a row of them along one side of my garden and they must have been ten feet tall when they bloomed. They leaves had to be picked off in order to keep the garden from being shaded. There was approximately a ten inch bloom on each of them which the redbirds ate before I could pick them. I had planned to eat the seeds myself.

To me, my garden was a great success. I did not put one out next summer because I was old enough to work in the big garden.

It was a chore to keep the weeds cut out, ground worked a little, bugs and worms picked off and keeping the wild animals out. A mole could destroy a garden very quickly by eating the roots of everything. Ground squirrels were also bad. Most birds helped to keep the insects out. The old dry land tarpons were hard on tomatoes. Mom raised a lot of frying chickens and they had to be especially watched during the daylight hours. They were penned up at night or something would pack them off.

MY FIRST SUMMER AWAY FROM HOME

There was a man who owned a small farm in Fintville (Woodford County) that did not have a house on it. He lived in Milliner on a larger farm. He asked me to work for him one summer. It would have taken me all day to walk to work and back home, so I moved in with my aunt and uncle for the summer. Therefore, I only had about a twenty-minute walk to the farm.

The farm was small with a little tobacco, corn, two or three head of cattle and a few hogs. My job was to perfrom any work that needed to be done. This man would come by in the morning and show me what had to be done. Most of the time, he brought someone along to work with me. He could come back in the later afternoon, pick my helper up and check to see what we had done during the day.

Living away from home was not much different than being at home. My aunt and uncle had two daughters and two sons. When I got paid on Saturday, half of what I made went to my aunt for room and board, same as when I was home. If her boys worked during the week, half of their pay went to her. May aunt and uncle also owned a farm, so the boys did not have much time for outside work.

Most things were about the same – lots of swimming, a little fishing and a lot of just roaming around the countryside.

There was a boy scout camp up the river and we spent a lot of time watching them. We could not join them because they were from town and had a different lifestyle from us.

On thing I liked about that summer was my aunt fed better. She had a refrigerator that operated off a kerosene motor. This meant cold water, milk, ice cream, jello, ice (at meal time) and a lot of things you could not have without one. She also had a big orchard consisting of apples, peaches, plums, cherries, strawberries and all kinds of good things to eat.

My uncle had a sawmill that was powered by a one-cylinder steam engine. It was a treat when he started it up because he was sawing a few pieces of lumber that someone needed. Sometimes he would use it to saw firewood. It was hard for me to believe that so much wood could be cut in such a short time.

The summer called for a lot of hard work. A lot of fun was had being with my aunt, including cousins for about three months. I was really glad to get back home and back in school at the end of summer.

FISH BAIT
(HOW WE CAME UP WITH IT)

A trip to the bait shop last summer stirred old memories of the bait we used back in the 30's and 40's and how we obtained this bait.

Worms were easy to collect. We had a spot where Mom threw all her dish water, where we could dig red worms and wigglers. A few shovel of dirt turned over on the riverbank would produce a full can of green worms. Crayfish, minnows, salamanders, go-devils and leaches were caught with a seine. Most times, these were easy to find in the creek of Anderson County.

We did not use many young wasps. Mainly because it was a big fight to get them. The adult wasps could sting and bite both at the same time.

Bag worms were only found a couple of weeks a year. They were found on red cedar trees in a silk cocoon and hard to remove. Snails were caught after a rain, when they came out. These could be saved for later use. Horseweed worms were a lava that grew inside the stock of a horseweed. They grew along the river bank and were easy to gather. Grasshoppers and crickets were good bait but hard to catch.

Dough balls were made of flour and cornmeal. They were rolled into a ball (marble size) and boiled in water to make them tough. A batch of these could be mixed, shaped into a block and used in hoop nets. This would draw in buffalo and carp. If the net was set in a good spot, this procedure was not needed. This was not used very often.

Locust only came around every seventeen years or so. There were plenty of them and real easy to catch. Tobacco worms were picked off the tobacco plants. They were not good bait but it was the only thing we could think of to use them for.

Sometimes we would take apart a rotten log and stump for grubworms. These were good for catching most fish. By fishing the creek, crayfish could be caught by hand. The tails were peeled and used to catch bluegill, warmouth, red-eye and bass.

The peddle fish (spoonbill catfish) would not bite on anything. The only way to come by one was to follow the Army Corps of Engineers up the river. They would blast the large trees that had slid into the river, so they could be lifted out by crane and placed back on the bank. The blast killed a lot of fish and we would eat real good for a while. They kept the river cleared for oil and sand barges that plied the river back then.

Getting bait back in the 30's and 40's was a lot cheaper and more fun to obtain than going to a bait shop.

GETTING TO WORK
(Three Miles Up River)

Pop ran the pump house for Ripy Brothers District, three miles up river from where we lived. If he drove to work, he had to walk a mile to get to the car and then drive about ten miles. He solved the problem with an aluminum boat and 5HP outboard motor.

It took him about twenty minutes to get to work by going up the river. If the river was up and had a lot of current, it took a little longer. The higher the water, the faster it moved.

Another problem was the boat had a round bottom and sharp bow. He liked to stand in the middle and steer it by leaning to the right or left. It worked and Pop was really good at it. The only time he touched the motor was to start or stop it or, as he called it, " taking off and landing".

It is well known that Pop did take a drink now and then. The drinking and showing off in the boat was known to get Pop wet. The boat would run circles around him until he could catch it or it ran into the bank. If he came home wet, we knew better than to ask him what happened.

In the winter time, when the river was frozen solid, he would skate back and forth to work. When the river was frozen too thick for the boat and too thin to skate on, Pop would walk. The car, when we had one, was used very little in winter.

He would leave the car parked at the pump house. On Friday, he drove to Lawrenceburg, got the groceries and brought them down the river.

Sometimes he used the trip up the river to check the traplines in the morning and bait them on the way home.

RABBIT HUNTING WITH POP

Pop was the only man I knew that could find so many rabbits, sitting still before they jumped up and ran. This gave him the edge because he knew which way they were going to run and was ready when they took off. Pop would never shoot one while it was sitting still. He would point them out to me and I would kick them out for him to shoot.

The reason for me being along was to carry the rabbits he killed. They were not very heavy because as soon as he killed one, he would wring the head off, cut them open and get rid of all the innards. This made them a lot lighter and kept them from spoiling. When we got home, all that was needed to be done was cut the four feet off, skin them and wash them real good. This he did while I was rowing the boat home. Most times we hunted on the Woodford County side of the river because land was not as steep and the hunting was better.

Pop was known to hunt with a 22 rifle. This was the only time he would shoot them while they were sitting still. I saw him kill them by throwing rocks (couple of small ones he had in his pocket for this purpose).

The one time I made Pop really mad was the day we were standing in the middle of a big field of dead grass. We were waiting for the dogs to bring the rabbit around close enough for a shot. I had a tobacco stick with me that I was using for a walking stick. I spotted a rabbit sitting under a clump of grass right in front of Pop. I whacked him with my stick and killed it. Needless to say, Pop was really upset because I had seen the rabbit before he did.

Sometimes our hunting trips were long (all day). The length of the trip depended on how many rabbits we went out for. Rabbits were plentiful back then and if hunting was good, Pop would shoot a couple for the neighbor.

Hunting was an art back then. The weather condition had a lot to do with finding them. Cold weather was better because if it was too hot, the rabbits would run into the first hole they came to and the dogs could not help. If the ground was covered with snow you could really track them. The snow made it easy to find them sitting still.

Different times called for a change in the way you hunted them and Pop knew them all.

OPOSSUM HUNTING AT NIGHTS WITH DOGS
(WE CALLED IT COON HUNTING – BACK BEFORE TV)

Hunting at night was one of our real down to earth froms of entertainment (winter or simmer). This was a real treat and also called a from of eating out.

We always had a couple of old hound dogs around. With a little planning, we were joined by a couple of neighbor kids with their dogs. Hunting gear consisted of a small bag of salt, hand full of kitchen matches and at least one one gallon metal bucket. Everything else needed was furnished by the countryside.

One favorite thing to do was go through a cornfield and everyone in the hunting party would pick about four ears of corn. (This was not called stealing back in my time, because everybody did it and no one complained). Sometimes we would use our own corn.

While we were waiting for the dogs to tree an opossum we would build a fire, boil the corn and eat it. (In winter we would gather dried corn and parch it). We also packed irish or sweet potatoes and baked them in the ashes. All the farmers kept chickens in the barns. The eggs would be gathered and boiled. (The barns were checked out ahead of time for location of nests).

Summer time hunting was much better because of the corn, turnips, tomatoes, etc. They were much easier to find and gather. Also, most of the hunting was much better.

If we were lucky enough for the dogs to tree a varmint, someone had to climb the tree and shake it out. Sometimes the dogs would come across a skunk and you stood way back. (This is a story in itself).

We never took a gun with us but if we were lucky, someone had a flashlight. Mostly we only had a kerosene lantern, which had to be replaced if we got into a field full of cattle. You had to sit the lantern down and run. The cattle would stomp the lantern, which was picked up the next day, and usually beyond repair.

This was also a time for checking out all fruit trees (apples, pears, cherries, peaches and plums). All farms had these scattered around mostly for the benefit of the wildlife. Winter fruits were wild grapes, persimmons, blackhaws, etc.

There was always something out there, year round, that was edible.

FISHING THE KENTUCKY RIVER YEAR ROUND

In the 1930's, fishing the Kentucky Rive, above and below Lock #5, is something I will never forget. There were a number of ways to catch fish of all kinds, but you had to work at it sometimes.

About the only way to catch a fish in winter was with a hoop net. There were always a few of them on hand. These were knitted, mostly by Pop, out of twine string with a mash of about two inches. This allowed the small fish to escape. Two throats were placed inside facing the large end of the net. This allowed the fish to swim in but no way to escape. The big end had an opening of about six feet.

After they were knitted and the hoops in place, they were dipped in a mixture of cold tar and something else (maybe kerosene) and heated almost to a boil. They were hung in a tree to dry because this made them last longer. They could be used all winter for fishing if the river was not frozen over. Catch was usually catfish, carp and buffalo. All game fish (bass and crappie) had to be released.

Summer fish could be caught with trotlines, jungle lines, hand pole, throw line or by hand (called cooning).

All fish of any size (two pounds an up) were up for sale. What we did not sell, we ate. They were cleaned, cut up, rolled in cornmeal and fried in hog lard until brown on the outside. The following fish were eaten: bluegill, crappie, bass, paddle fish, alligator gar, catfish and eels. It was really a bonus if we got a large snapping turtle. We also fished farm ponds and creeks for bluegill and yellow belly cats (called pond cats).

Jingle lines were about three feet of twine with hook on the end. This could either be tied to a short stick and stuck in the bank or tied to a limb/brush and dropped in the water with bait.

The throw line was not very popular because it took about fifteen feet of line and two hooks, Definitely did not catch many fish.

Trotlines were used a number of ways. One was to stretch a line across the river (bank to bank) with four or five size rock for sinkers. Place about fifty or sixty hooks on twelve or fourteen inch twine string. Bait about twenty hooks out from each bank for catfish or white perch. Middle hooks were baited for buffalo or carp. Another way was to run the trotline up one bank. You would go about twenty feet out any length or up the middle of the river, anchored on both ends with a large rock and guidelines to service with a bowie.

GROUNDHOG MEATLOAF

It was a real treat when Mom would announce she needed two groundhogs for meat loaf.

In the summer, we would take to the wood and shoot two groundhogs. If it was winter, and they were hibernating, we had to dig them out. Sometimes this would take all day. We knew where they were but sometimes they would be hard to get at.

With the hogs on hand, they were cleaned. All the meat was taken from the bone and put through the food chopper or grinder with an equal amount of back (hog jowl bacon was best, but any bacon would do).

Everything was mixed together along with salt, pepper, breadcrumbs, and I believe, a little milk was added. I am not sure what else was used. This was put into a pan, in the oven and baked. Baking time depended on the size of the meat loaf. There were never any leftovers.

Winter time was really a big chore getting a groundhog. They were hibernating and would stop the hole or den up behind them as they went in. You had to determine which way the den went and approximately how deep. When you started digging you hoped you had guessed right. If guessing wrong, you had to start all over again. Once you got it right, it was just a matter of putting him in a sack and keeping him away from the fire. If he got warm he would wake up and the problems started because he was mad and mean. The best thing to do in this situation was to let him go and start hunting again.

BARREL OF PICKLES

It seems that when I was growing up we would spend most of the summer storing things away for the winter (kind of like squirrels).

Most of the meat for the winter was hunted or trapped while the staple items were stored.

One thing that I remember most were the dill pickles. The dill was grown in the garden along with a large patch or two of cucumbers down close to the river in sandy soil, where they grew best along side the peanut patch.

I don't know where Pop got the barrel from but it was about the same size as a whiskey barrel. The only difference was that the barrel was not burnt on the inside like a whiskey barrel.

The barrel sat in the middle of the smokehouse. When the cucumbers grew to the right size, they were picked daily. After being processed, they were placed in the barrel one layer at a time until it was full. The top was slipped on and there it sat. When pickles were needed, they were taken out and used in the kitchen.

The amount of pickles were used were entirely too many to be put in jars. The jars were saved for bread and butter pickles, sweet pickles and green tomato ketchup. The ketchup (mixture of sliced green tomatoes, onions, peppers and a mixture of spices) was made in the fall before frost killed the tomato vines.

The reason for remembering this so well is because I never liked dill pickles but I did eat a lot of them.

Our family was living proof that a person can survive on one acre of land. The farm was thirteen acres and there were twelve of us.

Approximately half of the farm was river cliff, which provided for a lot of things we needed at the time.

BLACKBERRY PICKING AND WHY

From age six until about sixteen or seventeen, I was on the blackberry picking team for the family.

Starting around the first of July, when berries began to ripen, the crew would start picking. The crew knew where every berry vine was located in Anderson and Woodford Counties. Every three or four days, we would rotate to our favorite patches. Instead of picking them by the gallons, we would use lard cans, five gallon buckets and even wash tubs to pick in.

The rules were very simple - the sooner we could get one hundred half-gallon jars and one hundred quart jars canned for the family cellar, the sooner we could pick a few gallons to sell for spending money.

Being a large family, the half-gallon jars were used for cobblers all winter. Quart jars were cooked down and made into jelly, one at a time.

The jelly was basically used for school lunches by spreading on home-made biscuits (wrapped in brown paper or newspaper). These were placed on a shelf at school until lunchtime. When weather permitted, lunch was spread on the ground. (Sometimes a lot of trading took place among the kids). The girls were in a group and the boys in another group (most times on opposites sides of the playground.

Blackberries were not the only wild berries. We also picked a few gallons of raspberries, dewberries, strawberries, and other wild fruit. There were also used during the winter.

The picking had to end before noon because of the intense afternoon heat. Mom and the non-pickers would spend the afternoon boiling jars, washing, cooking and canning berries.

One of the benefits of being the berry picking party was getting the afternoon off. After cutting the firewood and getting the fire started, the pickers got to go swimming in the river. This was the only way to get rid of the chiggers we had accumulated. They (chiggers) had to be drowned before they got buried under the skin.

This is one of my fondest memories of growing up in Anderson County.

MUSIC

I can remember back in the 30's when music came only on special occasions. We had a battery-operated radio but not much music on it except on Saturday night when the Grand Ole Opry was on.

Had a hand-cranked Victrola but a limited number of 78 RPM records. Mom and Pop were the only ones allowed to play it. The needles wore out fast – after only a few records.

Later it was the juke boxes in the places where we hung out. They cost a nickel to play one record and nickels were hard to come by. Someone would play one now and then and everyone got to listen.

Early in the 40's we moved to Franklin County and had electricity and the radio had more music on it. We could listen to it if no one had the soaps on. Mom had to hear her soaps every day. Then at night, Pop or one of the older kids had to hear their serials (Gang Busters, The Shadow etc.).

Then we got a phonograph and it would play 78 RPM and 33-1/3 RPM records. Later they came out with one that played the 45 RPM.

First tape was the reel to reel but could not afford one of them. Then things got a little cheaper with the 8-track tape but they would not last very long because about a year and they would come apart. The cassette is a little better.

The Compact Disc (CD) made listening a lot better and they hold up better and longer.

The set up I have now plays them all except 78 RPM. Only problem now is that the last time we moved I have not gotten all of it hooked back up just right.

The stereo, radio, amplifier, turn table, 8 track tape, reel to reel and the CD players all work fine but have got to work on my speakers because only one of the four works.

All cars now have AM & FM radios and so many stations that they are hard to count.

I can sit for hours with just the music on – any kind of music (country to Bach). Not too much on hard rock but liking it a little all the time (maybe someday).

PENNY CHAPEL

Drove down to Penny Chapel in Anderson County a couple of years ago. I was taking the wife to some of the places where I grew up.

Spent a few summers in this area with my brother and his wife, working on the farms in the area. I believe that about everything in this area was owned by one of the Drury families. Brother was a Baptist preacher and preached at Penny Chapel (probably had another name in the 40's).

The church that was there was a wood building and has now been replaced by a concrete block building on the same site.

Brother was also a share cropper during the week. When he had no work for me, I would work on other farms in the area. There is no flat land in this area – just hills and hollows.

Just over the hill from the church was a stream called Little Beaver Creek. This is where most of my spare time was spent. Fishing and turtle hunting were good. Lots of frogs for gigging. Also, lots of hickory trees, so squirrel hunting was good. They raised a lot of hay, so rabbit hunting was okay.

Now, brother did not allow guns of any kind in his home, so hunting had to be done the hard way. Rabbits were no problem because you could follow the mowing machine and catch the rabbit by hand. They cannot get around on new cut hay and were easy to catch. Squirrels were another story - this took a piece of barb wire, use the dog to put them in a knothole, climb the tree and twist them out. The problem is that they are mean and when you pull him out of the hole he is at his meanest. It was my job to get him out of the hole and on the ground and I left the dogs to handle it from there.

Spent three or four summers in the area between Rt. 62 and where the Bluegrass parkway is now. This was before we had a Beaver Lake in the area.

Worked the milk trucks during this time. It was also operated by the Drury families. There were about three generations of them and they had all the milk routes.

This was also one of my learning periods because I was too young to take much of an interest in the girls. Spent all my time working, fishing, hunting, or just roaming the countryside seeing what I could get into without getting caught.

ANDERSON COUNTY CAVES

Have paid a visit to Mammoth Cave in Kentucky, Carlsbad Caverns in New Mexico, Carter Caves in Northern Kentucky and a number of caves in Virginia. Now, if you are into crawling around in caves, these are all good places to visit. Only problem is – a lot of people have been there ahead of you.

Growing up in Anderson County was a lot different. Crawling around a cave that nobody had been in was one from of entertainment for us kids.

Panther Rock was one place that had two caves. My favorite one is about half way up the face of the ledge (where the panther was said to live – that gave it the name Panther Rock). Had to crawl out the ledge to get to it. There was a small entrance but a-piece back in it there was a large room with a stream of water running through it – we called it a river. This water was the water that came out at the bottom of the ledge, down the cliff and emptied into the river, just above the scout camp on the other side of the river.

The farm we lived on, just above Lock #5, had a lot of caves. The entrance to them was up on the top of the hill and went straight down. Only way into them was with about a 50-foot rope. I never went down this one but some of the older brothers did.

We were digging out a groundhog, just above the house, when we worked a large rock loose. It fell in a hole and we found there was a cave there with about a 20-foot roof. Well, out came the rope and down the hole went three or four kids. We went in both directions but did not find much – just a normal cave. I do believe all the caves in that area are connected.

About a year later there was a group of cave explorers came up the river by boat. Showed them all of the caves and they did explore them. If they found anything worthwhile, they kept it to themselves. All the farms on Lock Road have a number of sink holes. They tell me that these holes are from the caves that are under the ground.

Never did hear anymore from the cave explorers. The caves are still there and the farmers still use the sink holes to dump everything in. A lot of them are full of rock that they have picked off the land they use for crops.

Oh, and we never did find the groundhog that we were after. Even the dogs lost interest in the hole.

ANDERSON COUNTY CREEKS

Lived on the Kentucky River most of my life – close enough that the river had been in most of the houses where we lived. My interest was more on the creeks that emptied into the river.

The house Pop built at Tyrone was right at the mouth of Wild Cat Creek. A very short creek, as the headwaters was up around Stringtown – someplace. This was not a creek for fishing, except where it emptied into the river. It was okay for catching fish bait (crawfish and minnows) and for skating in the winter when it was frozen over. By the time I finished second grade, I knew every rock in Wild Cat Creek.

On the other side of Tyrone where the bridge was, Bailey Branch emptied into the river. This creek had nothing in it and was a dead creek – weeds would not even grow in it. The thread factory in Lawrenceburg dumped al the wastewater into Bailey Branch. It ran a different color every day. Something in the dye killed everything. You could go up to where Cedar Brook Creek ran into Bailey Branch and here you could catch bait.

The branch that ran into the river at the Old Camp House where we lived did not have a name and was only about a mile long. While we lived here, we had to go about two miles across country to Sharps Branch. This one started somewhere around Lawrenceburg and was a good place to catch bait and had some holes of water that were good for fishing and swimming. It emptied into the river just below Sims Camp – below Lock #5.

By the time I was through the eight grade and we moved down the river to Franklin County, we all knew Sharps Branch like the back of our hands.

The other two creeks were used for catching bait and night hunting (Anderson County side of the river) were Turkey Run and Little Benson Creek (both ran into the river below Clifton). These two were not used much as they were too far away and if we used the john boat, we had to go through the lock. Most times we borrowed a boat that was below the lock.

All of the creeks except Bailey Branch were good for turtle hunting. Some of them had go-devils in them. Sharps Branch had the shiner minnows (red stripe down each side) that were an excellent bait for crappie or bass. All had chub minnows that we used for catfish bait.

HEDGE APPLE, HICKORY AND LOCUST TREES

Growing up, I can remember a lot of thing the hedge apple tree was used for. The first thing that comes to mind is they were set close together and in a couple of years you had a fence, thick enough that a rabbit had trouble getting through.

A small limb of about 3 inches in diameter was cut and used for signal trees – when using one horse to pull something (sleigh, one horse cultivator, a log out of the woods, etc.). One of 4 or 5 inches was used for making a double tree for use with a team of horses or mules. This took a double tree and two single trees (used with a wagon or a plow for breaking the ground with a team).

The hedge apple wood is about the hardest wood that I have worked with. Take a stick of the wood, season it good, put it on the wood lathe, stick a knife to it and it is like cutting steel. Knife had to be sharpened after a short spell. They make billy clubs that are good for a life time.

Fall of the year, the hedge apple tree was another good location for squirrel hunting. I guess the apples have some kind of seed in them that the squirrels eat. Have also heard that a couple of the apples under the sink would keep the roaches out of the kitchen. Have not tried this, so don't know if it works.

Cut the tree down, let the sprouts grow about 6 feet long and make a switch you could whip 6 men with. Cut the thorns off and you have a fine fishing pole for farm pond fishing for bluegill. This wood was also a good choice for wagon tongues, fence posts, sleigh runners, and handles for most tools (hammers, exes, pitch forks, grubbing hoes, etc.). Also works good for mallets used with wood chisels and pitman arms for the mower.

Another Kentucky tree that can be used for most of this is the hickory nut tree. The bark of the hickory can also be peeled off, dried and used to weave bottoms for kitchen chairs. A friend of the family by the name of Ralph Anderson taught me how this was done. The nuts from this tree can also be gathered, stored and eaten all winter – if you get them before the squirrels. The hickory was used a lot in the tobacco barns for rails to hang the tobacco on, along with another tree – the black locust.

The locust was mostly used for fence posts and when the electricity came through Anderson County, this one was used by a lot of farmers to run the lines on because most houses were a good distance from the light line. Has a lovely bloom in the spring that you can smell a mile away. Growing up, the locust had thorns that were hard on bare feet and hands when setting out the tobacco plants on the newly cleared ground.

STILL MORE TREES

I can remember that one of my most popular trees was the Mulberry. The fruit of this tree was great but you had to watch them close because if the birds got to them first there were not many ripe ones left.

Another one was the sassafras. This is the only tea that was served when I was growing up. Found out later when I went into the Army there was a tea leaf that was imported from somewhere and that tea was made by boiling it – just like the root of the sassafras tree. Do not have to dig up roots anymore or cut a bee tree down for honey to sweeten it with. There is a sassafras concentrate in a bottle now. Just a bottle of this and a quart jar of honey and I am set for months. Any time I want sassafras tea all I need to do is heat the water. Another use for the sassafras tree – find a thicket of them that have vines of some kind growing around them because it defroms them – and they make great walking sticks.

The paw-paw tree is another good one but hard to find and not much fruit on them. When ripe, it is a lot like a banana – just a lot bigger seed. The raccoons are partial to the paw-paw fruit. It is wise to pick them early, lay them up and let them ripen slowly.

The blackhaw tree was really a bush. I don't think it got very big but the fruit of this bush lasted most of the winter. Don't know of any wild animals that ate the fruit. I am sure that something ate it but never did catch anything eating it. The fruit was not real good but a couple of hands full of them would get you through the day, if nothing better was handy. The blackhaw is not a well-known fruit like some others and not many of them around. Does not grow well in the woods – just on the edge. The last one I ever saw were across the back of the parking lot of the Pic-Pac store on Second Street. Have not checked lately but they should still be there.

The hackberry tree is another one. The fruit of this tree is little ore than a seed – about the size of a small bead with a skin on it. Just a thin layer of pulp between the skin and the seed – was good but could not eat enough of them to do any good. Most of the trees were large and the fruit was hard to get to.

All this was taught to me by Pop and the older brothers. As I grew up, could not live on them but was good when out wandering the hills and hollows of Anderson county when there was not something better to eat. Most of them got ripe in the fall and took the place of blackberries, strawberries and things that got ripe early and were gone well before the fall of the year.

TREES

Growing up in Anderson County there must have been about a hundred different kinds of trees that grew wild along the river, creeks, river cliffs, farmlands higher up and everywhere crops were not grown. All were used for firewood, for cooking and heating, but most had a special use.

Fruit and nut bearing trees were used for the growing of food and only cut down when they died.

Oak trees were used for a variety of things. I was very small at the time, but can remember looking for days with Pop to find the right white oak trees to make the shakes for the house he was building in Tyrone (believe it was the only house he ever built).

They were cut into logs about 3 feet long, then with a special tool and a wooden mallet they were split and nailed on the roof. They were laid in layers to keep the water out.

Oaks made good lumber for about anything but got very hard to drive a nail in after it had seasoned out for a while.

The best use for an oak tree – most of them had some kind of acorn that grew on them – was to sit under with a shotgun and wait for the squirrels to come in for supper.

Knew where every persimmon tree in Anderson County and most of Woodford County was growing. Soon as the first frost fell it was time to eat the fruit of this tree. Also a good tree that was used for some types of hunting. There were times when out hunting at night, our so-called coon hounds could not find a coon to chase, or were just off somewhere chasing a rabbit, we could always check out a grove of the persimmon trees and find an opossum or two and the whole night was not wasted. Their hides were worth up to 15 or 20 cents each when shipped to Sears and Roebuck.

Never knew of the persimmon tree being used for anything when growing up, but read a story on it the other day and now know it is a member of the ebony family. It is one of the hardest woods to grow in Kentucky. It is dense, heavy and hard when used in making the head for the golf club called a driver. It is almost black in color.

The white oak was also used for making splits – used in making baskets or weaving new bottoms for chairs.

PINE TREES

I can remember back in the early 40's, a bunch if us brothers were out for a drive and we stopped at the entrance to Stewart Home School on Rt. 127 (Old Lawrenceburg Road now). There had been some pine trees transplanted at the entrance.

Now, a pine tree was a thing of beauty back then and a rarity in Franklin County because there were very few of them around.

We had been known to drive all the way to the mountains just to see the pine trees. We even brought a few seedlings back to transplant but never had any luck getting them to grow.

I cannot remember which of the brothers were in the crowd that day but we took pictures and the pine trees were a little taller than we were. The pictures are still around some place.

The wife and I drove by there a few days ago and the trees must be over 100 feet tall now.

Pine trees are everywhere now (even a few in my backyard). They have crossed them so many ways and there are so many different kinds and will grow just about anywhere.

Nothing will grow under the pine trees. The pine needles have some kind of acid or something in them that kills the grass and weeds that try to grow under them. If you rake all the needles up and get rid of them, the pine tree will die.

Not all pine trees are like this. Have found a use for mine here at the home place. Rake a few of them up, scatter them along the fence around the yard and this keeps the weeds and grass down and I don't have to use the weed eater on them.

Pines were known to grow straight and a lot of them were used for telephone poles or light poles.

Today, pine trees are used for everything from lumber to making paper.

PROS AND CONS OF THE WOOD CHUCK

I remember what we called the lowly old wood chuck (a.k.a. groundhog, a.k.a. whistle pig). Deserves much more respect from his human neighbors than they receive. It's very true that they will move into any neighborhood without the owner's consent. If the pickings are to his liking, such as your vegetable garden or cornfield, and just dearly loves red clover. Not to mention a multitude of other greenery. He also is not the least bit particular where he constructs his new home so long as it is underground. It may be under your home's foundation wall, barn post, or smack dab in the middle of your clover field, and he is never satisfied with just one. So he constructs one for summer, one for winter, plus any number or run in "danger shelters" in between. Then he spends the entire summer excavating homes, reproducing, sunbathing, and eating everything in sight to store up fat for the long winter sleep, and when winter approaches he just moves into his winter home, closes the front door, nice and snug, curls up in his nice warm bed, and goes to sleep until spring. Now, so far you haven't ready anything that deserves any respect, have you?

We humans – without his consent – have declared February the second as Groundhog Day. So just in case the sun shines on that day, we can blame the next six weeks of foul weather – which is sure to come anyway, on him, if the sun doesn't shine on his day. As usual the weather turns for the worst. Then we blame him for being a lousy forecaster. I feel sure that if old chuck could pick his own day it would be much later than February the second, that we picked for him.

If for no other reason than to show a bit of respect, consider when they are out feeding or just laying around, when danger approaches from any direction they will head for the nearest shelter at full speed. But before entering the safety of his own shelter, will stop, stand up, and give a loud "Warning Whistle" to his next of kin, or any other animal that happens to be within hearing distance. Now that's courtesy and should deserve a bit of respect.

They also loan out their summer homes and all run in shelters to the less fortunate animals for the entire winter, rent free, some of which must travel for long distances in winter to forage for food and would be in serious trouble without these rent free shelters. Even the birds seek shelter in them in extreme winter weather. Old chucks don't mind this infringement at all so long as they clear out when spring returns.

They will create numerous foot paths around steep bluffs and hills, making much easier walking for man or beast, when strolling in these areas, including but not limited to all hikers, plant admirers, rock hunters and bird watchers.

If you have a fat lazy dog lying around and old chuck moves in, things will never be the same, for the dog will spend hours every day trying to catch old chuck far enough from one of his shelters to head him off and latch on before he reaches safety. This rarely happens, as old chuck is a very good climber and also will not hesitate one second to seek safety by climbing a tree. If all else fails, most likely he will succeed in fighting his way to the nearest shelter, either way means a much healthier mutt, due to lots of good daily exercise. They become four-legged bush hogs all summer, consuming large amounts of weeds along fence rows thus reducing the number of weed seeds to contend with the following spring, saving his human neighbor both labor and fuel.

If you haven't gained enough respect for him by now to fence your garden against his persistent appetite, or planted a couple of extra rows of corn for him in the fields that are too large to fence and you feel that you must shoot him, don't degrade by hanging him on a fence by the side of the road for all the world to see – take him home and feast on him. You just might be surprised at the good eating inside that ornery looking hide.

Some folks eat the liver but I always save them until I go fishing because the catfish love them and I love the catfish. This way everyone gets a good meal. The following are three good cooking recipes:

"Baked Wood Chuck": - one wood chuck, six irish potatoes, three sweet potatoes, three onions, six carrots, salt and pepper. Cut wood chuck into serving size pieces, place in the kettle, cover with water, and bring to boil, lower heat and simmer until tender. Simmering time will vary according to age of wood chuck. When tender, remove from the kettle and place in baking dish along with vegetables, salt and pepper, and bake in oven at 350 degrees until vegetables are done. Serve while hot with lots of fresh ground black pepper.

"Wood Chuck Meat Loaf" – cut meat off bones of wood chuck and grind with equal amount of jowl back or pork sausage, add other ingredients from your favorite meat loaf recipe, and bake in oven at 350 degrees with lots of tomato catsup.

"Fried Wood Chuck" – to fry a wood chuck they must be young, not over half grown. After dressing, cut into serving size pieces, roll in flour that has been salted and peppered, then fry in cast iron skillet slowly until good and brown. This is wood chuck at its best and will give competition to fried rabbit, chicken, or pork chops any day.

"PS" – after cleaning, there is a spot of meat under the front legs that resembles a liver. This must be removed or it will give the chuck meat a funny taste. It should also be soaked overnight in a mild solution of salt water.

SCHOOLHOUSE MAINTENANCE

I can well remember maintenance at the one-room school that I attended on Lock #5 Road in Anderson County from Grade 3 through 8.

I don't remember the grounds ever being mowed. The children had to keep the weeds cut but the morning recess, lunch hour, and afternoon recess was spent keeping the weeds stomped down from the games we played.

Each morning, the boys in the upper grades were assigned the job of keeping the fire going in the big coal stove and water in the bucket from the cistern house next to the school. The older girls were assigned the chore of dusting and keeping the floor swept.

A lot of pride was not taken in the schoolhouse but when the inside or outside needed painting, the teacher would bring in the paint. The boys would spread the paint on where it was needed. Maybe not the best of jobs but it made it look a lot better. The building is still standing and being used as a house to this day.

About once or twice a year, the school board brought a bucket of oil (some kind) and a mop and we oiled the floor to keep the dust down. The road in front of the school was gravel, so we had a lot of dust.

The windows on the inside were cleaned by the girls and the outside by the boys. The teacher would bring everything needed for this including a step ladder.

All trash was gathered each day and burnt by the boys with the teacher's help.

I don't know why they did away with the one-room school, but sure am glad I was out grade school before they were all closed.

One big problem with schools today is that some company has to be called in for insect and varmint control. I guess we had flies, wasps, bumble bees, every honeybees and mice, but if they bothered me – I don't remember. I am sure we had plenty with outside plumbing and no air conditioning.

In today's time if a school gets a little run down, they just close it and build a new one.

WILD FIRE

For the last month or so, every news broadcast on television has focused on the forest fires in the mountains of Eastern Kentucky.

Growing up back in the late 230's or early 40's – in the fall after the trees had shed their leaves, they served as fuel for a fire.

When hunting a night, running a trap line in cold weather, skating on the creek that was frozen solid, going to or from school, or just out in the woods for the day, a good pile of dry leaves were what the fire was started with. Sometimes this was the only way to get warm. It was easy to get wet, feet stayed wet all the time when there was snow on the ground.

If the fire got out of hand and started to spread up the hill, no one tried to put it out, Sometimes they would burn for days before they went out. Cover the cliff from where it started to the nearest creek or ran out of fuel.

Don't know of one ever doing any damage. Maybe it would burn a few weed seeds or kill a bit of undergrowth. Don't remember a house, barn or shed of any kind burning down. Did not hurt the environment in any way that I can think of. Ashes all went back into the ground. It made walking the cliffs a lot less work and the fire only moved a few feet in an hour. The animals had no trouble getting out of the way. Squirrels would go up a tree, rabbits, groundhogs, skunks and opossums would go into a hole until the fire had passed. Birds would just fly off.

No one thought anything about this type of fire. Grown-ups as well as kids started these fires.

There were times when we would team up a couple of hundred yards apart at the river's edge, start a fire and see which one would get to the top of the cliff first. In order to do this, you had to pick a spot where there were no ledges.

At times you were asked to burn off a cliff in the spring so the vegetation would come up sooner and the cows, horses, goats, or chickens would have something to eat.

This was along the river and creeks in Anderson County. There were very few people around at the time. A lot of building has taken place in the last 50 plus years, so I don't think this is allowed anymore.

THE LOWLY 'POP' BOTTLE

I can remember from about age 10 to age 40, if you wanted to buy a soda pop of any kind, you put a deposit down on the bottle. Over a time of about 30 years, the deposit went from one cent to about ten cents, no question about it. If you did not have the money for the deposit, you drank it where you bought it and put the bottle back in the case.

This was also the case with beer. If you took a bottle home with you, a deposit on the bottle was called for.

Growing up, the only bottles that were thrown away were whiskey bottles.

If you wanted a piece of penny candy, the closest place to buy it was five miles or more away. By the time you walked that far, picking bottles up, you could turn them in and get the deposit, and get a pocket full of candy.

It was seven miles from the farm at Lock #5 to Lawrenceburg. Most of the time, you could find enough bottles in those seven miles to get a ticket to the movie and a bag of popcorn.

Later on when the deposit had gone up to a nickel – if you needed soft drinks or beer, you took empties to the store, traded them in for full ones, saved them each time for trade in the next trip.

Then they came out with the throw away and soon everything came in throw aways.

Now, this new thing that they call recycling – I tried. Picked up glass bottles for three days, broke them in boxes, got all my pickup truck could haul, took them in and got seven dollars for them (about two dollars a day). You could make pretty good money on aluminum cans – load was worth seventy or eighty dollars.

Big problem with glass was it had to be separated by color (clear, brown or green).

The day of the one-cent refund on a soda bottle is long gone. What I want to know if – what is this "NEW" Bottle Bill all about?

FIRST GIRLFRIEND

I was about eleven or twelve when I got to hanging out with my favorite girl.

It was really no surprise to anyone because I spent most of my time with the group of girls at school. It was more fun than fighting with the boys.

Edna May and I started hanging out together and got serious for a short time. We would hold hands a lot and even kissed a few times.

We talked about getting married and setting up housekeeping together. The subject did not amount to much because neither of us had any money. Summer was great, but summer turned to winter and we sort of drifted apart.

I only saw Edna May during school because she lived on the other side of the county. Heard a few years ago that she had married one of the Blackburn boys.

During summer vacation, the Lloyd girls lived just across the river in Woodford County. Lena was the oldest and Cora Bell was about my age. Never dated any of them but hung out with them a lot during the summer. They had a brother named Joe and I would spend a lot of time visiting with him.

Went to see them a couple of times after I went into the Army. Joe and I would do a little rabbit hunting but the girls were dating by this time.

They moved away when the Power Plant was built and I lost track of them and the rest of the family.

THINGS THAT WOULD EXPLODE

The other day I was checking my supply of firecrackers and bottle rockets and got to thinking about some of the things we did as kids to make noise.

Probably don't remember all the steps for it, but do know that we used a one-half gallon metal bucket that karo syrup came in, carbide and a little water. The top of the bucket had to fit tight and you had to put a small nail hole in the bottom.

Setup was a very small amount of the carbide and was put in the bucket along with two drops of water, put the top in, put the bucket on the ground. Set your foot on it and let about a minute pass and light a match and put it to the hole in the bottom of the bucket. If the load was right, this would explode and blow the top of the bucket off. If load was too big, or you waited too long to light it, the bottom and top would both blow out, ruining the bucket.

Pop worked at the pump house next door to the rock quarry at Tyrone and he always had a few sticks of dynamite on hand with caps and fuse. Now this is not recommended for home use. The older kids would take one-half stick of dynamite, cap and fuse and put it together with a long fuse, hang it from a tree limb and light it. The run until it went off. Made a big noise and at night a lot of fireworks.

Pop kept these materials on hand in case he wanted to go fishing and the fish were not biting.

One brother used the caps and fuse for firecrackers until he blew a finger off one day. This is not recommended.

We tried the dynamite one time for digging out a groundhog. We got him out okay but never could find him. After that even the dogs would not go with us to dig one out.

The one you had to work hard at was the railroad trusses at Tyrone and a big flat rock. Pack it out over the water and drop it over the side. Had to flip it when you pitched it over. Then hope that it hit just right. The report was about as loud as the half stick of powder. It would explode on contact but had to hit flat side down.

Big problem was the pump house where Pop worked was right under the trusses, so could only do this when Pop was not working. It would wake him up and he did not like that,

We tried gas but it had funny ways of exploding. Found the fumes traveled too fast and sometime it would be all around you when it went off. Could be set off with just a match.

Surprising that we all ten survived to be adults. Was more luck than anything, as we did not know how dangerously we were living.

VISIT TO LOCK ROAD
BROUGHT BACK SCHOOL MEMORIES

The wife and I drove to Anderson County a few weeks ago and took some pictures of the old Lock Road School and grounds. This is where I spent most of my time for six years.

It's hard to believe the schoolhouse is still standing, there have been a few additions made, but the main part of the house is the one-room school where I got most of my schooling.

The big oak tree, that was three sixty-five years ago, is still standing. It was a big tree then and now is a huge tree. It was in the stage of putting out new leaves and looks as if it may last another fifty or so years.

I spent six summers playing under this tree. From the big tree down to the rock wall (about half of the school ground) was covered with buck bushes and blackberry briars. This made a great playground and you were out of sight from the teacher.

We would get away with some things that we were not allowed to do when the teacher was watching. Most time we would make someone mad, and they would tell the teacher what we were doing and we got punished for it anyway.

The schoolyard had three corners, with the road in front, and it came to a point on one side. The wide side was where the big tree was, and that was where the boys spent their time. The girls stayed on the other side.

Lots of times I catch myself thinking about the people that were in the school while I was there.

The Hunter family had two girls and the McFarland's had two boys that went to school there. They were the lock tenders at Lock #5. Mr. Hunter was also the mailman for that area (he owned a car).

Just below the lock were the William's. I believe there was a boy and girl there. Just up the road was, I think, the Vaughn farm and the Sharp farm. They had kids, but I don't know how many. Same with the Sims family, who always had lots of coonhounds and kids.

Pop owned the farm just above the lock property. There were ten of us (nine boys and one girl) but only six of us went to this school.

The Blackwell family lived between Sharps Branch and Lillard Road.

On the big road (Route 62) on the hill just above Tyrone, was the Murphy farm. There was a girl named Edna May (I think). She was my first love when we were about twelve or thirteen. Our romance lasted all summer, but we drifted apart when winter set in. The Stratton family also had a farm in this area. They had two girls and a boy in the school. The Hughes family, I think, had two girls.

The Hopper family was in this area with one girl and two boys. The girl, Pauline, lived in Franklin County back in the 1970's. They had foxhounds.

Also on this road were some other kids, but I did not get to know them very well.

Down on the boys' side of the school, we made a boxing ring out of string, and this is where all of the disagreements were settled. This is also where I discovered that I was not a fighter, so I spent most of my recesses with the girls and teacher.

Just across the road was the colored school and we had some great ballgames with them.

We also had a good rock fight about once a month. I never knew who started them and there never was a true winner but it could take up a full lunch hour. I don't know of anyone ever getting hurt because they would wind up down on the farm each weekend fishing. We lived on the river where the fishing was the best.

I don't think the outside of the school was ever painted while I was going there. We did paint the inside a couple of times. We had to oil the floor at least once each year. The boys did this and the girls washed the windows. There was not much dusting to do as the oil on the floor kept the dust under control.

I cannot remember the grounds ever being mowed by the kids but one of the farmers always did it on the weekends.

I cannot think of a better way to get what schooling I had than in a one-room school with all eight grades and one teacher. You could not help but pick up some things. By the time you went from one grade to the next, you knew what they were going to teach you, if you just paid attention some of the time.

The same cistern that we got the drinking water from is still there and still being used from the looks of it.

Water from the roof is collected through the gutter system. The shed has been torn down, and the cistern probably has an electric pump in it. We got the water out with a gadget that had a crank and a string of metal cups on a pulley that brought the water up and was dumped into a bucket as the handle was turned.

It only broke down one time while we were in school. A new string of cups were brought out, put on, and we were back in business.

The big woods across the road, where we got all of our nature study, has been cut down for lumber. The field where we played ball, now has a house and horse barn on it, with a road right in the middle of it, all the way to the house.

The pond where we swam when we skipped school is full almost to the top of the dam with silt and not enough water for swimming.

The road has been blacktopped almost to the lock.

The colored school is not there anymore, but there is a building that may have been used for a school.

A lot of the houses have been torn down along with some of the barns that we hung out in during inclement weather.

The light line from the power plant goes right across the farm we lived on and looking down the river from the Tyrone Bridge, I don't believe anyone has built between the bridge and Lock #5.

From where we lived on the river to Lock Road was about a mile (could not be traveled by car) and then about two more miles to the school. This was the route we took to school each morning because we had to be there in time for classes.

When school was dismissed for the day it was out time and we had about ten routes we could take home. Some of them were just across country, up to six or seven miles. We had to be home in time to do our chores (get firewood and water, feed the animals and check and bait the trap lines, trotlines and nets). We never had any homework from school because this was all taken care of while we were at school.

There is no way to have as much fun going to school today as we had. I don't think I would have made it through all eight grades if I had to ride a school bus and study in a room with only one grade.

I have been fully retired for about twelve years, and to me, here and now are the good old days.

LYE SOAP

I have been planning for years to make lye soap and this is the year to get it done. Have everything on hand to make it. Found a fromula for it, so will be off soon to see if the wife and I can make it.

Mom made a lot of soap. All the grease she could not use for cooking was saved to make soap.

The lye soap was used mostly for the laundry and winter time when the bath was taken inside (wash tub). Lye soap could not be used in the summer time because the baths were taken in the river. She would buy Ivory soap because it would float. The lye soap would sink if you dropped it and someone would have to dive to the bottom to retrieve it.

Could always tell in cold weather who had taken their bath and had their clothes washed in lye soap. Put 30 kids in a school room, with the stove good and hot, and walk around the room and with one sniff you could point out who used lye soap and who used store bought soap. Could also tell who had put their long johns on in the fall and worn them all winter. There were a few of them around back in the 30's and 40's.

There were not too many brands of soap in the store. Can remember Ivory because it would float but we also used a brand called Lifebuoy. There was another one that was a big bar that Mom used for laundry – something like Octagon (?).

They did come out with an Ivory Soap Flake but it had to be used in a washing machine. There was some kind of a bar soap that was used on wash boards. The flakes could be used for washing dishes.

Now, they have bars, flakes, powders and liquids – must be hundreds of them. Used for baths, laundry, dish washer, dishes in the sink, washing machines and some with wax added for washing the car. A number of brands for the dogs, cats and horses. Also, no end to the kind of shampoos, rinses and such for the hair.

At one time, this was all done with the homemade lye soap.

The wife and I are going to make a batch of lye soap and run a test to see if we can survive a week of doing everything with only lye soap. This will probably be a test that we both flunk.

THE SEWING MACHINE

The one thing that every household had to have, back in the 30's ands 40's, was a sewing machine – hard to get by without one. There were 10 of us kids and that was a lot of rips and tears in shirts, pants and dresses.

Mom did most of her patching by hand with a needle and thread but there were times when she needed the sewing machine.

I can remember when nothing was wasted. Every rag was saved and used for something. Mom sewed a lot of quilt tops and could make one out of anything.

Mom saved old neck ties and everyone saved them for her. When she had enough she took them apart, sewed them back together and made a quilt top.

Pop rolled his smokes and used Gold Grain Tobacco. It was a nickel a bag and came with rolling papers. All the older boys used duke mixture – same size bag. Mom saved all the bags and took them apart, dyed them different colors, sewed them into strips, sewed the strips back together and had another quilt top. Mom made a number of quilts out of the tobacco sacks.

The socks, long johns, and linings out of coats were cut into strips, pleated together and made into a throw rug by sewing the pleated strips together.

Mom ordered the scrap material from Sears and Roebuck by the pound. Used it to cut out pieces for a quilt top. All the scraps left from this were sewn together in squares and made another quilt top. She called it a crazy quilt.

These quilts were not made for show. With 10 kids and only a drum stove to heat by it took a lot of quilts to keep warm in the winter. The quilts were used when there were not enough feather ticks to go around.

One of the first things that was purchased for the wife at Christmas was a sewing machine from Sears. She kept it around for a couple of years – don't think she ever used it. Someone came by and borrowed it and they loaned it to someone, then they loaned it to someone. That was 30 years ago and don't know where it is and don't care. Today, we get a rip or lose a button off a shirt – throw it away and get a new one.

HUNTING SEASON

I can remember back when Kentucky did not have a hunting season for deer because there were not many of them around – see maybe one or two a year. The dog would be chasing them when they came down across the farm and swim the river.

Went down and picked up my $5 hunting license this year. There is space on the back for logging 6 deer or turkey but I don't hunt anymore. Never went deer hunting but once in my life and that was with a Game Warden, out of season. Showed him where the deer was and he handed the rifle to me and told me to shoot him one. Someone had told me what he would do, so I just shot into the air and scared the deer off. He got mad and made me walk all the way back home.

Heard a story many years ago about a Game Warden that went out on the river with Bill Fint (over at Tyrone) to do some fishing with dynamite. The way I hear it was – Bill lit the stick of dynamite, threw it down in the boar and the Game Warden picked it up and threw it in the river. Don't remember all the story but they do say that Bill picked the fish up that were killed and took them home with him.

Never shot a deer myself but now and then someone will bring me one and the meat is all ground into hamburger. This is used to make my chili with (better than hamburger or sausage).

Can't believe the number of deer there are today – everywhere. Coming from Possum Ridge Boat Ramp at Taylorsville Lake about a month ago and saw hundreds of them along the road eating and just lying on the banks (from the ramp to the highway).

The deer is getting to be a real hazard on the road at night. Brother hit one about a week ago coming back from Beaver Lake. Almost got stopped in time but just nudged him a little. Did not knock him down but made him move a little faster.

Went fishing up at Cave Run last year and had an encounter with a black bear (I think) but did not see him. I was told they had been restocked up that way. There were not any lights at the boat ramp but they had been in the trash cans. Have now limited my fishing at Cave Run to daylight hours, and then only with a crowd.

HAND-ME-DOWNS

Growing up with five older brothers there was no such thing as new clothes except when school was ready to start a new year – some new clothes were brought. Sometimes there was just nothing left over to wear to school. Clothes with patches on them were okay and they did not have to fit to be used. Everyone got a new pair of shoes once a year – about the time the weather started to cool down. They were worn out by the time the weather started to warm up to where we could go without shoes.

Until the age of thirteen, I never had a pair of dress pants – but bib overhauls or blue jeans. When they got worn out really bad, the legs were cut off and used for patches and worn in the summer.

Hand-me-downs were a way of life when growing up. The one big problem they caused was that there were ten of us kids and next to the youngest was the only girl. For a while, baby brother got to wear dresses (have pictures of this). This only lasted a short time because by the time he started school he was in regular boys clothes.

Did not have hand-me-down shoes because they were bought big and were beyond repair by the time we outgrew them. Pop had one of the metal shoe horns on a stand and he could put on new heels and keep them together with a few tacks until they were thrown away. Any good part of the shoe that was left was used for hinges on the outhouses or barns.

Socks and underwear were not a problem. We did not have any most of the time. Just work socks and long johns in the worst part of the winter.

If there were any hats or gloves around, the first ones to get up and leave the house got to wear them – except Pop. No one wore any of his clothes because he worked to support all of us and he had first choice on everything.

Times were hard – so I am told. Did not know it at the time and don't ever remember having to stay home because we had nothing got wear.

FIRST SNOW

I cannot believe that something can give so much discomfort today that gave so much pleasure in the past.

The first snow of the season has me trapped inside. Only tracks in the front yard are where the mailman came through and where the wife went out to get my paper for me. The backyard has tracks where I put out seed for my birds and some scraps for my pair of opossums. One of the neighborhood cats has been by to check the deck to see if they could find something to get into. Also, a set of tracks that could be a rabbit or it could be from one of the squirrels that was looking to see if I put any peanuts out for him.

I can remember a few winters back when the snow started to fall that we would grab the sled, head for our favorite hill and sit and wait for the snow to get deep enough for that first ride. Temperature had nothing to do with it or how wet we got. We had to see how many runs we could get in before it got too dark. You just built a good roaring fire to keep warm by while you were waiting for your turn for a ride. Most of the time someone would have to come and get us when supper was ready.

This riding a sled took a lot of getting ready. First the sled had to be built – don't ever remember owning a store bought sled. The sled we had the winter before had been used for firewood back in the spring after there was no more snow. The track had to be cleaned of rock and any bushes that had appeared that summer and the wood for the fire had to be stocked ahead of time – it is hard to find after the snow falls.

It was good if the river was frozen over. If not, we had to use an alternate track where we could get stopped before we got to the river.

The old barrel stave sled was not much good in deep snow but a couple of slow turns to pack the snow down and they worked fine. You could steer them and as many as four could ride it at the same time.

With snow on the ground, the sled went everywhere with us, unless we were hunting. Pull it up all the hills and ride it down all hills and Anderson County was made of up and down hills in most places.

Used the roads most of the time, as there was no snow removal then and very little traffic.

THE ROCK WALL OR FENCE

The rock fences have been in the news a lot the last couple of years and they keep calling them rock walls.

Growing up in Anderson County there were not a lot of rock fences. They were not easy to build on a lot of the Anderson County acreage. Along the river and creek, a rock fence was not needed and they were not used often.

The good thing about a rock fence was you never had to replace them and the cattle could not break them down.

Some of the bad things were they were hard to build and they took up a lot of space and the snakes (all kinds) loved them as a place to take up residence. They were rather hard to climb over when you were hunting and it was about impossible to move one.

Good thing was there was plenty of rock around for building them and it was cheap because you owned the land – you owned the rock.

The farm Pop owned next to Lock #5 property had a rock fence from the upper end all the way to the lock property. Most of it was down and in need of repair except right behind the house. The fence separated the river bottoms (used for crops) from the river cliff and the road that ran behind it.

During the season, all the land was used for crops and gardens. The house and barn were on one side and the horse and cow (if you had one) were put out to pasture on the other side. The places where the rock fence was down, we put up barbwire fence.

They tell me most of these fences were built by slaves.

The portions of the fence that we had missing were used in the foundation of the house we lived in. Some were also used in the fireplace and chimney. Every house that I lived in for the first 18 years of my life had a rock foundation under them. The basement walls were also built out of rock. Back then we called them root cellars. They were only used to store potatoes, apples and the fruit jars that had been filled with good things to eat during the winter.

Another bad thing about the rock fence was it could not hold the goats we raised. They could also handle the barbwire fence. Had to keep them tied most of the time.

I believe the rock fence is a thing of beauty that will last forever if someone does not tear it down.

TOILET PAPER OR SUBSTITUTES

The roll of toilet paper is something that is not given much thought to, until you run out. It comes in a roll of around four hundred sheets. The wife gets the twelve roll quilted pack and it is a double roll. The last package she got, she pitched it on the floor of the linen closet in the downstairs bathroom. The hot water heater sprang a leak in Saturday and the water went under the wall where the twelve pack soaked it up. By Monday, when the toilet paper needed to be moved, I could not pick it up because it must have weighed close to forty pounds. I was going to spread it in the backyard to dry but it has rained or snowed every day now for over a week. I decided to just throw it out.

I was in my teens before my first experience with toilet paper – had heard of it but that was all. With no inside plumbing, there were a number of things used as substitutes for toilet paper at home and at school.

The Sears Roebuck and Montgomery Ward catalogs were the favorite – would have been great if we had phone books. Newspapers were okay – used a lot of them at school. Also, all school paper that was to be thrown away was used. Brown paper bags from the grocery were used in emergencies.

A lot of people tell me that the corncob was used but don't know about this because I never used one that I know of. At home, they were used for starting a fire in the stove.

It was a different story if you were out in the woods hunting or fishing the river. A hand full of green leaves was the number one choice in the summer. In the winter, a few dried leaves were about as good. Grass was okay if it was green but not so good if it was dried.

When stationed out west in Arizona, Texas and New Mexico, things were different. Everything that grows out there has thorns on it, so it was necessary to pack something with you.

Got addicted to using toilet paper when in training at Ft. Knox. Only had to revert back to the things that were used as a kid when at home on leave.

This item is kept in the survival kit on the boat. When out fishing these days, the bathrooms at the lakes are not always stocked with paper.

NOON WHISTLE

The noon whistle was something I had forgotten about until I recently read a piece in the paper about it. It really brought back memories of long, long ago when the noon whistle was one of our time pieces.

All the factories and distilleries had a steam whistle that was blown at noon and again at quitting time. There were enough of them around that one of them could be heard about anywhere in Anderson County.

At home, we had one clock and most of the time Pop had a watch. Saw him take it out a number of times and look at it when the whistle blew.

First wristwatch that was ever put on my arm was one that the Army issued to me.

When growing up, the only thing we had to keep time by was the sun. If we were out hunting, on the river fishing, or just roaming the countryside, and the whistle blew and the sun was low in the west, that would be the quitting time whistle. We knew it would not be long before Pop would be home and the chores needed to be done. Whatever we were doing, we dropped it and headed for home. This also let us know that it was about supper time.

If you got home late and had to chop the wood for the kitchen stove by the light of a kerosene lantern a couple of times – made you want to be on time the next day.

The noon whistle also let the school teacher know that it was lunch time. Her watch did not always run just right.

The train whistles at night would carry for a long distance. This was another way to tell time at night. The only problem with this was that train was not always on time.

When working at Lock #5 – if one of the oil barges was coming up or down the river, they would blow the horn about a mile away and we could be ready for them when they arrived. Could not mistake the boat horn or the train whistle for the noon whistle because they all had their own sound.

A lot of the larger boats that went up and down the river had horns. Mr. Hunter, who had been the lock tender for years, could tell you what boat it was just by hearing the horn. He also took his watch out and looked at it each time the noon whistle at Ripy Brothers Distillery was sounded.

NOODLING

Just watched a show on noodling for big catfish (blues, channel and flat heads). Growing up in Anderson County, KY, and fish being a big part of our menu, there were times when we had to go this route to get a mess of fish.

I don't ever remember catching one that went over two pounds other than a carp. The farm ponds had a good crop of the smaller pond cats (yellowbellies) and most times you could get one out of every cow track in the mud. We only did this if we had no hook and line with us or if we could not find any bait.

Bluegills were normally our big catch. They were a lot easier to catch than the catfish. They would hide under anything and were a lot easier to corner.

Caught a lot of snakes this way but as soon as you knew it was a snake, it called for a quick release – better known as catch and release.

Could catch a turtle this way but I was never brave enough to try this. You could take a stick with a nail in it and find them but someone had to catch it for me.

In the creeks it was easy when you could just turn the rocks over and catch them by hand. This took two people and one of them had to be rather fast. First you had to identify what was under the rock and then catch it before it got away.

The big challenge was catching the large carp in May when they were laying their eggs. They would swim through the driftwood and brush along the bank. Made them easy to find, but without a net they were not so easy to catch. When you did get hold of one, most times he would make you bleed all over the sharp points of his fins. Had to want a mess of fish really bad to catch one this way – with a lot of patience and a little luck, you could catch one this way.

Salt River had a lot of big flat heads and I saw a lot of them caught by hand. Never did get in on this first hand but helped to eat a few of them.

There are a lot better ways to catch a catfish. It may take a little longer and cost a little more with the price of tackle and bait these days, but then they tell me it is a lot more sporting.

THE FUNNIES

Today, they call them the comic strips – good name for them. Back in the 30's and 40's, we called them the funny papers but don't know why – because not all of them were funny.

Captain Jammer Kids – they were funny most of the time. Popeye was funny and Alley Oops (cave man) was funny. The best one was Li'l Abner and Yokeman. Always liked this one because of Daisy Mae and the Sadie Hawkins Day chase. Mommy and Poppy Yokeman were not always funny. The little fellow that always had a rain cloud over his head was good. He brought bad luck. Cannot remember his name. It was good when the Schomes showed up in Dog Patch.

Dick Tracy, Tarry and the Pirates were not meant to be funny, along with Little Orphan Annie. Andy Gumps, Little Lou Lou and Oh Henry were funny. Never understood them, but always read them – all but Henry. He never said anything – sort of had to fill in the blanks with him. Plus he did not have any hair – never did understand why. Snuffy Smith was another good one. More life than most. He was always making moonshine and drinking it, playing cards, shooting dice, stealing a chicken or pig and spent a lot of time in the local jail. Rest of the time he was sitting on the porch sleeping.

Never can remember reading the one called Mary Worth but the wife did.

Always read Flash Gordon first. They also had a short at the movie on Saturday on Flash Gordon. This is what got me into sci-fi. Still read a lot of sci-fi books.

Had Dagwood, Blondie, son Alexander, daughter Cookie and dog Daisy. They are still in the paper each day. The colored section of the funnies was saved at the time and used as wrapping for any Christmas gifts. Also used as wall paper a lot of times.

This was one of the tools for learning to read. Not used in school but a lot at home. Then they came out with the comic books. Now, they were used in school at times. Each time someone spent a dime on one, it was passed around at school all the next week and used until it was worn out.

The comic strips are in the paper every day these days but growing up they were only present in the Sunday paper. Should write a story on each one of these characters but that would be boring, so that will have to do for now.

THE CROWDED CLASS ROOMS

I have seen and heard a lot on the crowded class rooms in the schools these days. Think the problem is too many children or not enough rooms and teachers. Sounds like that should be easy to solve – just hire more teachers (pay an excellent salary) and build more schools (one has been completed and two more are under construction).

Growing up there were between 40 and 50 students in a room. The school I went to (Tyrone School) had two rooms the first two years. The rest of my schooling was in a one-room schoolhouse (Lock Road). All eight grades in the same room with only one teacher. She taught all eight grades and all subjects. Was assured free schooling for the first eight grades but believe we were short changed on subjects (reading, spelling, math, history and geography). I did okay on most of the subjects except spelling. Still have to have the dictionary handy (plus the wife) just to write a letter.

Our gym class was taken care of during lunch hour, recess and the three-mile walk to and from school. This also included the chores we had to do each and every day when we got home.

Have a 5-year-old great grandson that can read, wrote and add better than I could going into third grade and he is only in kindergarten.

First book I ever read was my First Grade Reader. Had to leave it at my desk as it was shared with the other students in the first grade. There were only 5 books in the eighth grade and they were left at school at all times. Some of the girls took books home but not the boys because we would leave them some place.

I was a drop-put after the eighth grade and went to work. I was 36 years old when I got my High School Equivalent (GED) by going to night school while stationed in Arizona. I was married and had two children and there was not enough money to do anything. Therefore, I went back to school at night and took the GED test.

Big problem with the classrooms today is there are too many students and too many subjects. There must be about twenty (plus or minus) different subjects for the students today. We only had five subjects. There is just not enough time in the school year to teach all of them.

If I went back to school today, they would most likely start me in the second or thirds grade and then I would probably fail at the end of the year.

FISHING THEN AND NOW

Back when I was growing up, you got a break and time to go fishing. The following things had to be decided: what we were going to fish for, the bait that was needed, where the fish should be and the weather.

Going for bluegill, you had to dig the worms, catch the young wasps, strip a lot of horseweeds (for the small worms inside), gather a bucket of bag worms (in season), or a bucket of crayfish (large ones – peel the tails). It took about half a day of work just to get the bait. Now we just stop at the bait shop and pick up what is needed.

When going for catfish, best bait was the soft craw or the gizzard out of the shad. Could spend all day snagging the shad for just enough bait for a couple of hours fishing. The soft craws called for a couple of nights in the creek with a light catching them by hand. Then they had to be kept cool so the shells would not get hard. You could also get a few catfish on green worms, which were easy to find along the river bank. Problem was, they were also liked by the white perch (drone) – good to eat but hard to keep alive. Today, you just pick up a few buckets of chicken livers, stroll over to Wal-Mart for a bottle of crawfish scent to spray on the liver. This makes the catfish think they are getting soft craws.

For croppie or bass, we had to have live minnows – a long walk and seining for the minnows – wherever we could find them. Now it amounts to a trip to the bait shop.

Buffalo and carp called for dough balls. Mom always made them and there were some on hand most of the time.

Turtles just called for a turtle hook and a lot of looking, mostly in the creeks and farm ponds – always had a hook around. Frogs called for a gig, light and some night work. Most times we had no gig and no light. Catching them by hand was a big job.

Tackle has gone the other direction. As a kid, it was just a cane pole, line, couple of hooks and something to use for a sinker. Today, it calls for a couple of hundred dollars worth of rods, reels and tackle plus a boat and a truck to pull it.

Fish the lakes these days. Growing up it was river, creeks and farm ponds in Anderson and Woodford Counties. I can only remember fishing Herrington Lake once as a kid and fished all night but did not catch any fish.

THE MAILBOX

I can remember as a very young lad that we had a mailbox – everyone had one. This is the only thing that we always had. It may have been on a post along the road, fastened to the house or one at the Post Office. It was our mailbox and no one was allowed to touch it except us and the person that delivered the mail.

We were taught at a young age that we were not to touch any mailbox except ours. If you walked by one with a package hanging on it, it was okay to knock on the owner's door and infrom them that they had a package on the mailbox. You were not allowed to take anything out of someone's box or put anything in the mailbox.

Growing up – about all mailboxes were about the same. Today, it is hard to find two that are anything alike. They look like everything from a house, car, truck down to a pet. Mine looks like a thirty-pound catfish. They are in bunches now at apartment buildings, trailer parks, etc.

I did break the law one time – a fellow made me mad and that night I shot a hole in his mailbox with a 22 cal. Rifle. I felt so bad about it later that I helped him fix it.

No mailbox is safe anymore. People have come up with dozens of ways to destroy them. A few people have encased them in brick or rock to protect them. A few on Cardwell Lane are made out of heavy gauge steel pipe. I bet that would ring your chimes if you drove by and whacked it with a bat or pipe.

Worked on a lot of mailboxes when employed by the Transportation Cabinet on road maintenance crew. The mowing crews in the summer and the snow plows in the winter were murder on mailboxes and one of my jobs was putting them back up. If they were damaged beyond repair, had to pick up a new one at Yagel's and replace it and a lot of times the post also.

Interfering with someone's mailbox is still a federal offence but very few people get caught at it.

HILLSIDE PLOW

Spring of the year, I was out in the truck – pulling the boat – on the way to see if the fish were hungry. There are very few fields that have been plowed and ready for the crops to be planted. A lot of farms have gone to no-till for corn, soybeans, etc.

I can remember working the farms in Anderson, Woodford and Franklin Counties back in the 40's. Now, a lot of the land in Anderson County is level and normal farm land. Down around Sinai area, level land is at a premium. Most of it is ridges and hollows. Roads on top of the ridges take up most of the level land.

Cannot plow this land with a regular plow. You must have a hillside plow. One furrow along the bottom, flip the blade and back the other way.

Cannot plow around the field. It must be plowed from the bottom to the top with the hillside plow. This must take about ten or twelve inches off the top of the hill each time it is plowed.

Looks like, that sooner or later, all the soil would end up at the bottom of the hill, along the creek bank.

Never heard of anyone starting at the top of the hill and turning the furrows up the hill to keep it in balance.

Back when all this was done with a team of horses or mules. Most hills were too steep for working with a tractor. With the tractors these days, most of the hay is worked with a tractor.

Guess most of them have gone to no-till except for tobacco. You could plow all of it in the same direction. By plowing one furrow, raise the blades, drive back across the field with the blade up. That should work but would add a lot of extra time and driving.

I am sure they have worked something out, but back in the 40's there was no other way of doing it.

Would say the hillside plow is a thing of the past except where the farmer has his mailbox mounted on them. Saw a few of them on the way to Taylorsville Lake to go crappie fishing.

CHAPTER SEVEN

STORES IN MILLVILLE

I can remember when growing up there were three stores in the Millville area. All were just plain old country stores (well, maybe not quite).

If your watch stopped running, had a clock that would not run, or a gun you hunted with had a broken or worn part, you got these services done at the Davis Store. This was located at the south end of Old Taylor Distillery. Mr. Davis also had about everything you needed including candy bars and soda on ice. I believe all three of the old store buildings are still standing. Mr. Davis would also trade for a few fish and sometimes he would buy the fish because he knew we were going to spend it before we left the store.

Most of the time if we just wanted candy or a coke, Mr. Tutt had these and his store was the one closest to the house. Mr. Tutt also sold gas and oil for the car or boat. Sometimes he would let us have things on credit. He owned a big farm and liked to let us work it off when he needed things done on the farm.

Days that we were going some place to work all day, we would stop at the Ruby Store. He had a meat department in his store with all kinds of good things. He also had a gas pump where we could get gas. One stop – he had everything we needed – couple of pounds of cheese, pound of bologna, box of crackers, loaf of bread, dollar's worth of gas and quart of oil. Get it all on the way to work, then pay for it on our way home that night. Mr. Ruby also had free air if we needed it for tires and most times we did.

Friday or Saturday night, when most of the kids in Millville would get together, ten to twenty of us (boys and girls) going to Mr. Ruby's store was the longest walk and we wanted to be together as long as possible. This was prime time for courting. If we had a little money to spend we always went to Mr. Ruby's). The ones that did not have any money would sit on the rock wall at Old Taylor and talk.

From our house on the river to Mr. Ruby's store there were about thirty-seven homes, two other stores (for a total of three), two churches and two big distilleries.

Kids of all ages were allowed to join in. If they could not walk that far, they were carried home. A few of the older kids had bicycles that worked and everyone took turns on them.

The old Tutt Store is now a body shop. Davis Store has sat empty for years now. The Ruby Store has changed hands a few times – had a pool hall at one time, video store and has had a restaurant added to the side of it now. No one sells gas anymore. The new store across from the old store is nice but don't stop there very often.

SHIPS VOYAGE

I was 17 when I was put aboard a ship for my first ocean voyage. If I had known what I was in for, I may not have taken it.

It was a troop ship operated by the Navy and I was in the Army. I was made to go by Army regulations as well as Navy. Not an easy thing to do as sick as I got a few days out.

Don't know how many troops there were on this ship but there were a bunch of them. Took 16 days for the crossing to Japan and I spent most of it in the chow line.

Got a little sleep at night. Had us stacked 4 deep in the hole – no room to sit down any place. You stayed in the bunk or stood up. When we were on deck this was about as bad because you were only allowed on some parts of the ship.

Was all right the first day or two, then I got seasick and was bad for about 3 days. Then made up my mind if I was to survive the trip, I had to get over it and after that everything was all right. Stayed on deck in good weather and below in bad.

Had a good trip once I got over being sick. A little time, now and then, for some cards. Did a little reading. Got the chow line down after a while and everyone was eating. Spent a few hours on deck sunning.

Was no work to do – too many people and not enough jobs. I did work for a few hours in the galley. A little time chipping paint but most time we just laid around and did nothing.

Only hit one bad storm and that was an experience I will never forget. Either the front or the back of the ship was out of the water at all times – one end out and the other end coming down. Hit hard and then back up and the other end hit. About 40 hours of this and no one could go on deck and could not take a shower. It was like riding a bull every time you went to the head.

Trying to eat was something, with the metal tables and metal trays. Sometimes you could eat out of 3 or 4 different trays in one meal.

Took a lot of voyages after that. Total of 5 across the Pacific and 4 across the Atlantic. Piece of cake after the first one and never got sick after that first trip.

Out of Seattle on 3 trips and back into San Francisco twice. Out of New York twice to Bremerhaven Germany and back twice.

CLIFTON

Cannot remember the ferry at Clifton and don't know what year it was closed. But I do know that there was a road all the way to the river on the Anderson County side and one on the Woodford County side.

For a while there was a boat tied up on the Anderson County side of the river. This was like a large houseboat but it was a bar and I think they sold food also. Hung out there a lot with an older brother.

This was a good place to go with a date just to drink a few beers – not a rowdy place like some of them.

The reason I liked it so well, they had a penny slot machine. Just as much fun to play as a nickel or dime machine and could play all night on a dollar. We would take turns at playing, so no one ever lost more than a dollar. Sometimes, we came out a dollar or so ahead.

Don't know if they had trouble with the law or what. Maybe just wanted a new location and new customers, but they moved across the river and tied up on the Woodford County side.

Was drinking a little beer by now and brother had a car. We would get a few people together, drive up and have a few beers.

Could drink a few beers here and get home down through Millville without getting out on the main highway. Sometimes the driver would have more beer than he should have. If things got bad, we just pulled over, parked, and slept if off and went home the next morning.

I did not drive at the time – was too young. Drinking a few beers I could get away with as long as Mom did not find out about it. This is what got me into a lot of trouble one night while drinking at Clifton.

About half way up the hill, coming out of Clifton, was a spring with very cold water year round. Someone had built a big round pool about 10 feet across and about 3 feet deep and put a pipe in the spring and ran the water in this pool – staying full at all times.

Had a beer or so too many one night and got silly as I did when I drank more than I should. Brother could not take me home like this, so he stopped at the spring, and they threw me in the pool to sober me up. That did the trick all right but we all ended up in the pool soaking wet.

Was in the fall of the year and the weather had cooled down a little. We all got back in the car to get warm. About half way home the car quit running and we spent one miserable night. Sun came up and we fixed the car and drove home. That was the last time anyone put me in the spring.

SWAMP LAND AT TRUMBO BOTTOM

I don't suppose the swamp can really be called a swamp because it was more of a wet land. Just a hole of water that has no way to run out and into the river. To most people it was just a mud hole, good for nothing. This could be, but if it was ever drained, it would take away a lot of memories for me and a lot of other people.

Growing up, this hole of water was a lot of things to a lot of people. Some of our special uses for it was fishing. Summer time we could fish, swim, wade, and just spend the day there.

Winter time it was a special place because when it froze over we used it as a skating rink. Froze quick as it was still water and not too deep. If the ice broke, which it did a lot of times, you would get wet and have to build a fire to dry out. This was all in a day of playing.

If the weather was right and it froze over hard and went a few days with no snow, you could see right through the ice. Turtles would float up off the bottom to the ice and you could take an axe and cut them out. This was a great source of meat in the winter. Have come out of there with 3 or 4 gunny sacks full of turtles.

Fish were the same way when the river got high and flooded over into this hole. When it went down, it would leave a lot of carp in this hole. Chop them out just like the turtles. Made a lot of people in town happy. We would go in, full the trunk of the car full of fish, and take them to town and give them away.

Had a brother that lived in one of the houses on the Dunn Farm for a while and I used this swamp a few times for duck hunting. Never did find anyone who knew how to cook a wild duck to where I could eat it, so I did not waste much time on this.

Don't know the fellow that owns the place now and he has it all posted – No Hunting or Fishing at all. Have talked to him a few times and he is not a bad fellow. He says people do too much damage so he just tries to keep them out. Can see his side of it but it is a shame that the kids today cannot use it they way we did when we were young. Not many kids that want to do things like that today anyway, but a few of them around.

Mr. Dunn let us use the swamp because we worked for him a lot in the hay, tobacco and corn. He had rules though – no cutting live trees, use the gates, and no climbing the fences. Most fences were just a few strands of barbwire and you could crawl under them. We had to be real careful with fire – no big ones because at night he could tell if we had a big one.

ROCK BAR AT MOUTH OF GLENNS CREEK

The mouth of Glenns Creek, where it empties into the river, has always been a favorite hangout for a lot of people, for different reasons.

I can remember in summer when the water in the river was low, this was where everyone went to swim. There was about two feet of water between the bank and the rock bar that showed above the water.

Anyone who came out from town and wanted to go swimming – this is where we went. Could walk up the bank or go up by boat. Just a short walk and it was a great place to swim. Small kids, who could not swim, stayed on the inside of the bar while older ones who could swim on the outside. It dropped off real steep into deep water and if two people wanted to be alone, it was a short swim to the big, flat rock along the other side of the river.

This has always been a good place for fishing, high water or low water, back in the 40's. The three distilleries on the creek ran a lot of stuff in the creek (cannot do that anymore) such as caustic soda and lots of sewer water from the drying house. All this made for a nice fishing hole at the mouth of the creek for snagging buffalo and carp. I could never get the hang of this kind of fishing but had a brother that was an expert at it, and Pop was pretty good also. This was done with five large hooks on the end of the line, big reel on a cane pole with eyes taped to it, throw it out, let it sink to the bottom, then when a fish swam into it, it would move the line a little, and you would snap the end of the pole hard and set the hooks. Have seen my brother land them up to forty-five pounds and could be hooked any place.

At night the fish would move up the creek and this is when we would sneak in real quiet, with a gas lantern or light of some kind and gig them. Took a little more skill this way. Very hard to hold a thirty-pound fish on the end of a stick (usually a broom or mop handle). Also got everyone in the boat wet.

The rock bar was also a hazard for anyone traveling up and down the river in a fast boat (not too many of them around but a few out of Frankfort). When the rocks were above the water it was not too bad, but a few inches below the water – look out. Would stop a boat dead still, no matter how fast you were running and everything in the boat – people included – would land up to thirty feet out in front. Only saw this happen once and that was enough.

The bar is still a good place to fish and a good swimming place if you wear your shoes. A lot of people use the creek for a dump and everything they throw in the creek winds up down stream on the bar – so waders beware.

TRAIN TRAVEL

Have crossed the states a number of times by train but my first train ride was the one I remember best. The shortest of them all but being my first time on a train that did not matter.

My oldest brother and I got aboard at the depot in Lawrenceburg and rode to Providence Crossing just past Salvisa. Cost us 15 cents each. I was working for my brother at the time and also lived with him and his wife.

Second train ride was a little longer. Got aboard the train in Louisville and changed to another train in Cincinnati. From there to Seattle, Washington, I had a sleeper which was a seat during the day and let down for a bed at night. Compartment held 4 people and made 4 bunks at night (two up and two down).

Army had issued me enough meal tickets to have 3 meals a day. These were taken in the dining car. Two or three choices at each meal. This was a very enjoyable ride and took about 3 days I believe.

Not much to see until we got out west. It was December and I believe the mountains in Washington State, with the snow on them, were the prettiest things I had ever seen.

My next train ride was from Oakland, California to Chicago. Had been discharged at Camp Stolman. Bought civilian clothes and traveled as a private citizen.

The train was called the California Zephyr. A compartment for sitting and sleeping in, but also had seating in the glass dome on top of each car. This one had a dining car but it also had a cocktail car. This car had to close when we were in some states but stayed open most of the time.

Up through Feather River Canyon in California was a lovely sight.

Had a lot of people on the train that were going to Colorado to go skiing. Made the trip very entertaining to just out of Denver where they got off. By now I needed a rest anyway. Slept the rest of the way into Chicago.

This was my best train ride to this point. You have not really lived until you have crossed the country by train. Can see things from a train you cannot see from a car or bus.

Traveled from Maryland to Washington State and from California back to Louisville a couple of times but none of them could come close to my trip on the Zephyr.

GARDNER HOUSE ON GLENNS CREEK ROAD

The Gardner house became our home when we came down river. It was smaller than we had been used to. Consisted of three rooms downstairs, one upstairs, three porches and a garage. Couple of the older kids had left home by now, so we had plenty of room.

One end of the house was a log cabin. The upstairs was really an attic. Had a large rock chimney with a fireplace in it, so the attic got a lot of heat from the rock in the chimney. They would stay warm most of the night after the fire had gone out.

This is the one house I can remember where we could have a stove in each of the rooms downstairs – cooking stove in the kitchen, wood stove in the middle room, and a fireplace in the other. Firewood was everywhere. Railroad ran right by the house which meant good source for coal (could be burned in the kitchen stove or the fireplace).

This place had everything. The road ran right by the front of the hose, river just over the bank (sometimes during high water it was too close for comfort), good spring right behind the house, (if it ran low, was one just up the river which ran all year). This was also close to Pop's work and he could walk up the railroad, which took about 10 minutes.

Lots of farms around on both sides of the river where we could pick up a few days work when we needed it.

Best trotline and hoop net fishing I have ever run across and still is.

School bus picked the kids up right at the house and then dropped them there at the end of the day. This was a new experience for all of us.

This place even had a level garden space and we had a nice garden every year we were there.

Not so far from town – just 7 miles by road and about 5 miles if we walked down the railroad. The only problem with the railroad was we had to go through the tunnel at the end of Broadway. Could also go by boat.

Rent was kind of high – a total of $8.00 a month. Sometimes this could be worked off as the landlady raised corn and tobacco.

Lots of wild berries close on both sides of the river. Could sit on the porch and see everything that went up or down the river.

All but 2 or 3 of the neighbors within a couple of miles were nice neighbors.

The house is still there – the only one left in that area. It has been rebuilt a number of times and has been under water a number of times. Has been enlarged and has a bathroom and everything now.

THE BOTTOM

When growing up, if you went down Broadway and turned right on Washington Street, you were in Craw. We called it "The Bottom". First building on the left was a Church and second building was Peach Tree Inn. This was my favorite hangout because they had more girls to dance with plus they had beer and a juke box like all the other places.

Started rather early, at age fifteen, but I did not drink beer. Just liked to hang out, drink cokes, listen to the music and watch the people. This was always with Pop or an older brother or two.

Each Friday night we made all the places during the night. A couple of beers in each one. Cannot remember the names of all of them but a few were Tip Toe Inn, Blue Moon, Dew Drop Inn, and Twenty Grand's. Can see Grace as clear as day sitting behind the bar eating chili and smoking a cigar.

The one thing I did not like about these Friday nights was the fact there was going to be a fight – sometimes more than one. Could stay out of them most of the time but did get whacked now and then. Did not have to be in the fight – just in the bar where it started.

The one that started the fight would get put out and go to another place. After a while everyone involved in the fight would follow them and it would start all over again. As a rule, this could take place in three or four establishments. As soon as everyone got whipped real bad, everyone would sit down and have a beer. No one was mad at anyone by closing time. Go back the next week and do it all over again. I believe it was a way for them to get rid of the tension that built up over the week. Sometimes it was brother against brother.

Sometimes the fights were over a girl but not always. It could start because someone took a drink out of the wrong beer, sat down in the wrong booth, walked in front of someone at the wrong time, did not get everyone a fresh beer, or got one beer too many. Fight could start over anything.

Someone could pull a knife and everyone in the place was on top of them. Even the ones that were in that bunch. Knives were a no-no. If anyone ever had a gun with them, they kept it hidden – never saw one. Even the guy behind the bar only had a club and he was the only one allowed even that.

Know now that the bottom was not a good place to hang out. But outside of a few sore heads and a little skin missing on Saturday morning, cannot remember anyone getting hurt real bad. I am sure they did but I was never around when that happened.

FIRST RIFLE

Tried to buy a plinking rifle the other day but could not buy one. All the things you have to go through today to get one, I would rather just do without. Just wanted a 22 caliber rim fire to shoot a few targets with.

Back at age 15, I was working regular and went and had me a Mosburg 22 Cal., semi-automatic put on lay-away. You guessed it – at Western Auto on Main Street. Took me about 4 weeks to get it paid for but when I picked it up to take it home, the clerk gave me a box of shells FREE of charge (50 rounds). I thought this was the greatest thing that anyone could do.

Did not get this to hunt with, but used it for what we called plinking. Just sat on the porch and shot at whatever came floating down the river – a stick or a tree leaf. Three of four of us just wanted to see who could hit the closest to it.

This was my rifle but everyone had to buy their own shells.

Used it for hunting some. It was great for hunting groundhogs or squirrels. Shotgun was better but a good shot could get a squirrel now and then. Rifle shells were a lot cheaper than shotgun shells.

Kept it in the boat when fishing and used it to kill a few turtles. Even tried it on fish a few times. Don't think I ever killed one though. Could drive the gars crazy when they were floating on top of the water.

Had a younger brother who was not allowed to use the rifle because we caught him shooting at birds with it. Blackbirds were fine to shoot at, but someone caught him shooting at robins.

Packed this rifle for hundreds of miles. Took it everywhere with me when I was not working or going to town. The only time I know of misusing it was when I shot a hole in a fellow's mailbox because I was mad at him. Felt so bad about it, that I helped him fix it a few days later. Did not tell him I did it though. Just agreed with him that it was a terrible thing for anyone to do.

I was trying to date one of his daughters at the time.

FIRST BICYCLE

I can remember the first bicycle better than I can remember my first car. I was living with my brother and his wife in town and working on East Main Street.

Got paid one Friday and went in and paid my board for the week. Walked up town to Western Auto on Main Street (about where the bakery is now) and picked out a bicycle I wanted. Gave the clerk all the money I had (about half of what I needed) and told him to hold it for me until the following Friday.

To my surprise he wrote down what I owed him and told me to ride it home and just come in the following Friday and pay the other half. This was my first experience with credit. Worried about it all week until I got him paid, which I did the following Friday.

Now you talk about a happy fellow. Jumped on that dude and rode it 7 miles to Millville. I was so tired and out of breath when I got there that I could not talk for 30 minutes.

Mom was real proud of me but Pop was not so happy about it. He just knew he would have to pay for it.

Made me very popular for a while. I was the only kid around with a new one and everyone had to ride. It just about got worn out the first couple of weeks I had it.

Had me a rack on the back of it and a second rider could ride there. The girls could ride it sidesaddle style. (This was when all the girls still wore dresses or skirt/blouse).

After I got it paid for and had a little money in my pocket, it made a lot of trips from the river all the way to the Ruby Store in Millville. Not always with me on it but everyone used it for this purpose.

Always rode it back to town on Sunday night and back home on Friday night. Sat most of the week because we all walked to and from work and when I got home I was too tired to ride it.

I cannot say that having a bicycle changed or improved my life all that much. Big thing was I could get places a lot faster and that gave me more time for other things.

Did ride it to Versailles a few times but a long trip that way. Was a lot easier and faster if I caught a ride with someone. Could not ride it fishing because could never get through the weeds and bushes if I had fishing poles with me – better to walk.

Thinking back on it, I bought the bicycle just to show off with it more than any other reason.

Bicycles did last a year or so with a new tire/tube now and then. Back rack, fenders and chain guard all went one at a time. Finally sold it cheap for a few dollars – Spending Money.

DRIVE-INS

Frankfort has another drive-in eat at and someone told me that here you can order and they bring the food to you. Makes me think of the carhops years ago. Frisch's on the eastside of town is where everyone would hang out. Sometimes we went to Jerry's on the Versailles Road.

Places to eat were fine but the drive-in movie was the one I liked the most. It was a weekly thing for us to go to the movie at the drive-in.

All the brothers that had a car went to the drive-in on Friday or Saturday night.

Had two of them but most of the time we went to the Starway on Louisville Road at Bridgeport.

Left home as soon as everyone got home from work on Friday. I would load up with brother, his wife, and most times a kid or two. Drive out, get in line and wait for them to open – still had an hour or two to wait. They could not start the movie until it was dark. Always parked close to the snack stand. Got the speaker set up and listened to music until movie time. Lots of trips to the snack stand for popcorn and drink. Most times we would eat hot dogs and candy also.

Had the second drive-in movie off Holmes Street – Valley View. Did not go to that one much. Was living on Gayle Street (just up from this one) but liked the Starway better.

Did not make any difference what was playing. Only went to movies in Frankfort area so it was a different movie playing each week.

It was much better when they started to show two movies on Friday night. Got more of a crowd in and it took a little more maneuvering to get a good spot and sometimes we did not all get to park together.

Went to a few drive-ins in Texas and New Mexico. This was not the same because the rest of the family was not there to share the fun.

In the 40's this was the only time I can remember getting in a traffic jam. About 1 or 2 o'clock, when the movie was over, all cars in the drive-in took off for the exit. There was only one exit out to Louisville Road. This was a sight to see and almost as good as the movie. This was a bad time to be traveling Louisville Road. Best to just pull over and wait until most had left. Don't remember any bad accidents. A few fender benders but nothing serious.

Both drive-in theaters are gone now. They turned one of them into a trailer park and entertainment place. The one at Bridgeport is an amusement park with race car track, miniature golf, etc.

Plenty of drive-ins for food around. Just pay for it, drive up to the window and pick it up – no carhops. I don't think the food is as good.

FIVE AND TEN CENT STORES

I can remember when Frankfort had two dime stores, Lawrenceburg had one, and Versailles had one. To me there was something magic about the dime store.

Could go to town with Mom. Pop would park the car on Broadway and go get him a beer. I would go with Mom and we would walk up St. Clair Street to the dime store that had a soda fountain. It took us from noon until around 3:00 p.m. to have a soda because we had to look at everything in the store and sometimes would even buy something. On the way out, we would get a bag of candy – (the only place you could get this kind of candy).

Sometimes we would check both stores. Then we stood outside the rest of the day and talked to people we only saw on Saturday when we went to town.

Mom would get me a ticket, send me to the movie and when I came out, Mom would still be there talking.

Just before dark we would meet Pop at the car, drive over to the A&P Store on Second Street, get the groceries and go home.

This was every Saturday, rain or shine, and all winter. Sometimes I got to go with Pop, but all I did was sit around and drink cokes and watch the pool games.

The older kids who had cars would drive around the block for hours (Broadway, St. Clair, Main and Ann Streets) and burn half a tank of gas. Some Saturdays I rode with them a few times, but to me walking was more fun.

The dime stores had too many treasures in them. People just could not stay away. Many times I have bought a bottle of perfume or a piece of jewelry for my girl at one of them for 10 or 15 cents. Got carried away one time and paid $3.50 for a diamond bracelet just to impress a girl.

Frankfort does not have a dime store these days. You cannot drive around the block any more because the streets are mostly one-way and there is a mall and you cannot drive on them at all.

No one goes to town on Saturday anymore because there are no movie theaters. The theaters are all out in the shopping centers where you can find a parking place.

The last time I was in a dime store was about ten years ago while I was visiting in New Hampshire. Ran across one and went crazy. Bought all I could pack (did not need it but bought it anyway). It was having a going out of business sale.

BEFORE FAST FOOD

Still a few good restaurants around. In the late 30's and early 50's, things were different. Back then there were places where you could go in, sit down with your feet under the table, order your meal, and drink coffee while you waited on your food.

Still a few of them around. One holdover from the 40's is Saylor's Restaurant and Lounge on Louisville Road. Same location, different people run it now, but the food is still good and service is great. Prices have gone up a bit but good food makes it all worthwhile – always did. Cliffside was an early one. Do not eat there much anymore but a good place for breakfast.

Some that are not around anymore – Downtown on St. Clair Street. The Wagon Wheel, owned and run by Mr. Yancey. This was where we would stop late at night on the way home. He put out a great hamburger – one was enough to get me through until morning. However, he was known to use cabbage in the hamburger if he was out of lettuce. Made no difference to me because they were still good.

On of the places I liked to eat was on Broadway called Home Restaurant. Got its name from the food – more like home cooking than you could get most places.

Mucci's on Main Street was a good place to eat. Depending on what you wanted to eat. Everyone had a special. Wanted spaghetti, you went to Putt's and saw Mamma Benassi at corner of Ann and Broadway.

Wanted a good country fried steak with lots of white gravy, had to drive out to Jerry's on Versailles Road just before you got to Jett.

A good steak or two meant a trip to Saylor's. They also had lamb fried – something you could not get at any of the other places.

In town alone, just wanted a hamburger, go to the Little Hawk on St. Clair. Got crowded at times (was so small) but put out a fine hamburger.

Just about all of them served a good bowl of chili with lots of oyster crackers. Could get this at the Pool Room on Broadway or the one on St. Clair.

My first experience with White Castle hamburgers was on Main Street. The White Light on Second Street – a good place to stop and eat. Also had a pinball machine you could play while waiting for a seat.

White Signal on Bridge is still there but has another name now. Pete's Corner on Second and Bridge Streets was a hangout for most. I did not eat there much but was a good place to get a shake, malt, and local gossip. Do not have room to cover all of the good eating places but a few others were: Powell's, Knotty Pine, Capitol Bar and Lounge, and Green Mill.

Only know of one place where the cook pats out the hamburger, cooks it on the grill and puts on all the trimmings now – I do this at home.

CATCHING SOFT CRAWS

Back when we caught soft craw-dads to fish with, it took a lot of time, patience, nerve, work and a lot of luck. You could go out with a seine in the daytime and get a few, sometimes. They shed the hard shell at night and it did not take them long to get it back. It was best to hunt then at night and catch them by hand.

This may sound easy, with a good light, as they were usually in shallow water and did not move fast but that is wrong. Soft craws were food for a lot of things like snakes. This made it a little harder because you had to look for the craws and snakes, both at the same time. A good pair of boots would keep them off your legs and that made for another problem. When creek water is warm, it makes the rocks slick and slimy and could cause you to get wet real quick and sometimes more than once a night.

After catching them, special care was taken in keeping them alive and soft. We took damp newspapers and placed craws between layers and then stored them in the refrigerator crisper. This would keep them alive for days. As long as they were cold, the shells would not get hard.

It has been forty plus years since I have gone out and caught any soft craws and they cannot be purchased at bait shops.

Soft craws were great for catfishing in what was called the deep hole in Elkhorn Creek (at Bates Bottom almost at the backwaters of the creek). If you knew where to fish, they were good for catfish and white perch in the river.

One brother had to keep it quiet when he had the craws because an older brother would treat them like shrimp when he found them, and make a sandwich out of them (when no one was looking).

This was a very special bait and not used often because it took a full night to catch enough for a few hours of fishing.

Today, everyone just goes to the bait shop and buys bait. A lot of fish can be caught with soft craws but the calling is just not there.

COAL FOR HEATING AND COOKING

Today there are not many railroad tracks around because trains are beginning to fade out. The ones around have either diesel or electric engines. Most kids today have never had the pleasure of spending a few hours at the railroad station watching the old steam engines going past. These were all powered by coal.

Most people did not know that a large lump of coal could not be placed in the firebox. If this was done, the fireman on the engine was in trouble. It would burn okay but would not turn to ashes or cinders that could be removed later. Coal that was too large would turn into a clinker (stick to the firebox) and had to be removed after the fire was out and the firebox had cooked down.

We could not afford to buy coal for heating or cooking so we had to use wood. Living close to the railroad tracks was a plus for us because all the coal too large to burn was kicked off the engine by the fireman.

Approximately once a week we went out with sacks, buckets or bushel baskets to pick up what coal had been thrown off. One mile in each direction was as far as we were allowed to go because any further would put us in someone else's territory.

In winter there was enough for maybe one day of heating and cooking, but in summer it could last for two or three days for cooking. This was a lot of hard work but not as hard as cutting wood. We did not know it then, but I guess you could have called it recycling.

After we moved to Franklin County, the tracks ran within about fifty feet of the back of the house. There was only one train a day in each direction. We got to know the fireman and on the way out he would save all the large pieces and on the way back he would kick them all off at the house. Each day there would be a pile of coal on each side of the tracks. There was not much but it was a lot easier to gather.

Trains just ran from town to the distillery and back each day. Another benefit from this train was all the grain hauled. The doors of the boxcars were covered with what we called grain doors. A hole was chopped in this to let the grain run out. Pop worked at the distillery and a lot of the doors were brought home for firewood.

The old railroad tracks may have been taken out now but I will always remember the great way to get fuel for the fire on a cold winter's night.

MY FIRST WEEK IN THE ARMY - AUGUST 1947

When I got to the age of seventeen, everyone told me it was time to start training for something I wanted to do for the rest of my life.

Well, I worked at a lot of things. Had already made up my mind not to be a farmer. Construction was my choice until I was put on the crew that poured concrete. Thought about being a river man but the oil barges had stopped running the river, leaving little to do there. Tried factory work but ruled that out after a short while. That is when I decided to go in the Army for two years. Mom signed my papers and off I went to Lexington for a physical. After passing the physical, I was put on a bus with a group of people and sent to Ft. Knox. This is where we got our thirteen weeks of basic training.

The first day we got another physical (much more extensive), blood tests and shots if we needed them (which everyone did). The next few days we were tested, given a military haircut and pulled small details (all volunteered) such as picking up trash, cutting weeds and grass, sweeping sidewalks and parking lots and such.

They had us housed in a couple of old wooden barracks and taught us how to keep them clean. The Army never ran out of brooms, rags, mops, soap, buckets and paint brushes.

We all ate in the mess hall, which was run by people already in the Army. We ate three meals a day and also had to do a few chores in the mess hall. Chores included washing dishes and silverware, peeling potatoes, keeping garbage cans clean and all areas in and around the mess hall clean.

The second week was spent taking tests, going to classes on what the Army was all about and working. When they had five hundred of us (enough to from a training company), we spent two days being issued clothing and equipment. Moved into four two-story barracks, four platoons (125 to a platoon) and broken down into sixteen squads.

Then for the next thirteen weeks we had to know the following: (a) where we should be; (b) what time; (c) how long and (d) be available twenty-four hours a day. We were available for working, training, going to classes, drilling, learning to shoot, walking, hiding, fighting, seeing in the dark, crawling, driving, taking care of equipment, making a bed, scrubbing a floor, saluting, standing still, swimming, digging a fox hole, and ways to get to Louisville and back without being caught. I thought I knew how to do most of this until the Army got a hold of me. You learned all over again – the Army way.

All of this and more, we had to learn in thirteen weeks. We were paid $98.00 per month, which was a lot back in the 40's. It got a lot better over the next twenty years.

CUTTING A BEE TREE FOR HONEY

Gathering wild honey was a job for late summer when the bees had had all summer for making honey. Most of the time we had a few hives that were gathered in the fall and about half of that was left for the bees.

Cutting a tree meant the swarm of bees could not make it through the winter. Most of the bees were killed during the gathering of honey.

All summer while out in the woods we would find active bees and follow them. With a little patience and a lot of time you could locate the hollow tree where they stored their honey. We always tried to locate four or five a year. Most of them were in terrible locations. We left them alone if they were located over water because if the honey got wet it would spoil real quick. Trees could not be cut even on a rainy day.

I always tried to leave this to someone else because I always got stung ten or twelve times. The same thing happened when we gathered young wasps for fish bait.

Honey was used in place of sugar for cooking and for breakfast on hot biscuits. My favorite was to sweeten sassafras tea, and still is. Also, could be used to sweeten coffee.

The honey cone was also used. It could even be used in place of wax for some things.

The tree was also used for firewood, if close enough to make it worthwhile.

Bee trees were also graded. The best for taste were red oak and white oak. The worst for taste was walnut. Sugar maples were good. The in-betweens for taste were water maples, sycamores, box elders, ash, buckeyes, birch, poplar and hickory nut. Fruit trees (apple or pear) were never cut. I never found one in a pine tree.

Bee tree cutting was a lot of work and definitely a fight all the way with the bees. When winter came and the honey was used – it was well worth it (including the stings).

MOVING DAY CALLED FOR A TRIP DOWN THE RIVER

Moving was not unusual for us. When Pop sold the farm in Anderson and got a job at Old Crowe Distillery in Franklin County, he rented a house on the river close to his work and that meant time to move again. Simple move – not quite!!! Most everything was loaded on a truck. Mom and the kids (all but three) were put in the car and moved. The year was 1945. Problem was the leftover items: three dogs, two goats, flock of chickens, one cat and the john boat. I was fifteen so I was put in charge of two younger brothers. Our job was to get the boat and leftover items down the river about ten or twelve miles.

The lock tender at Lock #5 looked a little surprised when we arrived. He had heard about the move and was expecting the boat but not what was on board. There were three kids, two dogs (two of them very large), two medium size goats, a dozen chickens and one cat. Also, a lot of fishing gear, nets, poles, traps and such. I believe we even had all the family guns with us.

We had helped lock boats through Lock #5 but had never done it on our own.

Being kids, we did not know what it was to hurry. We knew we had all day and a lot of new territory to check out. We needed to know what kind of boat everyone had, count the docks, camp houses and houseboats. Also, we needed to know what crops were being raised on the banks, and how far the back waters went up each creek that emptied into the river. We also had to know where the good fishing places were, each sand bar for future swimming parties, and size and location of the river cliffs. A special was Lover's Leap, which we had only heard about but knew it when we came upon it.

We had a few anxious moments on the trip but about an hour before dark we arrived. As planned before hand, someone was on the rock bar sticking out in the river to flag us down.

Everyone slept well that night knowing that tomorrow there was new country to explore. Everything within five miles of home had to be checked out and stored in the memory bank. This way it could be called up and viewed when needed. (Memory bank, back then, meant our brain).

Things checked were: all farms for work, ponds for fishing, places for hunting at night, neighbors who had kids, berry patches, location of all fruit trees, tobacco barns, caves, etc. Also, the closest route, easiest and fastest way to get to everything.

SATURDAY NIGHT IN TOWN

I was taught at a very young age that to go to town on Saturday night – take in a movie, have a hamburger at the pool hall and a dish of ice cream at the drug store – meant part of the week working at whatever the season called for.

Working was no big problem in the spring because farmers were getting the grounds ready and putting crops out. Getting the tobacco beds ready for planting, then setting the plants (when ready). In the fall, tobacco was housed and stripped. This was all hard work but each one was a moneymaker. There was always plenty of work.

During the summer, help was needed to keep the weeds out of all crops. Also, help was needed for other things that had to be repaired.

It was a seven-mile walk to town. You always took a chance on catching a ride home, at midnight, either on the back of a milk truck or from someone with a car (if they had room).

Winter was a different story because of being in school. Things had to be worked out. We would
shuck corn, which had been cut and put in shocks. Shocks were used by most people who went coon hunting at night. Fur or five people could crawl inside and keep fairly warm while the dogs were on a trail until they made a tree (but that is another story). We were paid fifteen cents per shock. By really working at it, we (two people) could do about ten shocks on Saturday. I was always teamed with an older brother. He got ten cents a shock and I got a nickel. This meant I went to town with only fifty cents on Saturday night.

The fifty cents was spent as follows: movie (ten cents); popcorn and candy bar (ten cents); and hamburger/ice cream (30 cents).

With everything taken into consideration, this was not a bad Saturday night for an eleven or twelve year old.

The big problem in winter was if you took your girlfriend with you because it meant dutch treat. It never did cross my mind as to how she came up with her fifty cents (her dad probably). In the summer, you paid her way to the movie and ice cream afterwards.

Winter time was also a hard time for working on fences. One of the big winter chores was keeping the house warm and wood for cooking. Firewood had to be gathered daily. This was done with a chopping axe and cross-cut saw.

All chores had to be done at home before you even thought of going to town on Saturday night. Especially, since we lived on a farm most of the time.

THE GRAB BAG

I can remember the grab bag from sixty-five plus years ago. Each time we went to Lawrenceburg, one of the first things we checked was the counter in the Five and Dime Store that had the grab bags. If you had a couple of extra nickels or dimes, this is what was bought first – could worry later about what you were going to do with it.

The wife and I were at the Dollar Tree the other day and they had a lot of grab bags made up in brown paper bags. Someone ahead of me had opened most of them. This took all the fun out of opening the bag, so did not buy any.

Growing up, when you paid a nickel for a grab bag it was full of things that were worth at least a quarter. If you paid a dime for one, you got fifty cents worth of something. Really did not matter that it was something you did not need or want. It was a real bargain and you could spend the rest of the day deciding who you were going to give it to or what you were going to use it for.

One time, got one at the dime store in Versailles and got a bottle of nail polish along with some other things. Used it to polish my nails one time but did not like it, so gave it to a girl I hung out with sometimes. This day we were in the park, down behind the courthouse, using the swings.

Bough one in Frankfort that had ten boxes of caps for a cap pistol. Did not have a cap pistol at the time, but not a problem. Just took two rocks, laid the cap on one and hit it with the other rock. Popped just as loud as it did in a cap pistol.

Have bought grab bags all over the country but never did get anything that was what I wanted. Even got some of the nastiest candy and cookies that were ever made.

Took a while, but now know that everything in the grab bag was probably something that the store could not sell.

Bought a fifty cent one in Texas and got a two-dollar watch that had stopped running before it was put in the bag. Never did get it to run but did sell it for a dollar.

Paid a dollar for one at one of the dime stores in Frankfort. Must have been fifty dollars worth of hair bows and barrettes in it. Did not wear any of them but within a week every girl close to my age in Millville was wearing one.

THE CONCRETE MIXER

The wife and I sat down to supper the other night with brother and his wife. She had cooked up a pot of brown and white beans, fried potatoes with onions, platter of crappie, bash and catfish, and lots of fried cornbread. Now, that could be a story, with nothing more said.

Brother Donnie got to talking about the crew he works with pouring concrete footers for a house they are going to build.

My memories of the late 40's and early 50's came flooding back of the time I put in working for Horn and Goins Construction. (This was before they went into concrete business with the big trucks). They bought a one bag mixer for pouring basement footers, walls and floors.

Brother Carlos and his father-in-law, Mr. Hillard, had gotten me the job and they helped with the mixer. This was a great experience but would not want to do it again. The footers were not much of a job – could do two or three of them a day – but the walls were a full day because the gravel and sand had to be shoveled into the hopper with the cement mix, then dumped into the machine with water, mixed and dumped out the other side into a wheelbarrow. Pushed up the ramp, poured into the froms and then worked with a long 2x4 to get the honeycomb out of it. That was a full day with some overtime just for a small basement. It was also a job just to get the mixer, wheel barrows and other tools cleaned after a wall was poured.

Floors in the basement were also a big job and took a bigger crew for this, as it had to be floated down level, screts taken out as it was dumped and leveled. Then when everything was cleaned, everyone had to wait around for the concrete to start setting up. With the knee pads, floats and trials, a slick finish was put on the floor.

There were times when we used a little too much water and it would take all night for the finish job to be done right.

The part of this job that I disliked most was when the mixer was moved from one job to the next. The boss, Philip Goins, pulled it with his pickup truck and my job was to ride in the back of the pickup and let him know when he was going too fast and the mixer would start to bounce. First, it would run for a while on the left wheel and then the right for a while – very scary.

This was another of the jobs I did early in life and then moved on to something I liked doing better.

LOVER'S LEAP IN ANDERSON COUNTY

Between Shore Acres and Clifton, on the Anderson County side of the river, there is a large rock ledge called Lover's Leap. Lots of stories about how it got this name but they are all kind of hard to believe.

Fifty years plus in the past, this was a spot on the river that was my favored place to park the john boat and spend a day or two. The fishing in this area was about as good as it got in the four pools of the Kentucky River.

Set up for a couple of days and fish. Catch a few bluegill, maybe a bass or two, catfish or just a buffalo or a nice white perch (drone). Clean them, build a fire, fry them right there on the bank – no matter what kind of fish it was. It was fish at it's best.

Tired of fishing, grab the old ginseng hoe, take a walk around the cliff, and with a little luck you could find a patch of ginseng. Dig the roots up, dry it good and later send it off to market. Back then it went for $30 to $80 a pound. Today it goes for $400 to $500 a pound.

Never could find any in this area but brother Woodie always came back with a sack full. The only ginseng that I ever found was a nice big patch up on Clear Creek in Woodford County. Dug about one-half pound but did not sell it – used it myself.

When fishing was not good (cold weather), the cliffs around Lover's Leap were great for hunting squirrels. There were lots of oak trees and a few buckeyes. After a couple of hours hunting, you could always get enough squirrels to feed everyone. Just across the river were acres and acres of land for rabbit hunting.

I was in the area a few months back and all the farm land in the Woodford County side of the river is for special animals now. Saw some llamas, pot belly pig, wild looking sheep or goats and some that I could not get close enough to (either a musk ox or a yak). Believe they were the ones with the horns curved down – musk ox. Well worth the drive through if they are all outside. It is private land and you have to stay on the road.

The Anderson County of the river now has a winery. Don't know how this would affect the hunting on that side of the river. I must get up that way soon to see what the deal is there. It is on top f the hill, so should not hurt the fishing or hunting.

BLUE BONNET ICE CREAM

I can remember when the plant was just a hole in the ground on East Main Street and Winding Way. It is now a state building. Three of us went to work for Mr. Harrod. It was just a big mud hole and we started by building froms and pouring concrete for the footers. After froms were taken off, someone came in with a couple of truck loads of froms built out of 2x4's and plywood. This was my first experience with these. First they had to be painted with used motor oil, which made for a real mess when we started to set them. I believe the wall was 12 foot tall, maybe taller. Had to put the metal wires through them, then drive the metal wedges in each side to keep them from spreading when the concrete was poured in them. When they were all set, we spent a few days bracing the wall inside and out. This was when we lined the walls up and got them straight.

Don't remember who the carpenters were but the fellow in charge, when Mr. Harrod was not around, was a fellow by the name of Tracy – and he got things done. When all the froms were straight and braced good, they hauled in a number of truck loads of gravel, sand and bagged concrete. When they brought in a one-bag concrete mixer, operated by a small gasoline engine, the work got a little harder. Crew was a lot bigger now and the wall had to be completed once it was started. The mixer held about three wheelbarrows full. The process was: all had to be shoveled into a hopper, hopper was raised, dumping everything in one side of the mixer, water was added, and when the shoot on the other side was lowered, the concrete was dumped into the wheelbarrows, pushed up a ramp and around a platfrom, dumped in the wall and worked with a board to get the honeycomb out of it. When they got back, we had to have another mixer full and ready. Mix was one bag of cement, so many shovels of gravel and half as many shovels of sand. Gravel would work you to death, so we would trade around all day – rock, sand and cement. Man on cement bags had to operate the mixer.

Walls had to be poured, froms removed and cleaned. All braces and ramps cleaned, nails pulled and lumber stacked for later use. This is when we started to rub the walls with a stone to smooth them a little. This took weeks and by the time this was done, none of us had any hide left on our hands. The basement floor and the ground floor were poured. At this point we thought we had it made, as we were told we all had a job once the plant was in operation. On bad days, Mr. Tracy would take us over to Pete's Corner and we would work in the storage room. Pay was the same but they fed us a lot better.

We were setting the walls up when we all got fired. Guess we had slowed down a bit – work had gotten easier or they just did not need us any more. Have often wondered how I would have been at making ice cream.

STYLE

Thinking back on times past – some of the ways we dressed make me wonder about the way we dress today.

Growing up it was blue jeans and any kind of shirt from T-shirt to a white dress shirt and if you were lucky enough, a pair of penny loafers – this was the way boys dressed. The girls wore dresses or skirts and blouses, and oxford shoes (black and white, or brown and white) most times.

When I started dating, back during the big war, there were 4 of us boys about the same size and we had one suit between us. I was the smallest and it was a little big for me, but the oldest brother had a tight fit. It was a double-breasted blue serge zoot suit. We took turns wearing it on weekends and it sure felt good when it was my turn to wear it to town.

Also remember the bell-bottom trousers. Got to use them when brother was home from the Navy. Again, they were too big for me but I always found a way to wear them.

Went from bell-bottom trousers to the peg-leg pants, while the girls went from the poodle skirt to the mini skirt, and culottes to slacks. Don't see many dresses any more. Skirts went from mini to the ground and back up. Today, they are back down to the ground.

Men's styles are about as bad – from the dress suit, sport coat, suit with no vest, leisure suit (owned a couple of them) and then just pants and sport jacket.

Bought me a tux and only wore it a few times to fromal things. It still fits but is probably out of style now because it is black. They now come in all colors even pink.

Missed out on a lot of style changes when I went into the Army. Liked the unifrom so much that I just stayed in for 20 years and wore it. They changed a few times – from the Ike Jacket to a long tailcoat of a different color. Now, about all I see is camouflage and some times you see someone in dress blues. All have changed in the 30 years since my retirement.

As for now, I am back to my blue jeans, T-shirt and penny loafers and loving every day of it.

THE SPITTOON

The other day I was with a group of young people and the subject of smoking came up, and was told by one of them that smoking was a nasty habit. She was right; smoking messes up the walls, drapes, stuffed furniture, plus the ashes blow everywhere. The car is a mess all the time.

Growing up, there were a lot of smokers around. Most of them rolled their own or smoked a pipe because ready mades cost entirely too much – 15 cents a pack. That amount of money would have bought 3 sacks of tobacco and papers – enough for all week.

There were a lot more people that chewed tobacco. Now, that was a nasty habit and that is where the spittoon came in. Every pool room and bar in Frankfort, Lawrenceburg and Versailles had them sitting on the floor along the bar. They were used as ashtrays for the smokers and to spit in by the ones that chewed.

Now, you talk about a mess. As ash tray can be washed very quickly and easily, but a spittoon was a job to clean. This was one of my jobs when I worked at the pool hall in Versailles. At closing time, they had to be emptied and cleaned – if not, it was the first job the next day when the hall opened.

Clean them up – spick and span. First person in was a chewer and would mess them up first thing and they stayed that way all day. Lots of them missed and the floor was a mess.

I have known a lot of people that chewed tobacco in the last 30 years. With no spittoons around, they just spit everywhere. This made a mess on the ground. In the office, they use coffee cups for spittoons and then dump them outside. This was a lot worse than cigarette butts.

The spittoon has gone the way of a lot of other things now. They are one of the collector items found only in antique shops or at flea markets.

When I was young (at home), the fire place, wood stove or the coal bucket was used for a spittoon.

Did not see it, but heard a story about a fellow in Fintville who used his collie dog when inside. When they went out, the dog would roll in the grass to get it off. Don't guess it hurt the dog as he died of old age.

POWER LINES

I can remember back in the late 30's when a power line was stretched across Anderson, Mercer, Jessamine and Woodford Counties.

I was too young to work on the line but Pop and two or three of my older brothers did work on it for a while. One brother still talks about it.

First a crew had to go through and survey the property and get permission to put the line across a lot of farms. They drove stakes as to where the post had to be set.

Then a crew came through and dug the holes. Lots of them had t be blasted with dynamite. Pop was on this crew for a while and told the story about one farmer who made them move one of the stakes that was driven in his barn yard (right in front of the barn door). Pop said he had to move it because the farmer had a loaded shotgun.

After this a crew came by and set the poles, then the wire was pulled across the top of the poles and stretched with a team of mules. Most everything was moved in with mules and horses.

Brother tells of the time they had to lower the air compressor over one of the river cliffs, drill holes through the rock, then shoot it out so the pole could be set. All went well until they started to drag the compressor back up the hill – it got loose and was destroyed when it went back over the hill on its own. Can't remember if he got fired or just quit.

Pop was always talking about the cattle that were close when they set a charge off. He said some of them ran across three or four farms before they stopped. There were dairy cows that did not give any milk for up to two weeks afterwards.

A lot of the farms raised a few sheep at the time. Some of them were never found. Nothing would stop them once they got scared and started to run.

The blasting also affected the chickens at times – they would stop laying eggs. Some farms had their wells go dry. Springs would dry up. This was before people knew how to use dynamite and a lot of charges were more than was needed. Some of the holes were so big that they had to be filled back in – just so they could set the light pole.

The line was finished in time, and I do believe they even got electricity in Tyrone after a while.

THE MUD PUPPY

I was in the Bridgeport Community cooking catfish for the Bridgeport Ruritan Day, back in the summer; therefore the big topic of the day was fishing.

Now, I do a lot of fishing, so I call myself a fisherman. This tells everyone that I have been known to stretch the truth now and then – all fishermen do.

I had just told the story about the big one that got away a few days before, when a fellow stood up and told one that topped mine – hands down.

Seems back in the 40's or early 50's, he was fishing out at the mouth of Glenns Creek when he hooked something (on a hand pole). After an hour or so when he landed it, it turned out to be a large mud puppy – weighing in at 35 pounds. Well, I did not tell any more fish stories that day.

Growing up we called them water dogs (real name is necturus maculosus). Normal size is three to seven inches. The biggest one I ever caught would have weighed, maybe one pound – no more.

The mud puppy is very easy to catch, during the month of March when the river is muddy. I don't know why anyone would want to because I don't know of anything they are good for.

I will not name the fellow that told this story as I am sure that what he landed was probably a flat head, mud cat – a good catch anywhere. Believe the record for a flat head cat is about 105 pounds. I have never seen the record for a mud puppy, but there is probably one on record some place.

Caught a lot of mud puppies when I was growing up and made it a point to move to another fishing hole when they started to bite. Never knew of one biting anyone but was always scared to handle them. When one was caught, he left with the hook still in his mouth.

Will most likely hear from that fellow if he reads this.

A TYPICAL DAY ON THE RIVER

I lived about three miles above Frankfort on the river. On a day when the john boat was not in use, could get things together and spend the day on the river as everything was free most of the time.

Thins to take were a good sharp knife, ball of string, few hooks, hoe, can or something to put fishing worms in, set of oars, bathing suit or short britches, and anything to use for sinkers (nails, nuts, or bolts).

Start the day by finding a spot on the bank, dig a few green worms, and cross over to the other side where the brush piles were in the water.

Cut a willow pole, rig it and try for a few bluegills or warmouths. Only one house over there before the Big Eddy Beach. If anyone was at home and outside, stop and talk for a short time.

On down the bank, if the gars were on top of the water, could tie something on the line and try for them. A lot of fun if you can hang on. Then continue around the bend to the beach and swim for a while – longer if there was anyone around.

Next stop was the beer joint in the curve at the bottom of the hill. Get what infromation you could about who had been by and if there was any work for a day or two (store that). Then on down to Melody Park – always a good place to spend some time. Talk if anyone was around or just sit around and take in the beauty of the park. If you had a couple of coins, could cross the road to Cliffside and get a coke or something else cold to drink.

All the way down, all gardens and fruit trees or vines were checked for anything that was ready to eat. Never went below this point, as this would put you in town.

Cross back over and up the other side of the river, find a good mud bottom, slip over the side and gather a few mussels. There was no reason for this but they were there and fun to see how many you could find. If there were two of you, could see who could find the most or the biggest. Also, they made good bait if you got around to it.

Along this back was a spring, bubbling up right at the edge of the water by a big sycamore tree. A great place to get a drink. If you were lucky, our friend Whitie had put a few bottles of beer in it to cool and had missed a couple of them when he picked them up or just left them for later.

The last hour or so as you worked your way back up river, could gather wood for the kitchen stove – enough to cook supper and breakfast the next morning.

Could do about the same thing going up river but was a long row to Clifton and back.

WARDEN

Picked up my fishing licence the other day. I have been fishing for free for about four years now but the laws have changed. There was a time when we were kids, we did not need a fishing or hunting license.

There were lots of laws on the books and on occasions we used the laws as a game to outfox the game warden.

During time when the river was high and muddy, it was hard to catch any fish. This is where the old drag net came in. Just a long pole, half a hoop with a net made from chicken wire. Just hold it out over the water, let it down easy, then drag it out onto the bank. Hard to believe the fish you could catch this way, as a lot of them were close to the bank out of the swift water. This was not allowed and they were hard to hide when not in use.

I was home on military leave, early 50's, and my brother had made one out of half a hoop net. We spent a full day baiting a place. Then went up in the boat about midnight, slipped the net out over our baited hole, took up the bank with it and almost got pulled back in the river. The fish tore the net up and over half of them got away, but when we got the fish counted and weighed in, we had landed over 700 pounds in one dip. They were all buffalo except for one 22-pound carp. The other ones were from 10 – 42 pounds. Cleaned fish the rest of the night. That was a one time only because the river never got at the right height again or the right time of the year.

There was a law that forbade anyone to fish within, I believe, 100 yards of the mouth of any creek that flowed into the river. During the month on May, if you were fishing in this area and saw someone coming, just leave the poles and run.

Pop was the best when it came to fishing. If they did not bite on something or go in one of his nets, he would just light a stick of dynamite, drop it in the river, and then just pick the fish up when they floated to the top. He did not like to do this but he would if he needed a mess of fish.

My brother and I were at Taylorsville Lake fishing for crappie a few weeks ago and got checked by the game warden. Had a few short ones in the livewell and he made us put the 8½ inch ones back because he said they had to be 9 inches. We knew that but thought we could get away with a few short ones. After cleaning them, we sat down to a good dinner. Went back again and also got checked by the game warden.

BIG MISTAKE

Was living at the Gardner place on Glenns Creek Road. Brother Richard and two of the younger brothers were going to melt the tar out of a fifty-five gallon drum for some reason – to make a catch basin for spring water on the hill behind the house. All went well for a while. Got the drum up on the rocks with the bung out of the end so the tar would run out when it got hot, built a fire under the drum and sat back and waited.

Guess Richard was in too much of a hurry and bent over the hole in the end of the drum to see if he could see why the tar was not coming out. At this time, the flame from the fire picked the fumes up and the drum exploded. Burnt brother's eyebrows off, part of his hair, and blew his nose and mouth full of hot tar. This called for a fast run to the hospital and was enough that they decided to keep him a day or two. This was bad but it got worse.

He sent brother John out to get him a drink – said he needed it for the pain. Now brother John knew he was not to take alcohol into the hospital, so he got a pint, poured it in a thermos – worked good. Got to the room and was going to pour brother Richard a drink, but when he took the top off the bottle, it exploded. Brother John was rushed downstairs to the emergency room to have his thumb sewed back together. A sad looking bunch that night and brother Richard never did get his drink but the room smelled of alcohol for two days.

Another mistake – the house we lived in across from the church in Tyrone had the only yacht in Tyrone on the lot between the house and the river. Owner had parked it there during the last high water. This was the late or mid 30's. Boat was really a large cabin cruiser, all wood, and a great place for all the neighborhood kids to play.

One day when a group of the kids playing in it, someone had a big metal rod that they were using for a spear. When we were done playing, he took this rod and stuck it through the bottom in the ground so he could find it next time.

The owner of the boat got a crew together to put the boat back in the water to use that summer. They found the hold and had a man work on it for two days patching the hole. Got the boat in the water and it sank right to the bottom. Took about three days to get it pumped out and corked up enough so it could be moved down river, where it sank to the bottom again and never did get it back up.

The kids got blamed for it all, but it had sat there on the bank and dried out. Crack had opened up all over the hull.

THE PEACH TREE INN

The other day I received some new CD's (Country Classics) in the mail and after about three hour of listening in my music room, I had to turn the machine off. When Kitty Wells came on it really brought tears to my eyes.

I could close my eyes and go back in time to the 40's, back to the Peach Tree Inn. There were a number or places in Craw, but none of them could hold a light to the Peach Tree Inn.

The girls we danced with were the best looking, the beer we drank was the coldest, and the music on the jukebox was the best.

Not as many fights as the other places. Just a place where you could have a lot of fun and did not need a lot of money.

Everyone drank either Oertel's 92 or Black Label beer. They had other brands but sold very little of it. This was back when the beer was in long neck bottles.

The bartender and bouncer at the Peach Tree Inn was a second or third cousin and the law was not as strict on underage drinking. So, if you were good and did not cause any trouble, no one gave much thought to the younger boys drinking a beer.

The older brothers did most of the drinking. My reason for being there was to dance, talk and enjoy the music.

There is not a place in the State of Kentucky that is anything like the Peach Tree Inn. Now, they all have bands that are too loud. You have to bring your own girl if you want to dance. Don't have to have any nickels for the juke box. The beer is now about $3 a bottle and everyone you talk to wants to fight.

They had no places like this in Lawrenceburg or Versailles that I know of, but there were a couple of places between Frankfort and Lawrenceburg and three or four on Route 60 between Frankfort and Versailles. Most of these had the outlawed one-arm bandit. They were more fun than the dancing and they cost more. Only stopped at these places when we were on our way to someplace like Joyland Park, Fair Grounds in Anderson County, or the Roller Rink out Route 62 towards Sinai.

COFFEE OVER THE YEARS

I have been told by a lot of folks that I drink too much coffee, not so. They just do not know my history with coffee.

Guessing drinking coffee is just another one of my bad habits. I have been drinking it for as long as I can remember and that is back before my first grade in school. You could say that by the time I started school I was hooked on coffee.

There was only one way to make coffee – put coffee beans in a grinder, put them in a pot of water, set the pot on the stove and boil it. Now, that was coffee at its best. It took lots of sugar and milk to make it drinkable.

As stated before, lots of times a couple of homemade biscuits and a cup of coffee was breakfast. Only brand of coffee that Mom used was what Kroger in Lawrenceburg sold. I believe it was called Eight O'Clock. Later, when a door-to-door salesman came around, she changed brands for a while – Standard Coffee (I think).

They tell me if you drink coffee it will keep you awake. Again, not so for me, because I can sit, watch television, drink a pot of coffee, and go to sleep while finishing off the last cup.

Took most of the pleasure out of drinking coffee when they came out with instant coffee, but I could avoid this most of the time. During the war in Korea, this was all they had in the field rations. It was no trouble to make – just heat the water, open the bag, dump it in the water and presto – coffee. Not good coffee but did get by on it – never did like it, but got by.

Then they came out with Decaf. Now this really did coffee a disservice. They took everything out that coffee was drunk for – caffeine. Don't know why anyone would drink this. Hot chocolate would be better.

Bought me a cup of coffee in Lexington, back in January. They said it was Starbucks. Charged $2 for it and I had to leave it sitting. Don't know what it was – but it was not coffee. Coffee would have tasted better if it had been made out of acorns.

Have coffee in all flavors now. If you want some that taste like chocolate – get a candy bar. The latest, I think, is cappuccino. They say it is coffee but just won't tell you what it is made from.

There are still a few places around where you can get a good cup of coffee. When the wife and I leave the house on a trip, we take out coffee with us.

THE WASHING MACHINE

Well, there goes another high tech, best on the market, nothing better, labor saver, power saver, water saving appliance.

The washing machine just blew up. Put a new water heater in the day before and tomorrow a new washing machine.

I can remember when Mom was the only washing machine we had. She did it with a washing tub and a washboard. I was about 19 years old when we got electricity and Pop bought her a ringer type washing machine. From that day on the trouble with breakdowns have gone on non-stop.

Have bought about 20 of them over the years. They work fine for a while but by the time the warranty runs out, so does the machine. They have extended warranty you can buy. Tried it and by the time you pay for that, it is cheaper to just throw it out and buy a new on. Cheaper in the long run.

First experience with a real down home store bought washing machine was the summer I lived with Aunt Fay Brooks and her family. They had no electricity but were not quite as poor as we were. She had a washing machine that had a gas engine on it – was noisy and had to be used outside – but got the job done.

Also, had another first that summer. Aunt Fay also had a refrigerator that needed kerosene to run. Never did get it into my head how you could light a fire in something and it would freeze ice. Did not worry a lot about it – just laid back all summer and enjoyed the ice it froze.

Ran into a new type of washing machine in Korea. The Korean women used two rocks – a big and small one. Just lay the clothes on the big rock, soap them down and pound them with the small rock. Could never see how this could get the clothes clean but it worked.

The easiest way to wash clothes was taught to me by a sailor. Crossed the Atlantic and Pacific Oceans a number of times by ship. He showed me how to tie a suit of work clothes on a long rope, tie one end to the ship's railing and pitch them over the fantail of the ship and drag them for 15 or 20 minutes. Pull them in, hang them up to dry and you had clean clothes. Did not need any soap because the salt water would do a great job of cleaning them.

POOL TABLE

Back in the 30's and early 40's, the Sims Pool Hall in Lawrenceburg was the hangout for most people on Saturday night after a movie with the girls and a little hanging out in the cars on Main Street. The girls had all gone home by 10:00 p.m. and this was the time for another walk or two up and down Main Street.

This is when all the men and boys of all ages met in the pool hall. Most of the older men had been there all night shooting pool. The main reason for the younger ones to be there was to see if they could get a ride home.

The Sims lived at Sims Camp just below Lock #5 and they had a big flat bed truck they used for hauling milk to the cheese factory. Everyone left when the pool hall closed, piled on the truck. When it was time for someone to get off, they just knocked on the top of the cab. Truck would stop and they would unload. It was great in the summer time, but in the winter it was best to catch someone who had room in a car and leave early.

Was never allowed to shoot pool when young. First, it cost money and I never had much. Loser always paid for the game and for me I could never get good enough to win many games. Most times, there was a little money bet on the game, so I would just watch.

Later in life, brother John bought a pool table and had it in his basement (good gathering place). Still could not shoot real good, so mostly just watched these games also.

Did get into pool after winning a bumper pool table. Had it in my basement for a while, got pretty good at it, then had to get rid of if because the kids in my neighborhood were always fighting. The kids were always welcome to use the table anytime. Then it got to where every time they played they would end up in a big fight or a loud argument. I could not put up with that, so just sold the table.

Had access to a pool table most of my military life. There was always one in the day room where we spent a lot of our off time. Most of the time, all the tips were off the cue sticks or the sticks were broken.

ROAD KILL

You hear a lot of talk these days about road kill, especially at potluck dinners, road clean-ups and at restaurants – anywhere where food is brought in or bought. On the Ruritan Clubs road clean-ups, we find a lot of road kill. (This talk is all done in a joking manner).

This was not so years ago. There were not many cars and trucks on the road and not much road kill. Back in the 30's, it was not safe for a rabbit to sit next to the road and eat. Pop would run off the road and take a chance of doing damage to the car, to hit a rabbit or groundhog. If it was during trapping season, the skunk, opossum, fox, raccoon, mink, muskrat, or any animal that had a hide that would sell, was fair game. Hides taken with the car brought just as much as one that you had trapped all winter for. A rabbit hit with the car tasted just as good as one shot with a shotgun and the same with a groundhog. This was not the case if it was summer time. The rabbit was not to be eaten in hot weather. Don't even think of eating a rabbit until after the first frost. It had something to do with rabbit disease, but the others were okay all summer. The hides were not any good to sell unless they had a good winter coat.

Summer months we mostly ate fish. The Corp of Engineers would kill the fish when they blew snags out of the river. We would pick up all the fish they killed, clean them and eat them. This was also a sort of road kill.

Today there are so many cars and trucks that it is hard to find a fresh road kill. When I was working on the roads and we found a fresh kill (deer), we took it to the game farm and they used it to feed the animals.

Only road kill that we cook anymore is the mud turtle. Catch one crossing the road, when moving from pond to pond, catch him and bring him home and clean him. Guess you could call that road kill because he was trying to get across the road when you caught him.

Know of people within the last few years that have hit and killed deer. They have dressed them out and put them in the freezer – has to be during cold weather. If they are not hung up to cool out for a while, they are not good. Got me an eight-point rack mounted and hanging on the wall that was taken with a 1981 pick-up truck.

I have always said that the "Burgoo King" (Jim Conway) used road kill in his burgoo and that is why it tasted so good.

THE PENNY

The penny has had a lot of names over the years. Growing up, they were called coppers and penny. These are both wrong. We don't have a penny we have one-cent pieces.

As a kid selling blackberries, fish, animal hides or anything for a little change, we would deal for pennies. A handful would buy almost anything we needed.

At the age of ten, fifty pennies were good enough to pay for a Saturday in Lawrenceburg. This consisted of: ten cents for a movie ticket, ten cents for popcorn and a candy bar, fifteen cents for a sundae at the drug store, which left fifteen cents for a hamburger and coke at the pool room before going home. With a little luck, someone in the crowd had a pack of ready made cigarettes and you could bum a couple of them. If you had extra pennies, you could pick up a nickel bag of Bull Durham or Duke mixture complete with 20 papers and everyone could roll their own.

Now I know that smoking is not to be talked about, but 60 plus years ago it was cool, along with chewing, dipping snuff and such.

If you could come up with a couple hundred of the one-cent pieces, you could do your Christmas shopping with them.

Got me a few real pennies but they are not U.S. coins. Got them on one of my trips to Europe. They are a little bigger than a quarter and made out of copper. These have old dates on them back in the 1800's. This is the only true penny I know of.

Find a lot of one-cent pieces these days. Seems a lot of people throw them away when they get them in change and no one will bother to pick them up – I do.

Have a few Indian Head pennies (one cent pieces) and some wheat pennies (one cent pieces). These are hard to find these days. The last ones were minted in 1958. For collectors, they run from five cents to $800. Most of mine are the five-cent type. The Indian Head is the good one. They run from sixty-five cents to over a thousand dollars.

We had a large one-cent piece from 1793 through 1857 but don't think that I have ever seen one of these. The copper in my big pennies is worth more than the face value of the penny today. Can make more selling them by the pound. Not going into the one-half cent piece or the two-cent and three-cent pieces, only to remember they were cent pieces and not pennies.

If I had all the one-cent pieces that I spent while growing up, I could retire on them.

GREYHOUND BUS

I have seen a lot of buses on the roads these days – charter buses and a slew of school buses – but not many Greyhound buses. Back in the 40's, 50's and 60's, they way to travel was by train – from Frankfort to Louisville or Cincinnati. Since there were some places that did not have train stations – the way to go was by Greyhound bus. They stopped everywhere. If you caught the bus in Frankfort, you had stops at Bridgeport, Clays Village, Shelbyville and all points in between.

Traveled a lot from Frankfort to Ft. Knox by bus. If you took a train, you could only get a ticket to Louisville where you had a long layover or get to the bus station and catch a bus to Ft. Knox. The buses did not have dining cars or rest rooms but they did have rest stops along the way and it cost a lot less to eat.

When going across country to the West Coast, the train was the way to travel but on trips less than five hundred miles – the bus was the best. The Army used trains for most travel. When going across country, they issued a ticket for the trip and meal tickets for the number of meals for the trip.

Problem here was that they gave me tickets from New Jersey to Seattle, Washington, with a 30-day leave in Frankfort. Had no money and the closest stop they made to Frankfort was Ashland KY and then to Cincinnati. When my leave was up, this is where the Greyhound bus came in. Caught a ride from Ashland but took the bus to Cincinnati.

The train did not take the bus out but it did help. The airplane is what did away with most bus lines. Could fly from home to the West Coast so fast that you could stay at home 3 or 4 days longer when on leave. Still rode the bus a lot. Could not afford to fly and the Greyhound was a lot more fun to travel on. You could see the country from a bus and only clouds from the plane.

Have put in a lot of miles on a Greyhound bus – trips to and from Texas, Virginia, Ohio, Tennessee, Washington D.C. and other points. Last 20 years all travel has been by car – can stop anytime or anywhere. See a Greyhound bus now and then but not many of them and the bus station is a thing of the past. The stops now are just a small place somewhere. Guess some of the larger cities still have bus stations.

The last time that yours truly came to Frankfort by bus, they put me off somewhere on East Main Street – think it was an auto parts store. It was closed and I had to walk to Statesman's Lounge to find a phone. Don't know how many places the bus stop has been in Frankfort and don't know where it is now. The last time we picked someone up at the bus stop I think it was at Hardee's in West Frankfort.

THE SERVICE STATION

How many people out there can remember the ding dong at the service station? Run the car over that rubber hose, ring that bell, and the service man was right there to service your car – did not matter if you got a fill up or a dollar's worth. He popped the hood, checked the oil and water and gave a tug on the fan belt to see how tight it was, put the hood down and washed the windshield – all for a dollar sell.

Only a few of these stations are still around. Have run across a couple of them in Virginia. They stick the hose in the tank, start the fill up, and ask if you want your oil checked. Sometimes you have to show him how to get the hood open or how to get the gas cap off. For this the gas costs more than it would if you pumped it yourself.

Also, miss the green stamps and TV stamps that they gave out. Some gave dishes and glasses. Traded with one in Dayton, Ohio, that passed out cards. They would punch it each time you got a fill up and when you got all the numbers punched off, they took the seal off and whatever amount of money it revealed – that is what you got – up to ten dollars.

Most of them still have the free air and they have everything there to wash your windshield – if you want to do it.

The Spur Station on High Street was the one that put me to work a few times just helping the people that worked there. Never did get paid for it. The oil came in fifty-five gallon drums and had to be pumped out and put in quart jugs – that was my job to help with. If done right, you could get two or three extra quarts out of it. This could be sold and you could get enough out of it to go to the movies or get a hamburger.

Loved the gas pump at the Tutt Store in Millville. Had a glass tank on top of it. Just pump the amount of gas you wanted into this, then gravity fed it into the car. Most times it was two gallons of gas and a quart of oil. Never got too far from home in the car because if it broke down or had a flat tire, you had to walk home. Did not mind the walk in warm weather but in the winter it could get tough.

Don't ever remember going out of the state before joining the Army. Now days, we will drive to New Hampshire to go ice fishing. All the way to Texas for a bowl of good chili or to Old Mexico just to buy a hat. Have to pump my own gas and check my own oil.

MOM AND POP

My father, Kirby Bowen Fint, Sr., was born in Henry County, Kentucky, on May 1, 1895, and passed away on August 8, 1958. He was the son of Page Franklin Fint and Mary Ellen Palmer Fint. He married Lola John Herold, who was born in Anderson County, Kentucky, on December 22, 1899, and passed away on November 12, 1949. She was the daughter of Richard W. Herold and Mary Ellen Williams Herold.

Kirby and Lola were married on May 5, 1917, in Versailles, Kentucky. By April 1938, they had ten children – nine boys and one girl. The children were: Cecil Everett Fint (born April 14, 1918 – died January 5, 1993); James Carlos Fint (born January 9, 1920 – died April 1, 1989); Richard Franklin Fint, born February 28, 1924); Andrew Woodie Fint (born January 9, 1929 – died March 29, 1988); John Thomas Fint (born March 31, 1928 – died April 14, 1996); Kirby Fint, Jr. (born January 12, 1930); Maurice Hawkins Fint (born September 6, 1931 – died April 2, 1982); Albert Elwood Fint (born June 6, 1933); Irene Catherine Fint Cardwell (born December 22, 1935) and Donald Ray Fint (born April 25, 1938).

Pop was working the ferryboat at Tyrone in 1930 when I was born. He worked twelve hours a day, seven days a week. Uncle Willie was the night operator. I am sure they switched around a lot if one of them had something that had to be done. Pop made $75 a month and Uncle Willie made $65 a month. Uncle Willie was also a farmer. This was good money for the time because the Depression was in full swing and a lot of people were without jobs.

Mom was a housewife all her life. She never had a public job that I know of and with ten children to rear, who had time for outside work? The cooking, cleaning, laundry and watching the children (always four or five small ones at home) took fourteen or fifteen hours a day.

Pop worked the ferry until the new bridge was opened about 1934 or 1935. When I was old enough to start school, he had bought a farm on the Anderson County side of the river and built a house. By this time, there were nine children.

Pop was not a good farmer, so the farm did not last but a couple of years. He worked at a number of jobs such as the rock quarry at Tyrone and Ripy Brother Distillery.

We moved a number of times and then Pop bought another farm just above Lock #5. He did not give up his job. He still did not do real good at farming, but tried hard. He put in a lot of fruit trees and us kids were big enough to take care of the farm. We did okay for a while and then for some reason he lost his job and went to work on one of the oil barges that plied the river in the 1930's and 1940's. I never did hear where they picked the oil or gas up but know they would go up the river loaded (low in the water) and when they came back down the river they would be high in the water (running empty). Sometimes they would tie up close to the house so Pop could have a little time at home.

The war came along and one brother was drafted into the Army, one joined the Army and one went into the Navy.

There was lots of work to be found by now and Pop found a job at Old Crow Distillery in Franklin and Woodford Counties and we moved down the river to be close to his work.

When the war was over and all the boys returned home safe and sound, once again we had a full house. Only two had married and were missing from home and living on their own.

Mom passed away in 1949 and Pop got sick. He could not work and the family kind of broke apart. Three of us went into the Army, five were married and on their own, there were only two at home.

Pop lived wherever he could until 1958 when he passed away from an enlarged heart.

I still call the 1930's, 1940's and 1950's the good old days. I don't know why because living was hard. There was always enough to get by but we had to work at it every day.

As for me, I am almost seventy-four now and have been retired for thirty-four years from the Military and almost fourteen years from the State Government. Life is great because I do what I want, go to bed when I want, get up when I want and go fishing when I want. I have a few health problems and some would say I am old. I feel these are the good old days.

Mom and Pop had a hard life but they did a good job. All ten kids have had productive lives – one was a preacher, one was a plumber, one was an electrician, one had a military career, six or seven life-long marriages, and none of the ten kids have ever been locked up for long (no more than over night). They had a total of twenty-three grandchildren. I cannot keep up with the number of great-grandchildren, great-great-grandchildren and more. The children and grandchildren etc. are located in Kentucky, Ohio, Indiana, New York, Florida, Texas, Louisiana, Tennessee and West Virginia, that I know of.

THE TOOTHBRUSH

I was 17 years of age before the Army issued me my first toothbrush. Had seen a lot of them in stores and knew what they were but never owned one.

Don't ever remember brushing my teeth while growing up. Remember losing my baby teeth and my permanent ones coming in. I do not have a memory of ever having a toothache as a child.

I have thought about this a lot and cannot come up with an answer as to why we did not have any problems with our teeth. It could have been the water and the fact that we did not have a lot of sweets to eat. Possibly got a soft drink once a month.

Teeth were checked when I joined the Army but was years before they did any work on them. It was mainly a cleaning and a couple of fillings and over the years had to have a couple of wisdom teeth pulled.

Teeth got bad over the years and at about 46 years of age, toothaches got really bad, so had them all pulled. Got a complete set of false teeth but could never make myself wear them. Had to start eating different things. In place of eating a lot of things raw – had to cook them. I still cannot eat peanuts but peanut butter is good. New set of teeth are around the house some place in a jar. Keep them on hand so I don't have to buy another set.

I did not take good care of my teeth even after they gave me a toothbrush and paste. Did use the brush for a lot of other things. It was great for cleaning my rifle – could get the dirt and dust out of all the tight places. Got into a little trouble a couple of times and had to scrub the floor with it. They called it punishment and I called it wearing a good toothbrush out.

Times have changed over the years. Know of some children that have already had some of their permanent teeth pulled and they only had them for a year or so.

Can spend a month's pay on a toothbrush these days. There are a hundred different brands and each has a hundred sizes, shapes and any number with different types of bristles. A hundred brands of toothpaste, tooth powder, gels, flosses and just came out with a pad that can brush your teeth anywhere with it and throw it away. Then you come to the rinses. They have a whole section in the drug store with only things for taking care of your teeth.

WORK

I did not think much about work growing up. Only wanted to make enough money to get through the weekend in Lawrenceburg. Wanted to spend most of my time fishing, hunting, swimming, or just roaming the countryside in Anderson and Woodford Counties from daylight until after dark. To work more than one day a week was out of the question. Would work all week during the seasons for putting the tobacco crops out, housing them and then stripping, but this money went to Mom – except for enough for the weekend. Rest of the year, one day a week, working in hay, cutting the corn, shucking it and moving it to the crib was enough. A day now and then chopping the weeds out of the tobacco and corn. Most of the summers were spent gathering things to put away for winter.

About the age of 20 was when it was time to think of the time when we would be too old to work. From what was taking place with Pop – bouncing around from one house to another – trying to get by on his social security, I knew it was time to do something with myself and the family I had started.

The way it was supposed to work – was going into the Army for thirty years. Work for half pay and then draw the other half of my pay for the rest of my life. Well now, things don't always work out the way you plan them. About fourteen years into my Army career, the wife threw in the towel and asked for a divorce. Did not have much but came out of it with nothing.

After nineteen years in the Army, they told me they were sending be back to Vietnam for another tour as an advisor. I immediately put in my papers and retired with one twenty years. Came home and remarried. After about a year on odd jobs, went to work for the State. Worked 19 ½ years and retired for the second time, at age 60. Five years later, I started my social security.

Still have not saved any money but am doing okay – keeping the bills paid and eating pretty good. Back to doing the same as I did when younger. Lots of fishing and video games with some television and a little poker now and then. Legs will not let me roam the hills looking for ginseng or hunting. Do a lot of driving in the country visiting the places where I grew up.

Don't know why anyone would want as much as Bill Gates because it would drive me crazy just trying to keep up with it.

THIRD TOUR – SOUTH KOREA

I can remember that my third tour in Korea was not the best one out of the four that I served over there.

Started out bad. The engineer outfit that I was assigned to was at Ft. Hood, Texas. While I was home on emergency leave, the outfit moved to California before I could rejoin them. The boat ride was not the best but we made it to Inchon Korea (known as the best dammed port in the Pacific – had to go through a lock to get to the port).

After everything was unloaded, they gave me the job of driving the 20-ton crane to the new camp we had set up at Prong-Tech. We moved to this location while they were building the new compound. We lived in squad tents for about 3 months (winter time with lots of snow).

A little after Christmas, we moved into the new compound. The motor pool had the maintenance building up, but the barracks were not completed, so we were back in a squad tent.

They made me the number two man in the motor pool, right under the Motor Sgt. This meant that it was my job to get the work done or do it myself.

Things went pretty good until the spring of 1959. Someone in the motor pool ran out of money, took a truck load of gas to town and sold it on the black market, and got caught. This broke up the motor pool because about half went to jail. They could not tie me into it, so they transferred me to a security company at Camp Long, up near the 38th parallel.

They made me Motor Sgt. there. There were 5 vehicles in the motor pool and 3 of them were wrecks. The C.O's jeep and one ¾ ton truck were running.

The company's mission here was to guard a nikie missile site about three miles down the road. Every 8 hours, the guards and their dogs had to be changed. This is where the missile storage building burnt one night and we had the biggest fireworks show ever. The nikie does not fly too straight if it is not launched from a launch rail. No one was hurt and it only took us a few days to gather them all up. There was no explosion, as they did not have any war heads in them – just fuel.

Spent about six months there and did not leave the compound except when working the whole time there.

It was winter again when my tour was up. Just about froze on the trip over to the coast, where we caught a ferry boat back to Japan and then another troop ship back to San Francisco.

KOREA 1948

I can remember a little over fifty-four years ago looking for some kind of job with a future. With Mom's help, I got into the Army for a two-year hitch.

Going from an easy-going country boy to learning how to be a soldier took thirteen weeks of basic training at Ft. Knox. Got orders for reassignment to the Far East, and thirty days leave at home.

Took a train from Frankfort to Chicago, then another train to Seattle, Washington. I was put in a replacement company and sat around until there were enough of us to fill a troop ship – which took about a month.

A few days after Christmas, they put us aboard the USN H.T. Maoyo (not a big ship and not too fast). Took us sixteen days to get to Japan and most of the time was spent standing in the chow line. Have breakfast, go back on deck, get in line for lunch, back on deck, get in line for supper and back below deck for a few hours of sleep. Next day, start routine over. For the first three or four days, I was confined to my bunk with sea sickness.

We were put in another replacement company at Camp Zama, Japan. We were only to be there for a few days but someone came down with the measles and they put us in quarantine for three months.

Some of us boarded a ferry boat bound for Inchon, Korea, bus ride to Seoul and another replacement company for assignment to our permanent outfit.

After another three weeks, I was assigned to HQ & HQ CO, 32NC INF BN, 7TH INF DIV.

Took me six months to travel from Ft. Knox to the compound in Seoul, Korea, and this was without getting paid. A few times they had called me in for a partial pay o $15 or $20, so we could get a hair cut, couple of bars of soap and shaving equipment. Got a few cigarettes along the way from the Red Cross.

Took all my entertainment at the USO Clubs. These clubs were a Godsend. Being broke for six months really made a fellow appreciate the USO Clubs and the people that ran them.

After my assignment to a company, it was back into training. Six weeks learning Morse code and how to operate the radio and code machine. Got the code down good and could take and receive about twenty words per minute but never did master the code machine – always had to have a little help with decoding a message.

MY V.W.

I can remember my first new car, as it was a V.W. Beetle. Bought it while serving one of my tours in Germany, got tired of walking everywhere or bumming a ride.

Went down to the V.W. dealer in Karlsure and for $1,300 got me a brand new one right off the factory line – just the basics, no extras. Took about a week for me to get my insurance, driver license for Europe, passes and stickers to get it on Post and then had to go to the PX and buy a book of gas coupons. Could not go straight to the gas station and buy gas. Cost was about $3 a liter when bought at the station. Could get a book of coupons good for 100 liters of gas for $35. Only $.35 a liter when bought at the PX and the coupons were good at all gas stations in Europe.

Now, driving in Germany was a lot different from driving in the States. There was no speed limit when driving on the Autobahn (Germany's equivalent of the interstate here). Whatever speed you wanted to drive was okay. There was no such thing as a two-car crash because most accidents had from 30 to 90 or 100 involved.

Don't remember any law against driving drunk. I did get a ticket one time for taking a nap in one of the rest areas because I did not leave my parking lights on and it cost me all of five marks ($1.25).

Owning a car in Germany sure did improve my social life because everyone wanted to be your friend if you had wheels.

Took a two weeks leave and drove all over Germany (American and British sectors). Could not get into the Russian sector. Also, spent some time in Spain and France. The Black Forest in Germany was well worth the trip. This was the only way to see Europe.

Owning a car in Germany meant you could get out into the country to places most Americans did not go. The beer was the same but the people were different. Really got to know the real Germany.

Cost me $100 to get my VW shipped back to the States and had to have seat belts installed at a cost of about $40.

I was assigned to Ft. Lee, VA, on my return to the States. Picked up my VW at Norfolk, VA, and put about 50 thousand miles on it before it was traded in on a VW Camper.

TROOP TRAIN

I was shipped back to the States after being in Korea for 16 months. It took me that long to get enough points to rotate home.

After processing at Camp Stolman, California, they put two passenger cars of a train on the back of a civilian train headed for Chicago and loaded about 150 of us on them with one Lieutenant in charge. His job was to see that we stayed on the train when it made its normal stops.

Big joke – no way one officer can watch that many soldiers. It only took a stop of a few minutes for us to jump off, get something to drink and get back on. A couple of us would take off down through the civilian part of the train, while the Lieutenant was getting us back, others would jump off and buy beer or other booze – whatever they could get. Train would get under way and the Lieutenant would confiscate all the booze and lock it in his compartment.

About half way to Chicago, he had so much stored in his compartment that he could not get inside. He finally opened it and told us to go ahead and drink it – quite a party after that.

Now, you have to understand – we had all been in a combat zone for up to two years. We were now back in the States and rather rowdy.

When we finally got to Chicago our two cars were put on a side track. We were told that we would be there for approximately six hours waiting for a hookup on another train headed for Louisville. We all dressed and went to town.

Some one gave us the wrong infromation because the cars were only there for a short period of time and when we got back they were gone. Some of us got a bus, some hitchhiked, and some caught a plane to Louisville.

They had sidetracked one of the cars in Evansville, Indiana, and that is where some of us caught up with it. After one day, most had caught up. They hooked us to another train and took us to Louisville. We were two days late getting to the station in Louisville. No one was looking for us and we had to wait another six hours for buses to come from Fort Knox to pick us up.

Showed up about three days later and everyone was mad at us. The held us up for about a week before we got our leave so we could go home for thirty days. During this time, we were all assigned to our new post.

MY NASH RAMBLER

I was shipped back to Germany in the 60's and stationed at Warner Barracks in Bamburg. This was not one of my better trips overseas. Things had changed a lot since the last time I was stationed in Germany.

Went to the PX and ordered me a car. This time I got a Nash Rambler. It was built in England and they shipped it to Bremerhaven where I picked it up.

On the way back to camp, it began to run a little rough, so I stopped at a gas station to see what the problem was. Pulled the cover off the valves and two of the springs had come off the valves. They had been put together with no grooves cut in the valve stems to hold the locks in place.

Along with the mechanic, who spoke only German, we took a hand grinder, cut grooves in the stems and put them back on with locks from a Volkswagen. This worked well enough to get me back to camp. The PX put new valves in the engine.

Put a lot of miles on this car in Germany. The girl that I had met and dated a few times lived in Witter-Rourg (British Sector).

Her brother, father and uncle belonged to a shooting club and over the two years of spending most of my spare time with them, I got pretty good with an air rifle (only type of weapon they could own).

Spent some time at the guest house (that is a pub in England – bar or joint here). They also served some fine food but were known for their beer drinking. Lost every beer-drinking bout that we had.

Had enough rank by now that the government shipped the Nash back to the States for me. Picked it up somewhere in New Jersey while on leave at home. Brought it home and put it in storage, as I took an I.T.T. from Germany back to Korea. (I.T.T. means you transferred from one foreign country to another). Only had to come back to the States for my leave.

Still had the old Nash Rambler when my time was up and retired from the Army. Came home and got married.

MY GAS MASK

The lowly old gas mask had made a big comeback. I can remember carrying one of these for most of my twenty years in the military. This was one of the first things that was issued to me along with my rifle.

One of the requirements to get through the thirteen weeks of basic training was going to the gas chamber with this thing. I can tell it now – I never did do this while in training at Ft. Knox.

My first experience with any kind of chemicals was in the classroom where I was instructed on germ warfare with a vial of mustard gas. Just a little reading, then took the vial, looked at it and passed it on to the next fellow. Left the class room and went to the parade ground for a little physical training (PT). By suppertime, everywhere I had touched my bare hide; there was a big blister about the size of a quarter. Thought for a day or two that my arm was going to fall off.

Now with this memory of how bad that was I made up my mind, then and there, that I was not going to any gas chamber. I was going to get out of this by hook or by crook.

Made my plans ahead of time. Got the date for the visit to the gas chamber and the day before I goofed up so bad on everything. Got chewed out a number of times and gave the Sergeant a little back chat. True to form he put me on KP (Kitchen Police) the next day. Spent the day cleaning pots and pans. I did not go to the gas chamber that day nor any other day for the next fifteen years.

After fifteen years of working my way around this – went so far as taking a thirty-day leave once to get out of it. I was on duty at the firing range on Grafinburg, Germany, doing range maintenance and not thinking too straight. Spent most of the night out drinking with my friends and overslept. Got sent to the gas chamber with no way out of it.

You know, it was not all that bad – just made it look like you were crying the rest of the day. I just had a fixation about it and this was the one and only time I used my gas mask in my twenty years of military service.

SURVIVAL

Picture this – can remember very well back in 1951, 4 privates with little experience at combat, put on a train as train guards. Two train cars loaded with equipment that is being moved to our new company location closer to the front line for better support of the fighting troops on the front line. Issued lots of ammunition for the rifle and a number of grenades to each one plus three days rations.

Orders were for one man to be on the train car at all times, and awake – one sleeping and one awake. Sounded like a good job. No sergeants or officers around – just the four privates on their own. The perfect situation for disaster.

First night went well but when the sun came up we were sitting on a siding in the country with the engine still hooked up. Sat there all day and all night. The following day someone came by and told us that a tunnel up ahead had caved in and they were in the process of clearing it. The next day they did fire the engine up and we went backwards to a rail yard in a small village with no name and no military units of any kind in the area – which meant no mess hall. By now, the three days rations were gone.

This is where the fun began, as we had to start foraging for food because no one had any money. After a few field trips to hunt, we found out that you cannot bird hunt with an M-1 rifle – even a chicken was hard to hit.

It turned out that we were on that train for twenty-six days before we got back to the company.

Traded a lot of equipment we were guarding for rice, eggs, vegetables, or whatever we could trade it for – as long as it was edible. A case of about 100 raincoats would feed us for about 2 days and a squad tent or a stove was good for 3 or 4 days. A roll of telephone wire was good for 1 day. Came up with a coke burner to cook on. All water had to be boiled. Got lucky and we all 4 survived. We did not run into any opposing forces and a good thing as we had used up most of our ammunition trying to kill something to eat.

We were a ragged looking bunch when we got to where the company was, as they had moved again before we caught up with them. Lucky also that this was in the spring of the year and the weather was not too cold and we could bath and shave in a stream – two at a time because two had to stay with the train just in case they started to move.

No one said anything about half of the equipment that was missing, as they had given us up for lost. The company commander welcomed us back and gave us a day off to recuperate.

FISHING IN VIRGINIA

I can remember when I was stationed at Ft. Lee in Virginia. At the time I was dating a lady that lived in Williamsburg and she had a cousin who was a big fisherman. He had a boat and camp house in Deltaville. This was right at the mouth of the Rappahannock River where it emptied into the Chesapeake Bay.

Fishing this area was a lot different than here at home but Everett was a good teacher and soon taught me enough so that I could do pretty good.

I spent all my weekends there unless duty kept me on post. We would go up on Friday and the family would all get together for a two-day stay.

Everett would get the canoe and the crab nets and we would spent Saturday morning wading in the shallow water dipping crabs. The large jack or blue crabs were dumped in the canoe for cooking later but the soft crabs were put aside to fry for supper, and the peelers were for fish bait. By noon we were ready to go fishing. Sometimes Everett and I were the only ones that went but every once in a while the women would go along.

You never knew what was going to bite but got a lot of salt water trout, puffer fish, flounder, stripers, eels, sting rays, trigger fish, spots and a lot of oyster toads. The oyster toads and the sting rays were not good for anything, so they were thrown back and lots of others that I cannot name. Also, caught a lot of blues. These could be caught on lures and some of them two at a time on the same pole.

Saturday night the crabs were cooked and what was left over were peeled and the meat was put away for crab cakes later. With a good day on Saturday or Sunday, some fish were cleaned and packed in a can with salt for later but most were cooked and eaten when they were caught.

This was the only time I ever ate any shark. The 3 or 4 pound sand shark was cut in sections and good either baked or fried.

The time of year would depend on what kind of fish you caught. Some days when we were fishing, the ladies would go clamming and this made for some great clam chowder.

Have spent a few weeks back in that area fishing with Everett since I moved back home. Fishing is still good but we buy our bait (peelers crabs and blood worms) now. It is not as much fun this way but still have a great time each trip.

FISHING IN TEXAS

Summer of 1958 I was stationed at Ft. Hood, Texas with a unit that was being put together for movement to Korea.

The family was with me at this assignment and we had an apartment in Belton, Texas.

Crappie fishing a lake was all new to me. A rod, reel, crappie rig and a few minnows were all that was needed. Drove out to the boat dock and bait shop. Got a minnow bucket, couple dozen minnows, and paid $1 to fish from the dock.

The dock was about 100 foot square with an open center. Had a roof all the way around so you could fish in any kind of weather. Everyone sat around in a circle and fished in the center.

Now, I don't really call this fishing. I am sure it was baited because we were catching them two at a time.

Once when I dropped my line down to the bottom to pull it back up a few feet, I hooked a rod and reel that someone had lost over the side and it had two fish on it.

Went home that first day with sixty-two crappie and an extra fishing pole.

The fish were small, as the lake was only a few years old, but to me it was a good day of fishing.

Went back a few times but never did catch as many fish.

Spent some time fishing for bluegill and a couple of nights were spent on the shoreline with family and a few friends. Not many fish were caught on these outings.

Did some fishing on the creek that ran through Belton but outside a few small catfish this type of fishing was not good.

After almost 50 years, there should be some good crappie fishing at Belton Lake and some of the catfish should be in the 30 or 50 pound range by now.

YUMA PROVING GROUND

I can remember one of the times we tested out in the deserts of Arizona. It was a jet plane, no pilot and was remote controlled. It was launched from a ramp, guided over an area where it took pictures, then returned to a drop zone (spot we had cleared about one-half mile square). Most of the time we hit the drop zone but there were times we had to go looking for it. The motor was cut and the plane was lowered by chute.

Russ and I had the job of recovery with a small crane and a long trailer to haul it on. Then back to the lab and someone else took care of the rest of the job.

Got on to the test track one time in a tank. It was a lot of fun for a short time but it would bruise you in spots you did not know you had.

We had built a 60% slope for the tanks. It was just a big pile of rocks and dirt with about a 150-foot concrete ramp on one side. I don't think the tanks ever made it all the way up on their own. Always had a winch cable hooked to the front in case they stalled out. This kept them in place and let them back down slowly.

The most boring test we had was a fuel tank that was made like a big rubber tire. You would fill two of them with gas, hook a truck or tank to them and pull them around until you wore the gun out.

Got to go back to the Yuma Proving Ground in 1965. I was stationed at Fort Lee, VA, and assigned to the Army General Equipment Test Activity.

They put me on TDY with a group of guys for 45 days to test a 12-inch booster pumping station.

Was set up on the channel and working around the clock in shifts. I got to do a lot of fishing because could fish and watch the pump at the same time. All fishing was catch and release because we had no way to cook them.

Got me a heavy-duty Penn reel and rod, 50 lb. test line and all you needed for bait was a loaf of bread. Landed some carp that could go 30 to 35 pounds and a lot of smaller ones.

Had made plans to settle in Yuma when I retired but a lot can change in 10 years.

NAGS HEAD NC

While stationed at Fort Lee, VA, I became a single man, so I took to traveling a lot. In order to get out of the expense of motel rooms, I traded my car in and got me a small Volkswagen Camper with everything. I would just pull off the road, park, and spend a couple of hours or a couple of days. I could cook, sleep, or just hang out.

It was not far from camp to the outer banks of North Carolina and there are a lot of miles between Corolla and south to Cape Hatteras. You could spend your whole life and not fish all the good spots along this beach.

Stocked the camper with food, fish, fish bait and drinks. This was all that was needed for a weekend with a little gas for the camper and a bag of ice now and then.

Never did catch many fish in this area, mainly because I did not know what I was doing. Always had the wrong kind of bait, tackle or the surf was coming in so heavy that when you threw the bait out, the waves would wash it right back up on the beach. It was a lot of fun anyway because a weekend on the beach was worth the drive down and back.

Did a lot of swimming and picked up a lot of shells. Had my lounge chair with me, so just take a nap, get a little sun and salt air, and all was okay with me.

Must have been a hundred miles of beach and you could pull off the road anyplace and walk over to where the sand and water met. It has probably changed by now and need a permit or something. Lots of places where you could fish from both sides of the road.

My lady friend asked me one time to bring her some of the grain that grew on the dunes (looks like rice). She was making a picture out of it. Did not know until I got back that it was a five hundred dollar fine if you got caught picking it.

There were a lot of places along the road to stop (stands of all kinds) and a few places to charter a fishing boat.

I started to Myrtle Beach on one of the trips, but never did make it because I got sidetracked at Fort Bragg and my leave time ran out.

YUMA ARIZONA

I can remember my first experience with R&D (Research and Development). It was back in 1961 when I was stationed in Arizona for a couple of years. Have not written about any of this, as it was all classified at the time, but I am sure it has been declassified by now.

I was assigned to Army Ordinance Test Activity on Yuma Test Station – way out in the desert – about 20 miles out of Yuma. Had a lot of jobs but the big one was testing ammunition – everything from a 22 caliber to the 16-inch navy shells.

From the firing line down range was about 5 or 6 miles with camera sights every one-half mile or so. One employed civilian and I had the job of servicing the camera sights each night and they were all operated by generators, as there was no electricity in that area. Along with Russ we serviced the generators each night if they were used during the day. Did not get into the picture taking but do know that the cameras were fast enough to stop the artillery shells in flight and get a still picture of them – that was fast (thousands of frames per second).

At the end of the range was the impact area where the shells exploded. There were about 100 cameras set on posts about 10 feet tall and about 50 feet apart that recorded the shell when it exploded. Lost a lot of cameras this way but they were replaced by someone and they did get a lot of good pictures. We worked mostly at night and had a long pole and a few one-gallon jars in the truck. We caught snakes (rattlers and side winders) that curled up in the middle of the road where it was warm. This was a side line as the university would pay so much an inch for each of them.

This was rather a nice tour as the family was with me and we were living on post, working nightly, and the fishing was great. Also, got in with a group of rock hounds and spent a lot of time out in the desert looking for rock.

Imperial Lake was the best bass fishing I ever did and just for fun it had more of the biggest carp I have caught anywhere. The small carp (2-3 inches long) was the bass bait. They were crossed some way with gold fish and could be dipped out of the irrigation ditches with a net. This is the only place in the world that I ran across this.

Arizona was one of my better assignments because it was warm most of the year and no snow to speak of. It only rained about once a year and sometimes not at all.

KOREA – 1950-1951

Watched a movie called "Pork Chop Hill" the other day. It was not quite the way I remembered the war over there but that happened after I had chalked up enough points to rotate back to the States.

I did arrive in time to retreat south when the Chinese got into the war. The boat that I was on arrived at Hungnam in November and, after it was secured, I was assigned to the 4th SIG BN Unit of the 10th CORP.

Spent the first month putting a radio station on top of a mountain assembling two fifty foot towers and raising one of them. While working on the second one, the engineer showed up, set charges and blew up all our month's work. We were evacuated back to Hungnam.

Stayed there for a short time and after the Marines and Infantry broke out of Changin, the outfit was put aboard an LST along with what equipment we could get aboard and shipped south, where we landed on a beach somewhere around Samchok. This was the beginning of a trip in an open jeep in the middle of a Korean winter that was a humdinger. There were three of us in the jeep – Radio Operator (me), Platoon Leader and the driver.

Was in a convoy of the whole battalion, moving mostly at night – by compass and most of the time with no road. Moved inland a few miles a day. Set up every three or four days, then packed up and moved again. This was done most of the winter, moving back north. This was like going back to the 1920 and 1930 dirt roads. The only smooth ride was on the bridges. There were no road signs and no good road maps.

By spring, I had a three quarter ton truck and my job was to repair generators and take them to the unit that needed them. Most of the time I was told what unit to take them to and to go out, turn right or left, go so many miles and look for the unit, most of the time they had moved and sometimes I spent days looking for them.

Spent the summer and part of the next winter moving every month or so. We were set up and living in squad tents with heaters which was much better than the pup tent I was used to as housing.

Never did get into the thick of it except by accident a few times. I was put on a ferryboat somewhere north of Seoul and sent to Japan for shipment back to the States in February.

POINSETTIA'S

I read a story in the paper a few days ago about Christmas plants (very interesting) and it made me think of one of my experiences with one of them in Vietnam years ago.

Story said that poinsettias were from Mexico and I can' t argue with that. I saw them in Vietnam and they were twenty to thirty feet tall and you could climb them. I was so intrigued with them that I stopped a convoy to take pictures of them. I took about half a roll of film because I did not think anyone would believe me if I told then they were so big. I still cannot prove this because my camera got ripped off before the film was developed and I did not get back to take more after I got my new camera.

These plants were along Route #1 between Natrang and Cameron Bay on the coast. The blooms on them were about the size of a regular poinsettia; just a lot more of them, and all were red.

Guess some things just grew big over there. They had a cactus that looked just like the Christmas cactus we have here, which grew through the trees to fifteen or twenty feet, same stalks, only bigger. These I do have pictures of around the house someplace in one of my books.

Poinsettias grew year round over there. Have tried them here for about three months and they got so shabby looking that I had to throw them out. Working on two now which still have blooms but leaves have all fallen off.

The temperature in Vietnam was about that of a rain forest, warm all the time and wet most of the time. The flowering trees stayed in bloom all year round. You could pick and eat bananas the year round. Coconuts were available three hundred sixty-five days a year. Lots of other fruit around but could not eat most of them because I did not know if they were edible. Some of the bananas over there had large seeds just like the paw paws do that grow here.

SHOE FACTORY

After the Korean War, Uncle Sam sent me home for a little rest. I got married and took a discharge from the Army when my 3 years were up.

Tried a few jobs but they did not pan out. Someone suggested that I try the Shoe Factory on Warsaw Street.

It was a good job as you did piece work and the more work you did the more they paid you.

As I remember, they started me off at the bottom – putting glue on the soles (easy). About two weeks of this and I was making above my quota and drawing a little extra money.

I was moved to a tack machine – tacking straps to sandals. It was not too hard, but for the first week I drove about as many tacks in my thumb and fingers as I did in the shoes. It took a while to master the machine and only drive one tack at a time. About three weeks of this, I could make my quota and some above. Got moved up again.

Now here I had a table with a foot shape thing on it, a tool that was a hammer, pliers and tack puller. I was to pull the sides of the shoe over and stick it to the inner sole. Before the outer sole was put on. Glue was put on before and all I had to do was pull the side over, hammer it down so it would stick, without leaving any wrinkles in the side.

All things can be taught and I did get the hang of it and was doing okay after a while. Another move!

Asked the boss why this time and he said I was in training to learn every job on the floor. I counted the stations on that floor and believe there were about 36 of them. This would consist of 2 years of training.

I didn't think my body could take it, so I drew my last check, told them I was changing jobs and went to Lexington and re-enlisted in the Army for the third time. Fighting a war, now and then, seemed a lot easier than making shoes.

VIETNAM

I was stationed in Germany when the fighting got started in Vietnam. Being in the Army, and as my chosen career was fighting wars; I went right down and asked for a transfer to the country where the fighting was taking place. I was turned down then and there – this was the thing to do if you did not want to do it, volunteer for it and they could put someone doing it in your place.

Was rotated to Ft. Eustis, Virginia, and assigned to Research and Development. The outfit was put together and moved to Ft. Lee, Virginia (about half military and half civilians). Assigned me to test a lightweight rough terrain forklift that could be air dropped into a combat zone along with supplies.

Was sent to Battic Laboratories in Boston for training and then to the Cerlis Diesel Engine Factory in Detroit for schooling on the 3 cylinder engine.

After about a year of schooling, the forklift was delivered for testing and was put on a 2 year stabilized tour (time enough to give it a good test). Well, it did not work out that way because about 4 months into the test I came out on orders for Vietnam.

After 30 days at home, they flew me from the West Coast to Saigon, South Vietnam. Took a chopper from there to Plakue – a real garden spot. Up in the mountains so far, all the natives ran around with no clothes on.

Problem was there were 3 of us there to do a job that one could do in a couple of hours a day. After a while I was told to catch a plane and find a job.

Found one in Na-Trang, down on the coast a Maintenance Advisor to an Arvan Combat Eng. Outfit. We worked at building new roads and replacing bridges. I spent the next year riding shotgun for the Captain that was assigned to the unit.

Good thing here was the beach where you could swim every day, year round. Lived in a hotel, had a nice NCO Club and even did a little fishing.

When we wanted a little excitement, me and a Navy man would volunteer to go out on patrol at night on one of the swift boats and cruise around all night along the coast and search the junks. This was a lot of fun until one night we took 14 rounds from a 20MM cannon in the wheelhouse. After that we stayed at the hotel like everyone that lived there.

All good things come to an end sooner or later. My time ran out and they I.T.T. me back to Germany with a few days leave at home.

Could write a story for each day over there but that would be a book.

THE SHOPPING CART

The shopping cart is a four-wheel contraption with a handle for pushing it. It never works the way it should. The wheels all have flat spots on them and they never run straight. There is always one parked in my path of travel.

The parking lots are full of them. My car has numerous scratches and dents caused by the wind blowing them into it. They should have brakes on them so they will stay where you put them.

I can still remember my first encounter with the contraption called a cart. It was at a Piggly-Wiggly Market in New Mexico (Albuquerque, I think). I thought it was the greatest invention that anyone had ever come up with. All you had to do was take the cart, go into the store, get what you wanted, pay for it, and go home. This was fantastic.

Little did I know the trouble they were going to cause me. For example – I have been run over with them and knocked down. Some of them at Wal-Mart have motors on them and these you really have to watch out for.

Don't know if they push the prices up or not, but my guess is they do. I see them everywhere – over the banks, along the road and have seen people use them for hauling everything – miles from the store where they should be. Saw two in a playground the other day and kids were using them to ride each other. Don't know where they were from, as they did not have a name on them.

Can remember back in the 30's when I would go to Lawrenceburg with Pop. We would park the car some place close to the Kroger store on Main Street, take the grocery list and give it to one of the clerks. While he was putting everything together, Pop and I would go to Sims Pool Hall, where I could have a hamburger and a soft drink (grapette, coke or an orange crush – depending on what mood I was in). Pop always drank a couple of beers.

When we left there we went to the drug store, or western auto, to get the other things we needed, then back to Kroger. Paid for the groceries, loaded them in the car (most times in boxes), drive over to the coal yard to get ice, them it was a mad dash home. Would get 50 pounds of ice and by the time we got home, we had about 25 or 30 pounds left. A 7 or 8 mile drive took a while as the car was slow and the roads were rough.

Could this be one of the reasons people call them the Good Old Days?

REMEMBERING THE KING

Twenty-five years ago, a great rock and roll legend passed away – Elvis Presley. As many remember his music and style, I remember some of his tour in the Army at Ft. Hood, Texas, where I was also stationed at the time.

I was not much of an Elvis fan back in 1958. He had only been in the Army for a short time and me, well, I was an old-timer – having been in about 8 years. We were both at Ft. Hood for some advance training.

I was in training to be a Motor SGT. with an outfit on orders to ship to Korea as a unit. Don't really know what Elvis was training for. The only time we trained together was in a classroom, on the ground for our daily PT exercise or in a parade.

My company was just a few barracks down the road from his. He lived off post in Killeen, Texas – believe his family was there with him.

Had my family with me but we lived in Belton, Texas, some 20 miles from Ft. Hood.

The place where we lived in Belton was right next to City Park and a lot of times the kids and I would spend our Sunday afternoons in the park playground. Right next to the playground was a little stand that sold ice cream, chips and drinks. Twice while we were there, Elvis drove in to get him an ice cream cone. This was the only time we ever talked.

We were both in the Army and that was about the only thing we had in common. He drove a big long Cadillac and my transportation was a used Chevy (when I could get it to run).

He lived in a big house, just off post, and we lived in a 3-room apartment, 20 miles from post.

As far as I could tell, he was just a normal person. I was in the Army for the long haul and he was putting his time in so he could get back to doing what he did best – singing and swinging hips.

When our time came to move – they sent me to Korea and Elvis went to Europe (Germany).

BABY THINGS

The wife and I went out shopping the other day and walked into the baby section of the store. I could not believe the number of makes, models and styles of baby strollers they had for sale – must have been fifty different styles. How can anyone pick out the kind they want to buy? There were so many things to buy – cribs, swings, car seats and large toys for walking or riding. Back when my boys came along, there was not much of a choice.

Had a bassinet when they were small (now 48 and 43 years of age). Then there was a crib for them to sleep in and high chair for eating. When it was time for a stroller, you only had one choice. A stroller with 4 wheels, made of wood and metal with a handle for pushing (think I got it at Sears). They were all the same color – white and blue. The only thing that folded was the handle and it filled the car trunk up – if you had a car to put it in.

All buggies had four wheels and were made of wicker with a handle for pushing. Had to have a truck to haul it because nothing folded on this thing.

My two were never in a car seat that I know of. You held them or laid them on the seat.

The only riding toys were a tricycle or small metal car with paddles. Later it was a scooter or a bicycle – all man-powered – no batteries.

Things were bought for the first one and saved for the next.

This was all back before plastic – just wood, metal and rubber.

Today if you get the kid all the things that he needs before starting school and put it away for the next, you would need a warehouse to store them in. To list a few – bassinet, crib, stroller, buggy, swing, walker, car seat, tricycle, high chair, all the plastic, slides, pools, electric car, motorcycle, jeep, pick-up truck and all the accessories that go with them.

The toy box is also a thing of the past. Today, kids need a room just for toys (be they boy or girl) and this is all before they start pre-school.

HAIR ROLLER

As far back as I can remember anything; there was something that was used for hair rollers. Everyone who did not have a curl in their hair wanted it to be curly. Mom used everything from a stick of wood to a corncob and a strip of cloth to tie it up with. Some people would get a perm but you had to have money to pay for that.

While I was in school they came out with a roller made of metal with a clip to fold over to hold it in place. The girls would use then but they would not let anyone see them when they had their hair rolled up.

By the time I was married, they had rollers made out of rubber plus they had come out with a home perm – a real mess and you had to have rollers for it to work.

Then someone came up with plastic and the hair roller makers got out of hand. There are so many different sizes – from about half an inch up to four or five inches. Some of them came in a kit that you plugged in to heat them up. About this point is where the comb changed but I will not get into the sizes and shapes of the combs and hairbrushes.

Never could get used to the wife sleeping in curlers because it was like sleeping with a porky pine.

Will only say at this point, if you were on a weeks vacation, you had to have a special suitcase just for the hair which consisted of: rollers, combs, brushes, curling iron, hair dryer plus shampoo and rinse.

Never used a hair roller in my hair but if I had the money that I have spent on them, I could take it and buy me a new Bass Tracker and new truck to pull it with.

Saw on television the other day where someone has come up with a tool called an iron – used to make curly hair straight – will wonders never cease. I am sure one of them will wind up in my bathroom – just don't know when.

VW CAMPER

Bought me a VW Beetle when stationed in Germany and had it shipped back to Virginia. Drove it for a while. Had to live on post and did a lot of camping at Deltaville with my fishing buddies. Camp house got filled up every weekend, so I traded it in on a VW Van that had been converted into a camper. This trade was made because a beetle was not made to sleep in. The camper slept 6 with an icebox, stove, water storage, table, closet, but no bathroom.

Took me a while but got to where I could spend a week in it and have everything that was needed.

I was new at owning a camper but was one of my best moves. Could spend the weekend at the camp house, a few days down on the outer banks, or an extended leave at home (put no one out). Just make up the bed and spend the night anywhere.

Be driving and get tired, just pull over (off the road) and go to bed.

Put in a well stocked bar, had music but no room for dancing (had to do that outside).

I was sent to Vietnam and had to leave it at my sister's place.

Came home for about 40 days leave en route back to Germany. Drove the wheels off it for a while and left it with a brother while in Germany.

Bought me a Nash Rambler through the PX. Brother used the VW Camper for camping at Beaver Lake. He fell in love with it and I never did get to drive it again. After three years, I jut gave it to him.

Put a lot of miles of the VW Camper and so did my brother. I believe he sold it to someone. The last time I saw it, it was in pretty bad shape (rusted out real bad and the top was caved in where brother had put it on a rack for an oil change and forgot to take the boat off).

Hope the fellow that bought it had as much fun and as many good times with it as my brother and I did.

GERMANY 1953

I can remember my first trip to Germany – about seven or eight years after the war. To me, the Germans still could not be trusted.

They took me off the boat, put me on a truck and took me to the compound in Friedsburg, Germany, and that is where I stayed.

Took all my meals in the mess hall and if there was some drinking to do, it was done at the E.M. (Enlisted Men's) Club. Anything that was needed could be bought at the P.X. (Post Exchange).

Could not speak a word of German, so did my shopping on Post.

Did get a chance to leave Post a couple of times in the daytime. There was no way you would catch me off Post after dark. Walked downtown a couple of times just to take some pictures. There was a big castle that I wanted some pictures of.

Did not know what a good time you could have if you did your beer drinking in one of the guest houses (bars here and pubs in England). I did not discover this until they sent me back to Germany in 1961.

Had been to Korea twice by now but just could not bring myself to trust the people over there. Had to work with them. There was a German man that worked at the Post Engineer, where they put me to work. Really worked for him as he was in charge of the shop. He knew what had to be done and how to do it, so we worked for him and did what he told us to do. There was a Lieutenant over him, but don't think he was every in the shop.

Did knot know at the time what a scenic country Germany was or how nice the people could be. I was only there for a short tour – about sixteen months. I was only on a three-year hitch and had been in Korea for sixteen months, so they had to ship me home and discharge me.

BLUNTS CREEK, NC

I was stationed in Karlsrue, Germany, back in the early 60's. Had a fellow in my maintenance platoon that was from Blunts Creek, North Carolina. He came back to the States after getting his discharge and went back to work in the sawmill.

Told me before he left that if I ever got stationed close to visit him and he would teach me how to catch flounder (great eating when fixed right).

Well now, when I came back they stationed me at Ft. Lee, Virginia – not far from where he lived. After a few months I drove down and looked him up – another one of my big mistakes.

It was a little cool for wading at night and the flounder lay on the bottom, covered with sand. Only their eyes were above the sand – not easy to see. Dean had no trouble finding them because he had done it many times.

Flounders are rather flat and they get big. Step on one and it was about like stepping on a large soft shell turtle. I was wading in about two to three feet of water with gig in one hand, light in the other and boat tied to my belt so I could pull it along behind me. Got dumped three or four times before I gave up and got in the boat. I definitely do not recommend this if it is your first time, unless the weather is warm. I about froze to death.

Spent other weekends at Blunts Creek but took my fishing pole with me – more fun to catch them that way.

We got a boat load of fish the night we were gigging but Dean and the other fellow got most of them. Got a few little ones on my gig but could not hold the big ones.

THE GREETING CARD

It is that time of the year again, to get the Christmas cards addressed and in the mail. I did not get into special day cards a lot until about 1952 when the first wife and I tied the knot (known as getting married). When in school the only cards sent or handed out were Valentine cards. You could get a package of them for 10 or 15 cents and this was enough to give one to each of the girls in school.

Birthday cards were the big ones. I was away from home a lot, so I had to send out a lot of cards – with a big family like mine. Someone was due a card each week. Missed a lot of them, but always sent more than I received.

Got into Christmas cards early – only a few at first. A few years back, the second wife and I peaked at about 200 cards but now send a little over 100 each Christmas.

Growing up, if we had a few coins to spend on cards and mailing them – we would buy a gift, wrap it and make the card up on a sheet of paper from the writing tablet and deliver them by hand. The cost of cards today and the stamps to mail them is enough to make a car payment or a months rent.

So many kinds of cards today. When growing up, we did not have cards for the grandparents, mother-in-law, grandson or granddaughter, get well, anniversary, Easter, thanksgiving, 4th of July, St Patrick, Halloween, friendship, missing you, etc. They go on and on – have got stores that sell only greeting cards and get catalogs in the mail that only have greeting cards in them. Some are normal size and they have them as big as a tabletop. Also, some that have several pages like a book.

The card that is remembered most was a brown paper bag and the message on it was – "Happy Birthday, fill this up and send it back". This type was sent to a sister-in-law 5 to 6 times, and she always sent it back each year on my birthday. We used the same card for a number of years. There was never anything put in the bag but we saved a lot of money because we did not have to buy a new card every year.

Have got away from birthday parties with cake and things – just a card now days. Christmas and Thanksgiving still call for a lot of eating and a lot of toys for the kids. Some people still have green beer on St Patrick's Day but mostly it is cards. Still a lot of candy and flowers on Valentine's Day. This will never take the place of the joy you could get out of a ten cent card back a number of years ago and nothing will ever be like the look on the person's face when you hand delivered that card that came in a ten cent pack.

THE COAT HANGAR
(Wire, Wood, Plastic, Cloth)

Growing up, I cannot remember having coat hangars. I am sure they were around but we just did not use them.

Never lived in a house that had a closet to hang clothes in. We had a wardrobe to put clothes in but they had built in hangars and the clothes were hung on these. The back up we used was a nail driven about half way into the wall. Most clothes were kept in a trunk of some kind. We did not have summer and winter clothes – we just had clothes. Winter coats and long john underwear were worn in the winter, put away during the warm months, then passed on as hand me downs for the next winter.

One of the things the Army had to teach me was how to use a coat hangar. The dress uniform had to hang on a hangar on a rack on the wall behind my bunk. This rack and the shelf on top of it, plus my footlocker, had to hold everything that we had. Also had to be folded the Army way, put in its place and everything that had a button on it had to be buttoned. Pants had to be folded and put under the jacket on the hangar. The work clothes and all shirts had to be folded. All dirty clothes were in the laundry bag and hung on the foot of the bunk. Shoes had to be lined up under the bunk in order – boots, dress shoes, tennis shoes and flip flops – all highly polished with a shine. Had two pair of combat boots that had to be switched each day. One pair had an "X" painted on the bottom and the other pair had an "O" painted on them. When we assembled for breakfast each morning, they checked and you had better have the right pair on or you could wind up polishing the garbage cans for a few hours that night.

The coat hangars had to be spaced just right on the rack. Overcoat was on the first hangar, raincoat on the next, then the dress uniforms, pants and Ike jacket. The sleeve with the patch on it had to be on the outside and the patches or stripes all had to be on the same level. All the hangars in the barracks had to be the same.

Field gear, pup tent, mess kit, poncho, pistol belt, canteen, first-aid kit, pair of spare socks, etc., was packed in the field pack and laid on the shelf above your clothes. The steel helmet and lines and the entrenching tool was arranged on top of the field pack. Rifles were kept locked in a rack at one end of the barracks.

After the thirteen weeks training at Ft. Know, things changed a lot. Some places we had metal lockers and some places the lockers were wood. Some places we had a room all alone. This was when you could go to the wooden hangars and things were a lot less trouble to keep straight.

Today, the wife has gone to all plastic hangars. No market for wire hangars anymore. Last batch of wire hangars we had were used for welding rods.

EXCESS BAGGAGE

Growing up, if you were going somewhere overnight, or for a few days, you got together everything that you were taking, rolled it up into a roll, wrapped your raincoat around it (if you had one) to keep it dry, tied it with something (usually your belt) and threw it on your shoulder and off you went.

The first thing that I had to pack clothes in was what the Army called a duffel bag. Just a large bag with a strap for carrying it on your shoulder. This was issued to me at Fort Knox. Then for a few years, when they moved me from one location to another, everything that went with me had to be in this bag or my pockets.

This bag was only big enough for your clothes, toilet articles and such. All the field gear, bedding, weapons, gas mask, etc., were turned in when you left one post and on your arrival at the next post it was all issued back, not new, and most were well worn.

Later, they let me buy a flight bag. Just a large bag with zippers. Lay your clothes in it, fold it up, with two large pockets (one on each side). This was harder to pack than the duffel bag.

After about 10 years in the Army, I bought a large Samonsite suitcase. This is the bag that went around the world with me. Think it was bought while at home on leave. It went to Germany, back to Virginia, then to Vietnam, back to Germany, from there to Korea, then back to Virginia for a second time, then to Kentucky, where it was retired along with me. It was finally sold in a yard sale and was replaced with a matched set of luggage (first of a number of sets bought in the last 30 plus years).

Could not keep any kind of suitcase in the barracks with you. All non-issued luggage had to be stored until you moved again. This was so you could not just pack up and leave when you wanted to.

What made me think of this was the other day while out driving. I saw a hitchhiker heading south and he had all of his belongings in a couple of heavy duty trash bags – guess he was sort of camping out along the way. He had a tent and blankets in a roll; therefore, he could set up any place.

SHORT ORDER COOK

I can remember a lot of work experiences. Believe that I have tried a couple of hundred kinds of jobs. The one that stands out was in Dayton, Ohio.

Went to Dayton and worked for a while on a chicken farm – selling eggs. Went good for a couple of months until the company went broke and everyone lost their jobs.

Had an apartment across the street from a drive-in restaurant and while picking up something to eat one day, the manager asked me if I wanted a job. I said yes but should have said no because I did not know what I was getting into.

Started me off in the basement peeling and cutting potatoes up for French fries, hash browns and keeping the supplies upstairs for everything (meat, drinks, paper products, everything that was cooked, served, and lots of cleaning up).

After a couple of weeks they moved me upstairs and made me the soda jerk working the fountain. This included fixing all the drinks for the inside customers and the carhops (10 or 15 of them) that worked the outside. Kept me really busy, depending what day of the week it was, and after a while got to where I could do about everything right.

Got so good that they moved me to the grill and made me a short order cook. Now, this was a good job because it paid a little more and I could even pay the rent on time. We ate good. Could not cook at the apartment but we could eat all we wanted at the restaurant and it was free. This was one of the benefits of being the cook.

It was hot and very annoying at times with so many people hollering at you about orders. The big problem was the carhops. They were always in a hurry and a lot of the orders they turned in were a little hard to read. Some of them were impossible because the orders looked like I had written them.

After a while, I was offered a partnership in another field. We took it but it was not a good move. Worked at it for two months. Never did get paid and went into debt for about three thousand dollars. It was time to pack and moved back to Kentucky.

Tried to get my job back at the restaurant but they wanted me to start out in the basement again. I declined and moved back home. Went back to construction work again.

Being a short order cook is not a good career move – there are no long-term benefits.

PICTURE TAKING

Opened my table drawer the other day looking for something that was not there but the drawer had a number of cameras in it – kind you only use once, turn the entire thing in for development. Think they take 25 pictures.

I can remember growing up – there was only one camera in the house, which belonged to Mom, and she was the only one that used it. You knew better than to touch it until Mom told you to. This was a 620 Kodak Box Camera with only one shutter speed and you had to be outside with the sun shining before it would take a picture. After all the film was used – eight pictures to a roll – they were mailed to Sears for processing and them mailed back to you. This camera was used from the time I was a baby until I was 17 years old. I still have pictures that were taken with this camera. Don't know what happened to the camera but she was still using it when I went into the Army.

Got into photography for a short time when they stationed me in Arizona. Picked me up a studio camera (antique made out of wood), contact printer, enlarger, lights for a dark room, trays for chemicals, cans for the different size film, and everything needed for making my own pictures.

The camera did not have a shutter on it – you posed your subject, set up the lights, took the cover off the lens for x number of seconds (according to the speed of the film you were using). Film was square – about 3x5 inches. Had to be put in one at a time and place the black cape over the back of the camera. It took most of the day to make only a couple of finished pictures (black and white only) and never did get real good at it.

I was just getting into it when they put me on orders for Germany. Stored everything until that tour was over. Everything had gotten wet except for the camera and had to throw it all in the dump when it was unpacked.

Enjoyed the picture making but could not afford to buy new equipment, so I just got me another camera and let someone else develop and make my pictures for me.

It took Mom about three weeks to get her pictures made. I can have them in hand now within a couple of hours after you finish the roll and that is in color.

REMEMBERING FT. EUSTIS AND FT. LEE, VIRGINIA

The year was 1964 and I was stationed in Germany. In May the Army reassigned me to Ft. Eustis, Virginia, and back into R&D (Research and development) – just the job that was number one on my list. Got to go home for a 30-day leave.

Started me out on a troop carrier that was not a swimmer – but the test took place on the mud flat while the tide was out. Ran out of fuel one day, tide came in, and the only thing above water was the radio antenna. Took a week to tear the engine apart and clean all the salt water out of it (was a Rolls Royce engine).

After about a month, we moved to Ft. Lee and got a new name – General Equipment Test Activities – was Transportation Board. Here we really got into testing things, walked a lot in combat boots, wore a uniform 5 days a week – going from khaki to green. Tested a machine for making hot rolls – put everything in that was on the list, turn it on and thousands of hot rolls came out the other end – ready to eat. Also worked on some of the new rations – fixed different ways and packed in a number of different packets.

The Army promoted me to a test NCO for a lightweight air drop forklift. This could be dropped along with other supplies. Gathered up and stacked them in a supply dump (called sandpiper).

Sent me to Detroit, Michigan, for schooling on the engine (3-cylinder Cyrillic) at the factory that made the engine. I had never had any dealing with a 3-cylinder engine.

I was spending a lot of time at the camp house in Deltaville, Virginia, fishing and learning how to catch crabs and clams. Everett and Louis Johnston owned the camp house and by now I was dating her cousin. Went into Norfolk to pick up my Volkswagen that was bought in Germany. Had it shipped back after about a year. Took it down to Petersburg and traded it for a camper that I could live in on weekends. Then I started spending about every other weekend down on the outer banks around Cape Hatteras.

Worked with the Lark 5 at Virginia Beach until one day I sank it on a sand bar out in the bay. A little time on the 50-ton lark and some time on a 5000-gallon tanker that was a swimmer.

Got the sandpiper in and after about a month of testing, had to put it in the shop for new brakes. While it was in the shop, the Army cut orders on me and sent me to Vietnam. I did not get to finish the test.

THE CLOTH WATER BAG

I can remember when they stationed me in Texas, New Mexico and Arizona. If you were driving west to one of these states, you had to have a water bag to hang on the front of your car. I never did know exactly what the reason for this was, but it was almost the law that you had one – and had it full of water.

If it was for the car – there was only room for one gallon. This was not enough to fill the radiator up if it boiled over or the hose busted and it ran out.

Tried drinking it a couple of times but it tasted like swamp water. Hanging in on the front of the car was to keep it cool and that did not work.

Owned a number of them and none of them would hold water. A few hundred miles on the road and it all leaked out and had to be filled each time the gas tank was filled.

Back in the 1940's and 1950's, all the service stations west of Missouri had a rack full of the cloth bags with a rope handle out front. If you did not have one, and you were heading west, they would insist you buy one. If it was lost on the road, then at the next stop you had to buy another one.

These bags did not cost much but back in the 1940's a couple of dollars was a lot of money to put out for something that served no real purpose except it looked good hanging on the front of your car. Never saw one on the back of a car.

Bought about a dozen of these. Lost a couple on the road, a couple of them wore out and had a couple ripped off by someone that did not have any or the money to buy one. Ripped one off myself one time just for pay back for one of mine that someone took while we were eating at a restaurant one night in Yuma, Arizona.

Have not seen one of these cloth bags hanging on the front of a car in the last forty or so years. Guess a plastic jug has taken its place and is kept in the vehicle some place.

FORT HOOD, TEXAS

I was assigned to the 13th MED TANK BN at Ft. Hood, Texas, in 1952, to be a member of a tank crew and learn how to operate a tank and shoot the big gun – already had training on the 50 cal. mounted on the turret.

Well, it did not work out that way. I was there for about a year and was never inside the first tank of any kind.

Spent every Friday sweeping the parking lot, where the tanks were parked, with a push broom and dustpan, and there were acres of them. Rather hot concrete in the summer.

Had a two-mile course that we had to run about once a week. It was laid out on one of the tank roads and was about knee deep in dust from the tanks running on it. If it rained it turned into mud. You had to be hosed down after the run – be it mud or dust.

Texas is dry most of the time and about everything that grows there had thorns or horns. The armadillos did not have horns but they had a shell and could mess up your nights sleep if you were sleeping on the ground. They were strong enough to lift you off the ground when they went under you. The horny toad had horns – all over their bodies and there were lots of them.

It was not good to stay in the field over night except when you had a vehicle to sleep in, because there were rattle snakes, scorpions and a big spider called a tarantula.

Spent a lot of nights pulling guard duty and walking around the tank motor pool.

The wife joined me and we had to rent a house in Belton, 26 miles from Ft. Hood. Did not have a vehicle, so had to catch a ride or take the bus to and from work. She only spent a couple of months before coming home.

It was years later before I got the chance to ride in a tank – Arizona on a 10 mile course – to see how fast we could wreck it or wear it out.

PILLS, SALVES AND LINIMENTS

I can remember growing up there were not many pills around. Could buy liver pills that came in two or three name brands. Also, could buy aspirin that came in a small metal box of about two dozen. If you got a bad cough, you took a cough drop that you put in your mouth and let it dissolve. Any other medication that I can remember came in a bottle that you took by the spoon full. All of them left a bad taste in your mouth. Salves were rubbed on and some liquid that was a rub on. There were a few more pills around, but never did take any of them.

The Army was about as bad because they had pills but mostly they gave shots. They had a salt pill that had to be taken at the noon meal, if you ate. This was during hot weather. It made you drink a lot of water so you would sweat a lot. You were issued a bottle of about 50 water purifying pills, which had to be put in each canteen of water before drinking it – all that did was make the water taste bad.

Never took a vitamin pill before the age of 30 but now I have to take one each day. There are hundreds of brands and makes of them – good for everything.

Today, they have a pill for everything. Get a shot for some things but mostly it is a pill. Most shots are to keep you from getting something that you would have to take a pill to cure.

How was it possible for 10 kids to survive to be adults in the 20's, 30's and 40's? It could have been that the water and air were better. It's still the same water and same air bit it has all been recalled a number of times.

So many pills today, that if mixed (taken at the same time) they will make you a lot sicker than you were before you took them.

Got a book that will identify thousands of pills and tells what they are for. I must have a doctor tell me how and when to take them and how many to take.

Still take the aspirin for things that hurt. In place of the box of one dozen for 10 or 15 cents a box, they come in bottles of a hundred or more that cost enough to buy a good rod reel for fishing.

THE TOOTHPICK

Back in the early 50's, I was trying to do something big. It came to me while sitting in the foxhole in a combat zone in Korea. I had just had lunch and my teeth were full of string beef from a can of c-rations. Got my knife out and was putting a point on a match, to pick my teeth with, when the bell rang and lights went off in my head. I about went out of my head thinking of all the money that I could make.

Wrote a letter to the Diamond Match Company and suggested they sharpen the end of the matches and that would give them a double use – light the cigarette with one and pick the teeth with the other end. Explained to them that we had matches in the supply system but no toothpicks.

Sent the letter off and waited for the good news. Took about a month before I heard from them and it was not the news that I was hoping for. Was a long letter and it explained they manufactured the Diamond matches but they also made Diamond toothpicks. Could not make the match into a toothpick – something to do with safety. It would also cut down on the sale of toothpicks.

Thought that was the end of it but about a week later I got a box in the mail. Opened the box and it contained a case of Diamond toothpicks (twelve boxes with five thousand in each box). A note was inside that explained that it should be enough of them to get me through the war and back to the States where I could get the toothpicks on the market.

Gave the toothpicks to the Mess Sergeant for use in the Mess Tent. Everyone in the Company used them. I kept one box for myself and had a few of them left when my tour was finished.

Growing up it was no a problem not having toothpicks – just break a twig off a bush, grab a straw, splinter off a board or stick of firewood. Made no sense to pay good money for something that was around – everywhere you looked.

Have not needed a toothpick for about twenty years now because I have had all my teeth pulled.

Still have to buy toothpicks to use in cooking, crafts, for other people and other things. A box of eight hundred still lasts for a long while. There is one box in the kitchen and one box in the shop.

CHAPTER EIGHT

FAST FOOD

What is a fast food restaurant? Well, I can remember when they were around but there is no such thing anymore.

Went to a fast food establishment the other day because I was in a big hurry. The building was full and the drive-thru was all the way around the building. Another day without breakfast.

I can remember when we called it fast food at Frisch's on East Main Street. The big secret was the carhops – not really fast – just that you did not mind waiting when the carhops were waiting on you.

Only thing wrong with it back then – not enough parking places. It took about two hours to have a hamburger and coke – not really fast food – because there were three or four brother and myself in the car. It just took a long while to eat.

They way they were set up – the cars just drove around and around through the parking lot and back out on East Main then right back into the parking lot. Kinda like driving around the block down town.

You could also go to Jerry's on Versailles Road. The hamburgers were like nothing you can get today unless you cook them at home and bake your own buns.

By the time fast food came to town, everyone was in a hurry. Back in the 40's, we thought it was fast food because no one was in a hurry to go any place. If we did not get there, or get it done, we could do it tomorrow.

Can go to a couple of restaurants in town, sit down, order the breakfast bar, eat and be out faster than you can get a biscuit/egg and cup of coffee at some of the so-called fast food places and eat in the car.

They took all the fun out of fast food when they put in drive-thru windows and did away with the carhops.

Just too many people own cars.

THE USO CLUBS

Some of my fondest memories of the Army are the USO Clubs. All Army Posts of any size had one. No matter how down you were, a visit to one of these clubs was sure to raise your spirits. Did not need any money because everything was free.

There was something going on every night. About once a week they would have a dance. All you had to do was show up for a night of fun. Some nights they would have a live show of some kind, depending on where you were and what country you were in. The one at Camp Zama, Japan, would have all Japanese actors and actresses.

Any night you could find a card game of some kind to play (bridge, hearts, pinochle – single deck or double deck – crazy eight) or just a game of solitaire if that was what you wanted to do.

This was a good place to write letter home – everything but the stamps were on hand and free.

Had a library where you could read magazines or check out books.

The Hour Glass Club in Seoul, Korea, had an archery range – could check out bows and arrows. There were also bicycles to check out and go for a ride. Also, had golf clubs and balls to check out – just had a driving range.

Every club had a book to sign and a map you could put a pin in to mark your hometown.

Sis spent a lot of time at the one in Ft. Hood, Texas, playing music and hanging out with the crowd. She loved to play music and sing, so this was her thing.

Took me an overnight short leave in Honolulu, Hawaii, one time and looked for the USO Club but never did find it. I am sure they had one. They took us to town by the busload and dropped us off all over town. Saw a lot of Honolulu but was so tired by 1:00 a.m. that I caught one of the buses and went back to the ship.

Got to see a lot of big stars from Hollywood when they were on their tours. I saw Bob Hope approximately four times. His best one was the time in Korea when he had Ann-Margret with him and of course he always had Jerry Colona with him.

The people that ran the clubs were some of the greatest people because life without them would have been a lot less fun. It has been a lot of years since I was in an USO club but I am sure they are still around serving the lonely men and women in our military.

TELEVISION
THEN AND NOW

I can remember my first television very well. Stationed at Fort Belvoir, Virginia, and lived just outside of Alexander, Virginia. One of the guys in my company gave me a 13-inch black and white set.

Now, it did not work. Got me a set of rabbit ears, took the cover off and worked on it for a number of nights. Got it to work – sometimes. Had only 2 or 3 channels on it. Could not get a good picture on it but some shows could be made out enough to tell what they were.

Each time the channel was changed, the rabbit ears had to be moved and an adjustment made on about four buttons on the front and three on the back of the set – all at the same time. Never did get the cover put back on the set. It was still sitting there on the table undressed, with all of its tubes showing, when it blew up for the last time.

There was no disk or cable – just an antenna that had to be put up outside – as high as you could get it on a metal pipe. Some had a motor on them that turned the antenna when you changed the channel. Without the motor, you had to go out and turn the pole by hand when you changed channels.

If you lived in Millville (Woodford County) – which I had for a while – you had to go to the top of the hill, trim a tree, cut the top out of it and mount your antenna on the top of a tree. Some of the antennas in Millville were mounted over half-a-mile from the set. Lots of maintenance on the wire that went from the set to the antenna.

Not many television sets in Millville at the time and this was good. We all gathered around the sets on Saturday to watch wrestling (family time together).

The shows back then were much better than they are now. They were all new and there was no such thing as a rerun.

Like my television much better now. There are about 60 channels. Just sit in my recliner with the remote when the wife will let me have it, and surf all the channels each night. Sometimes I will watch a complete show and sometimes I even give in and let the wife watch her favorite shows.

AMUSEMENT PARKS

Went charging off to Florida a few years ago to go fishing. The usual crew – me, the wife, mother-in-law, Uncle Howard and a cousin from Louisville. Got a good day of fishing in at Ft. Myers and caught some large snooks. Next day we took across Alligator Alley headed for the Keys.

Mother got sick and we wound up at Clewiston on Okeechobee Lake. The wife stayed at the hotel with mother while the guys went fishing. Had another good day of fishing and caught bluegill, croppie and a few bass.

This was when Uncle Howard decided he wanted to go to Disney World. I got out voted, so we drove to Disney World.

We got in and bought tickets for five of the shows. First was the Safari Ride on the boats. Then we got in line for the Swiss Family Robinson Tree House, next in line for the ride through the Haunted Mansion (a good one). Had a candy bar, glass of orange juice and a short rest. Then it was in line for the Space Ship Ride to the Moon (okay). We had tickets for the Country Bear Show but everyone was worn out from standing in line most of the day, so we left, got rooms and sacked out.

Have no desire to go back again. Spent a week in Orlando a few years ago at a Ruritan Convention but did not go to Disney World.

Remember as a kid growing up that the only Amusement Parks around here were Joyland Park in Lexington and Fountain Ferry Park in Louisville.

Spent some time at Joyland Park. We would drive to Joyland just to ride the Wild Ca and look for girls.

I was only at Fountain Ferry Park one time. This was while I was in the Army and stationed at Ft. Knox – in my late teen years.

Have the parks everywhere now and the rides have gotten so fast and wild that they scare me – so just stay away from them.

Wanted to go bungy jumping a few years back but the wife said no and told me to not even think about skydiving.

THE COON DRAG

Growing up, one of our most joyful things to do was go coon hunting. Never owned a good coon dog and cannot remember ever catching one coon while night hunting. Spent a lot of nights in the woods and enjoyed every one of them. Even the nights that we spent up a tree – treed by a herd of cattle.

We would hunt until we were tired. Then we would find a hay loft/hay tack, sometimes just a fodder shock where someone had cut their corn – all would curl up in a pile and sleep till daylight when we could find our way back home. Sometimes the dogs would join us but most times they would be at home when we got back.

I was only involved in one coon drag. Brother had given me a shotgun for catching him a live coon (another story). We put the coon in a gunnysack and took him and dogs to the woods just after dark. One of the brothers dragged the coon about 2 miles and put him in the fork of a tree – close to where we were holding the dogs.

Turned the dogs loose and they ran the two miles right on track. Found the coon in the sack, which had fallen out of the tree. They had killed the coon before we could stop them.

Was to teach the dogs – as a coon will mark a tree along the trail by going up one tree then cross over up in the tops and come down a hundred yards away. They will tree him up the tree he went up most times. We tried this on them but it did not work.

Tried to tell my brothers that they were tracking him but no one would listen to me.

Think the coon drag was a complete waste of time and it took up most of the night – plus it took me all day to find the dead tree where he lived – chop it down and put him in a bucket and wire the top down before he woke up.

A large coon can whip two large dogs and will drown them if he can make his stand in the water deep enough that the dog cannot stand on the bottom.

Caught a lot of opossums while coon hunting and had a few run ins with skunks but never brought a coon home. The coon is a smart varmint. It is hard to catch them in a trap and they will put up a fight even when in a trap. We caught a few of them in traps but not many. Could get a good price for the coon hide and he was rather tasty on a platter if cooked right.

BEFORE THE BIG ROADS

I remember in the early 40's when five of us got together to take a trip to Ft. Campbell to visit a brother stationed there.

We left Millville early and got about two miles to Trumbo Bottom and the car broke down (something to do with keeping a charge on the battery). Took all day to round up parts and get the car running. We had to spend the night in Frankfort.

We left Frankfort the next morning. Our route consisted of: Route 127 to Lawrenceburg, Route 62 to Elizabethtown, 31-W to Bowling Green, Route 68 to Russellville and Route 78 to Clarksville. After a lot of stops (gas, oil, low tire, food and bathrooms), we arrived at Ft. Campbell sometime early Sunday morning.

Located our brother and the following sleeping arrangements were made: brother and his wife slept in the car while our brother sneaked the three of us into the barracks.

The day being Sunday, we all ate at the mess hall, visited for a few hours and then started back home.

We got as far as Clarksville and broke down again. I cannot remember if it was the drive shaft or axle that broke. We did not have enough money to have it fixed.

We pooled what money we had left. Two brothers stayed with the car while my older brother, his wife and I got bus tickets and came back to Frankfort (arriving sometime on Monday).

The older brother got the money together and wired it to Clarksville to have the car fixed and got back home. I believe they finally got home late Wednesday or early Thursday.

This trip took place about fifty-five years ago. The only four-lane road at that time that I can think of was from Versailles to Lexington.

It was a great trip back then and I enjoyed every mile of it even with breakdowns and bus ride home.

Travel back then took you through every little town and community with lots of things to see and more places to stop and browse.

Today it takes about four hours, each way, but all you can see is the road. The only way to see anything else is to exit the big road.

CATCHING A LIVE RACCOON

As I remember, when an older brother announced that he needed a live raccoon to train his dogs with, the hunt was on. The reason being that whoever got him one would get the double barrel shotgun he no longer needed.

I knew where they were but catching one alive and getting him home was a problem. There was one that had raised a family of young ones in a big dead tree up the hollow behind Crow's Nest. This was the area where the Distillery built a shelter (cooking pits and tables for having cookouts and parties).

About noon I knew if he was there he would be resting, so I took an old yellow hound, chopping axe and a large bucket with a top on it. We went out not knowing what we were going to do, hoping things would fall into place as we went.

When we arrived at the tree, it took about an hour to chop it down. After it hit the ground and split open, out rolled the biggest raccoon I had ever seen and he was really mad. We did not have to run him down because he took right after us. He had the dog whipped when I got a light lick in with the flat side of the axe. When he finally came around he was in the bucket with the lid tied down.

No one believed me when I took him in and demanded my shotgun. It was up to my brother to get him out of the bucket and in a cage. This was handled very carefully because by this time, the raccoon was really, really mad.

A few days later, the raccoon was put into a burlap bag, dragged about two miles across country and placed in a tree. Dogs were put on the trail and were supposed to tree the raccoon.

Luck ran out for the raccoon when he fell out of the tree and the dogs killed him before anyone could stop them. My brother said it was a waste because summer hides were no good to sell.

I was a happy kid because the raccoon had been caught alive and the double barrel shotgun was mine.

I never did tell anyone that I knocked the raccoon out to put him in the bucket and to this day some still wonder how I got the large raccoon in the bucket.

ST. CLAIR MALL

I still remember fifty years ago when downtown was downtown. This was before the shopping centers were invented. St. Clair Street had everything. The drug store on the corner of Main and St. Clair Streets – complete with a soda fountain. A couple of eating places where you could get a good hamburger or bowl of chili with oyster crackers or a full meal of roast beef, mashed potatoes and gravy on an open-face sandwich.

Pool halls where you could shoot pool, have a beer, or something to eat. Clothing stores, movie theater and a couple of places where the older folks could just stand and talk and have a drink – called bars.

Had two dime stores with everything and this is where the wives gathered on Saturday to shop and talk.

Many a Saturday we drove out a half tank of gas driving around the block. Could drive down Main Street turn onto St. Clair Street, then right turn onto Broadway, right turn onto Ann Street and then back onto Main Street. For a change we would go all the way down Main Street to Washington Street. Four right turns would cover Washington, Broadway, St. Clair Street and back onto Main Street.

All this driving did was let all the girls know that we had a car and we could drive them home when the day in town was over. Never did work that way though because we only had one car, which was owned by an older brother. The younger ones would wind up walking home on Saturday night and the older brothers would go to Lexington or some place.

The drive around town was always the high point of Saturday in town and it had to be a lot of fun, as every young man that had a car did it. Sometimes we would go down St. Clair, cross the Singing Bridge, up Second Street, cross Capitol Avenue Bridge and back on Main Street – but only if you had extra gas. Money was pooled to buy the gas and everyone had to help with this purchase or you had to walk around the block. Bad part of this was, if you were walking, you had to stop and talk to the girls. In the car you could holler or whistle, blow the horn, but you did not have to talk to them and make up reasons as to why you could not go to the movie with them or treat them to ice cream or a soda.

Today about all the young people have cars – boys and girls. If we still had a downtown and no St. Clair Mall, there would not be enough room downtown for them. Put them all downtown on Saturday and no one would be able to drive any place.

The young people still like to show off their cars and one of the most popular places today is the parking lot at Juniper Hills – times when it is full. Sure there are other spots where they gather, but there is no downtown center for them to drive around the block. Most streets are one-way and you have to drive straight through town.

PLUTO
DOG THAT CHASED ROCKS

Dogs were a part of our family as we grew up. We always lived on land that bordered the river. This meant we had to have at least one flat-bottom john boat or more, if possible. Having a car was not a priority because we did most of our traveling on the river or walked.

Now, back to the dog. We had a big longhaired white dog (mixed breed) called Pluto. He did only one thing and did it well – chased all kinds of rocks. All we had to do was get the rock moving and Pluto would go after it and continued until it stopped.

He started out with small rocks or sticks and would retrieve them all day. However, to make it more interesting we would start a small one over the river cliff. True to form, he would chase it until it stopped or went in the river.

Then we went to bigger and bigger rocks. Any flat rock we could stand up on edge and start to rolling over the cliff, Pluto would take after it. Sometimes he would get going too fast and end up passing it.

Cliffs were two hundred to three hundred yards or so from top to bottom. In places, they were almost straight up and down.

This is where Pluto's real talent came in. From this point to the bottom of the cliff he had to stay ahead of the rock or dodge it.

I cannot remember Pluto ever being hurt from his favorite sport but it would sure tire him out fast. There were times when he got back to the top of the cliff and we had to let him rest before we started another rock.

To this day I don't know why he liked to chase rocks the way he did. I never saw him, even once; try to eat the rocks (even the ones he caught).

1942 OLDSMOBILE

Been driving for about 48 years now but when I bought my first car did not even know how to start it.

Was discharged from the Army in 1949 and had a little money saved from buying War Bonds each month. No one owned a car at the time, so a couple of bothers talked me into buying one.

Took all my bonds to the bank, cashed them in, and we went car shopping.

Found a slick looking 1942 Oldsmobile. I believe it was the first one to come out with an automatic transmission. Figured this would be easy to drive. Older brother could drive it until they taught me to drive.

I believe I paid about $800 for it. Then brother drove downtown and got all the paperwork, went and got insurance for a year – about $32 worth, oil and gas, and we were ready to go.

Things went great for a while but as always my money ran out. That meant I had to go to work or stay at home. Car went every day but most time I had to stay at home. Pop even drove it a few times. He did not like the car be he would drive it.

First time I got to drive it alone, hit another parked car and dented the front fender of the Oldsmobile. Guess that started the rash of accidents we had in it. One brother stopped in front of a fellow one night and he ran right up on the trunk of the Olds – tore the bumper up and caved the trunk in. We were never able to get the spare tire out again.

I hit a gate one day and tore the driver's side up from the front fender all the way back to the back fender and knocked both door handles off. Lots of small accidents between the big ones. Everything on it was dented except the top and the grill was still in the front.

A brother took care of this one day out. We had worked on the brakes. When we got them fixed we found out that we did not have any brake fluid to fill the master cylinder with. Brother said this was not a problem. We would just drive to Jett and get some – big mistake.

Took off down the hill from the parking area at the old Quire House and got about a quarter of a mile. Mr. Tutt had parked his pickup across from the store and a tanker was sitting in the road pumping gas into the gas pump. Did not want to hit the gas truck, so brother put the Olds in reverse. This did not help because he stripped the gears in the transmission and hit the pickup at about 30 mph. Took care of the front of the Olds and also put a hurt on the pickup.

A few days after this, we were parked on Broadway (downtown) and a fellow parked next to us offered to trade cars, even swap. I believe he had a 1939 Buick, one seater with a rumble seat. Trade was made and we took off. Never did hear how the fellow got the Olds home, as it had no reverse in it. We pushed it out of the parking slot when we got ready to move.

THE QUIRE HOUSE ACROSS FROM CROW

My first experience with the Quire House was years before we moved the family there. The storehouse next door had been taken down and the house had no one living in it. It was furnished complete with clothes, bedclothes and everything. Seems the last people to live there just up and left one day and did not come back.

Whomever the house belonged to had taken what they wanted. With all the good things they had left behind, this made the ideal place for kids to hang out.

Was in the Army when the family moved into this house so I did not know what all there was in it at this time.

This house put Pop a little closer to work. Could sit on the porch and see where he worked right across the road. Had a lot more room and it was right on the road.

Some things were not so good. It was about a mile from the river, had no garden space and no source for wood (had to be hauled in). Pop went to a coal stove and an oil stove.

Was a short walk to the Tutt Store and we did have the creek close by if we wanted to go fishing or turtle hunting. Also, a couple of good swimming holes close by.

Kids still in school were now going to Millville School. Still had school bus service. It was just across the county line in Woodford County.

Still had a boat at the river as brother and his family had moved into the Gardner House.

The Distillery had an eight-foot chain link fence around it. I cannot remember even one time being on the inside of the fence.

The Quire House is no longer there. It was taken down and a sub-station for the Power Company was put in. Lots of the houses in that area have been gone for years – out of seven on the Gardner farm, only one is still there. The other houses up to the Davis Store – only four of them remain. I believe one has been built in that area in the last fifty years. All the buildings over around Crow's Nest are gone. All the farming in this area has stopped. Seven hundred acres – all grown up in bushes, blackberry briars and weeds. Road to the dump is still there – about the only place you can walk.

The old Quire House was the last place where we all lived together in Millville. Still a lot of the family lives in the Millville area. All the houses that are not there anymore are missed. Each time I drive that road, I can still remember them and the people that lived in them.

SPECIAL SWIMMING HOLE

The beach at Big Eddy is still there and always will be as long as the bend in the river is there to create the eddy that drops all the sand in that spot.

Me – I was just as happy swimming on a mud or rock bank. Just swimming made me happy.

What drew us to the beach at Big Eddy were people. Always more fun when there were lots of people around.

Most people went here on weekends. Some would come up river by boat and some would drive a car. We went down river by boat or walked down the railroad and swam across the river.

We would swim any place, but on a date would drive out to Red Bridge – out of the way. To me, this was not really a good place to swim because the water was not deep enough for diving and no rope to swing on. Could swim or just lay around and stay cool or could sit under the waterfall. Good place for a quiet swim but most times we liked to show off a bit.

The dam behind the Taylor Distillery was nice with a big hole of water and about four foot deep in spots. This has filled up a lot over the years. A lot of trash, cans, and glass have been added to it. Still a lot of people swim there. I still use it for fishing with the kids because there are lots of bluegills, warmouths, bass, suckers, catfish and a carp that weighs up to thirty pounds.

The hatchery at the Forks of Elkhorn was a good swimming hole but did not swim out there much. Lots of good places along Elkhorn to swim. Old Covered Bridge at Switzer was used a lot by swimmers.

Today, swimming is pretty much confined to the river, from a boat in deep water. There is no danger of stepping on something.

Now, lots of people have pools at home and the city has two large ones.

Don't enjoy swimming anymore, because my legs won't let me, but I still go to the pool to watch other people swim and still enjoy that.

CHAPTER NINE

CINCINNATI REDS

I can remember around 1946 going to Cincinnati to watch the Reds play. This was not so simple because you had to find someone with a car that would make the trip – was the big job. Next you had to get them to invite you along. This only took place once a year and only so many could go.

Tickets had to be arranged for in advance and money had to be put away for the trip. Do not know why but we had to have a new outfit for this trip – pants, shirt and shoes (if we could afford them). Got a new hat at the ballpark.

Ballpark was the Old Crosley Field – somewhere in Cincinnati. Only the driver had to know how to get there. Got to Cincinnati by going down Route 24 – was no big road. This was the only way to get there. To Georgetown and follow it to Covington, cross the river and from there on in I was lost.

There was nothing like a ballgame at this time. It was like planning a two-week vacation now. Always someone around to take your place if you did not get ready for it. If you were bad and got out of hand on anything, you got left at home. Everyone remembered from year to year if you got out of hand when going to the game or coming home. You did not get invited to go the next trip. Sometimes we would have to take two cars – could not get everyone in one car.

Big problem was the ballpark at Crosley Field. A lot of people had to sit behind a post and there were lots of posts in the stands. This was my seat a few times. Hot dogs, popcorn and drinks were handy. Some guy was always close with a tray full of them. Bathrooms were not as handy as they are now. You could smoke in the stands.

This trip would start early in the morning and it may be time for Church on Sunday morning by the time we got back home. After the game, it was everyone back to the car, get back over the river into Kentucky and then look for a place to eat (this you had to do). Could never come on in without eating.

Could spend the whole day at the game for which a ticket costs now plus. Don't remember ever going to a game that I did not enjoy. The ones we won were best but the ones the Reds lost were still a lot of fun.

The only times we went was when the Reds and St. Louis were playing. This called for a lot of fans rooting for both teams and there was always a crowd on hand. Stadium was always full and tickets had to be acquired early. As soon as you found out when these two teams were playing, you ordered tickets. The only game better than the Reds was when the local boys at Old Taylor and Old Crow were playing each other.

WEEKENDS AT BEAVER LAKE

There was a farm on Route 62 that surrounded one of the slues of Beaver Lake. The farm was rented by kinfolk, so all the family were welcome to use the road that went down the hill across the end of the slue to a point that jutted out into the lake.

After retiring from the Army in 1969, I got married and settled down. The wife and I were invited to join in on the weekends to do a little fishing.

Sometimes there were eight to ten vehicles to spend the weekend. Everyone showed up on Friday and left on Sunday.

All the guys would head to town on Saturday for fresh bait and maybe a few beers. The gals would stay at the campsite to sunbathe, clean things up, get things ready for supper and catch some fish for the guys.

Bluegill fishing was fantastic but trying to catch a catfish was really hard. This was mainly due to the fact that we did not know what we were doing.

Frog gigging was fair, but hazardous. The catfish had all the bluegills up close to the bank and nervous. When you put the oar down close he would come out of the water at full speed and land in all kinds of places. Some would jump over the boat and land in the lake on the opposite side. Came in one night with a couple of frogs but a mess of fish that had jumped in the boat (43 to be exact).

We started out sleeping in the car, then went to a tent, and eventually bought a camper.

Most weekends were fun but I think the best ones were when it rained. It was a real sight watching everyone trying to get out on Sunday. First one hundred yards of the road were dirt (yellow clay by this time and wet, which was just like driving on ice). By the time everyone got out, the mud was a foot deep in places and everyone looked like they had wallowed in to (which they had). It took about two days to dry everything out and get it cleaned. Sometimes it was as hard to get in on Friday, as it was to get out. A few of us always showed up – rain or shine.

Clear weather was nice because you had a big fire and fished all night, if you had enough clothes to keep warm and you needed plenty.

The wife and I spent about six years at this, every summer. Some say we were a little crazy for doing this but it was our way to enjoy a weekend and spend very little money for entertainment. Cooking out made things taste so much better. The tasty things were: things out of a can (especially pork 'n beans – hot or cold); potatoes baked in the fire; corn on the cob cooked with the shuck and wrapped in aluminum foil; and sometimes fish.

KIDS AND CATFISH AT BEAVER LAKE

The memory of the weekends at Beaver Lake still come back on Friday nights when are fishing there now. Only now we do not camp out like before. We take the boat fishing at night and come home.

Back when 7 or 8 families gathered for the weekend, a few times I got to take the boys with me. Sometimes there would be 10 or 12 kids there.

Now, one of my kids could catch a fish anywhere. The youngest one couldn't care less about fishing and would not take a pole with him most times. The two of them did hang out together most of the time and this did create a problem sometimes.

The oldest boy found a place around the lake where the catfish were biting. Hooked a nice one and after playing him for a while, got him right up to the bank where the youngest one jumped down the bank, grabbed the line to drag the fish out and broke the line. Took me a few minutes to get them apart. I really believe that the oldest one would have drowned his younger brother if I had not been there.

The following weekend, the oldest showed up with a broom handle for a pole with a twine line (about 600 pound test), large hooks and went to the same spot. Put on a big chicken liver for bait and pitched it out and sat down with the pole.

Took about an hour but he got a bite and when he set the hook he took up through the woods and dragged the fish out on the bank. About a four pound catfish. Got a bear hug on the fish and took off back to the campsite with it. May have been the same one that got away the week before.

That summer he caught a lot of fish in the same spot but he would never take his brother with him after the week that he broke the line. I fished right beside him all summer and never did get the first fish out of his fishing spot.

The oldest boy can still out fish me most of the time but we have watched him over the years and picked up a few of his tricks of the trade. Now and then I can catch more than he can, but most times he still gets the big one.

Youngest one still doesn't fish much. He just never did like to fish. Always wanted to go camping and be there with us but did very little fishing.

KIDS

I cannot remember the day that I was born but have been told it was cold in January 1930. The only thing I knew how to do was eat, but everything after that was taught to me by Mom, Pop, and older brothers (with a few pointers from aunts, uncles, and cousins). It took them months to teach me how to walk and the first thing I did was walk over the edge of the yard. Fell over the riverbank and about killed myself. Don't know exactly how old I was at the time but do know that I was still in diapers.

Kids today are not like we were. Mom and Dad waited months for them to get teeth and then yelled at them every time they bit someone. A few more months are spent on teaching them to walk and then when they walk over and get into things, that is another no-no.

When they learn to eat by themselves, goes back to the beginning. Everything that a kid picks up for the first few years goes into their mouths and they try to eat it. The second big thing for me was swallowing a jack (for people that don't know what a jack is – it's a small toy – about eight to ten of them have to be picked up with a small ball that is only allowed to bounce one). The jack has a lot of prongs sticking out of them and they are hard to swallow. Pop was working the ferryboat at the time and lots of excitement took place before they got him up the hill. When he arrived, he turned me upside down and shook or beat the jack out of my throat.

Now days when a kid starts to walk, the first thing mom does is purchase them a pair of eighty dollar running shoes, then chases them all day on Sunday explaining why they should not run in Church.

Parents cannot wait until kids say their first words. Some will follow them for week trying to get their first words on tape or video. Then spend the rest of their lives telling them to shut up every time they say something. Spend months teaching them that cute little thing to say, and then scold him when he says it when you have company – especially when the Minister and his wife are visiting.

Just remember – a three year old does mot make up these bad words. If one tells me, "Paw Paw, you are stupid for smoking that old cigar", I don't scold them. I just think – now who could have said that where they could hear it? If you are gone from home a few days and want to know what happened while you were gone, don't ask. Just listen to that four year old and he will tell you – maybe add a little – but listen to him.

The schools have made some big changes with the kids. Today, by the time they are out of elementary school they know things that I was not taught until after I joined the Army at seventeen. Lots of classes have been added since my time and I think one more should be added – "What Not to Learn While In School".

THE RUBBER BOAT

About 30 years ago, shortly after the wife and I got married, Uncle Howard (Howard L. Black) bought a rubber raft. He said we needed it to get out in the middle of the pond in Shelby County, where the fishing was the best.

This raft was sold as a two-man raft but by the time we got Uncle Howard in it with all his tackle, bait and oars, there was not much room left for me – but the room was made because I did the rowing and he did the fishing. This was when we found out there were no fish in the middle of the pond. They were all around the bank in the moss that grew on the pond. The only thing that lived in the middle of the pond was a huge snapping turtle about the size of the top of a whiskey barrel. Uncle Howard hooked him a couple of times but there was no way you could land him. He had claws like a bear and would tear a rubber raft to shreds without trying.

The old raft made it to the pond numerous times with a few patches and a lot of patience. The wife made a one-man raft out of it. She was pumping it up once, while I was getting everything ready for fishing, and blew the outside air compartment in half. Still used the inside half until it got beyond patching. Hooked up with the granddaddy of turtles a number of times fishing from the bank. Could get him in to where he got his front feet planted on the bank and that was as close as he ever came to being landed. Suppose he is still in the pond.

This pond was on the Biagi Farm, Route 53, just out of Shelbyville. Take warning, if you plan on catching that turtle; don't try it in a rubber raft.

Caught a lot of bluegills out of this pond. Two of them are mounted and hanging in the living room. The wife caught one of them and Uncle Howard caught the other one.

BICYCLE EXPERIENCE

I can remember back when the wife and I bought us a camper. Needed it to stay in on weekends when we were fishing because we could not afford a camper and a car. The camper was used for everything – car, truck and camper.

We spent a lot of weekends at Greenbo Lake State Park. It was a long walk to the boat dock from the camping grounds, so I bought bicycles for wife and I. Now, they are what this story is all about.

Got a rack and mounted it on the front of the camper for hauling two bicycles.

They went everywhere we went and for some reason the wife always came up with a reason for not riding hers to the boat dock – we still walked.

Returning from the second trip to Florida – one of them all the way to Key West. This time when I asked her why she had not ridden her bike one time – she told me that living in town all her life, she was not allowed to have a bike and did not know how to ride one.

My answer to this was a set of training wheels – which were bought and installed on her bike. She worked hard at the training – riding the bike in the basement – wore the training wheels out. She still could not get the hang of how to balance the bike to where it would not fall over.

Gave up on this and sold the bicycles in a yard sale. Found and bought a bicycle built for two. Back into training but this time outside. After losing a pound of skin off my knees and elbows, gave this up as a bad move.

Now with me it is hard to start something and not finish it but put the two seater up for sale and bought a unicycle. This should be a story all by itself, as there was a lot more of my skin scraped off but could not master this myself and sold the unicycle.

Don't have the camper anymore but replaced it with a pickup truck and car.

Working on something new now. Trying to get the wife to buy us a couple of motorized scooters. We would really look cool riding them around the block.

CAMPING

The wife and I took up camping out on weekends shortly after we got married. Camping out on weekends was the only thing that was really affordable.

Started out sleeping in the car. Took a little fishing tackle, little bait, food and a few soft drinks. Any cooking had to be done on an open fire – roll the potatoes and ears of corn in Reynolds wrap, bury them in the ashes for a short time, then cook the hot dogs and it could turn into a great meal.

After a summer of this, we bought a tent and sleeping bags. This was a big move up in camping out. Still fished most of the night and got very little sleep.

Brother had a small john boat, so we could put out trot lines, use it for frog gigging or just go for a ride.

After a couple of years of the tent, we went wild and bought a camper – complete with stove, refrigerator, water storage, bed and dining area. Had a radio, television and heater. With this we could go to different places way off – even to the Florida Keys. Fishing was a lot better but could never get used to this kind of camping.

About the time we settled into this type of camping, wife's mother started camping with us and this put me outside sleeping again.

We used that old camper a lot over the nine years we had it. Made five or six trips to Florida and a couple to Virginia. Also made a 17-day trip to Mexico with side trips to Grand Canyon, Petrified Forest, Painted Desert, Las Vegas, Sand Dunes in California, back by Boulder Dam, through Colorado, Iowa and spent every night of the trip in a motel and took all our meals in a restaurant. It was also used for a car, truck and camper.

Besides a lot of weekends at Beaver Lake, also spent a few at Greenbo Lake State Park, couple at Lindville Lake in Renfro Valley, one at Carter Cave and one at Jenny Wiley.

Camping was a lot of fun and a good way of life when we were younger. The older you get the less you enjoy it. Now, a night of fishing on the boat is about all we can take.

Spent a lot of time camping out when putting my time in as a soldier in the Army (20 years) and it got a little rough at times. A lot of fun most of the time. This camping was for longer periods of time – sometimes it would take months and the weather was not always good.

ROAD WORK

The other day I was at the Highway Maintenance Barn, getting material for an Adopt-a-Highway Project. Things have really changed in the last 30 years. I cannot believe some of the equipment they have.

I can remember the first winter on this job. Believe we had 3 or 4 dump trucks with snowplows on them. One or two of these stayed broken down most of the time.

Worked with salt during the first snow but after that we used mostly cinders. This called for two men to ride on the back of the truck and spread then with a scoop shovel. This was only done on the hills. Sometimes we had a little calcium chlorite to mix in and sometimes it was mixed with sand or fine gravel. Salt was only used on the main roads, around town and interstate.

The Flat Creek Road was the only one you definitely did not want to get assigned to at night.

Brush along the road was cut by hand with a bush cutter and axe. Weeds and grass around the guardrail were taken care of with a weed hook.

Putting up the guardrail was a real job. Had a little motorized driver that was moved around by hand. Believe this is all done by contract now, as well as the mowing. We had 4 or 5 tractors with mowing blade on the side and a bush hog on the back. Had one tractor with a butterfly mower on it, which was only used on interstate.

When resurfacing a road, it took every man in the crew and any others we could round up from other crews in Shelby or Jefferson Counties. I can remember doing this on Route 60 from Woodford County Line to Shelby County Line. Some of the smaller roads we did were: Bridgeport-Benson, Bryant-Benson, Bark Branch, Evergreen and all the roads in Peaks Mill and Switzer areas.

The road from Peaks Mill to Elmville was a real dilly, no matter what you were doing on it. It was really not wide enough for two-way traffic.

St. John Road was another one. Would put out a few inches of extra blacktop on it each time we worked. Now the fence posts on each side of it are right against the pavement. Also, some trees are pretty close.

PROGRESS

Picture this (circa 1940's) – you are in town on a Saturday with your girl. When the afternoon movie is over, you want to take her for a coke. Choice to make is a trip to the soda fountain at the drug store or go down the street to the café and get a bottle of coke.

Now days you are in town with your girl and want a coke – find the nearest coke machine and stand around drinking it. Not quite the same.

Can remember the first coffee machine that came out. There was no way you could get a cup of coffee out of it on the first try. Most times the cup would come out upside down and the coffee went down the drain. First coke machines were about as bad. A fountain coke without ice was not much to talk about.

I cannot remember all the times that I have put my last coins in a cigarette machine only to have it keep my change and give me nothing. I believe that these have been taken out because of underage smokers.

Machines for candy bars were about as bad. If you were lucky enough for the machine to drop the candy bar. It could hang up somewhere and the machine got a good shaking – then it could not work at all.

Get just about everything in a machine these days. If you want stamps to mail a letter, it is best to drive to the Post Office. Want a Lotto ticket – got them in a machine that works most of the time. It used to be if you wanted a newspaper, you got one from the newsboy selling them. Now, you find a box, put your money in, and hope there is a paper left. The bubble gum machines have always been around and they were the only ones that took pennies. Now, they are as much as a quarter.

Growing up, the only coin machine that worked was the slot machine. (One Arm Bandit). Put a coin in one of these and not get anything – that was expected. At least with them you knew you were taking a chance and that you were gambling.

These machines are everywhere now and most of them work. Still cannot get a good cup of coffee out of one. Most soft drink machines give you what you pick (in a can). Just look around because it is surprising what is in some machines.

There is a machine at Wal-Mart that dispenses live fish bait. Will have to wait on this one and get my information from someone because I am not going to put any of my money in it.

CABIN FEVER

Well, here it is late January and the weather has me holed up with only the wife and television to keep me entertained. The television is not much help because of all the reruns. Reading helps but can only do that for a short time. The music has run out because I have now memorized all my new CD's. What I have is called "Cabin Fever". All my fishing tackle is sitting in the living room, well oiled and new rigs on everything – but too cold to take it out of the warm room.

I can remember when cabin fever did not exist because you had to go out and gather firewood for cooking and keeping the house warm. Today, you just turn a knob on something. Most of the day was spent gathering some kind of meat to go on the table with what was put away during the summer. Could have been rabbit hunting or just running a trap line, with dead falls or a few snares. If we came up with nothing, it meant a couple more chickens lost their heads or another shoulder of ham left the smokehouse.

School was not canceled in bad weather. There were no school buses, so the three-mile walk each way was the same – a little harder if the snow was deep. Maybe a little late for the first class but that was because we had to pull a sled the three miles. This we had to have during lunch hour and recesses (morning and afternoon). Also, could ride it most of the way home after school.

There was no boredom at night because when all the chores were done, supper over and everything cleaned up, everyone was tired enough that going to bed was the only thing everyone wanted to do. There was no television and homework but maybe a few minutes of something on the radio. Sometimes we had popcorn that was popped on the kitchen stove before the fire went out. A bucket of walnuts or hickory nuts were brought out and cracked on the hearth in front of the fireplace. We did have a checker board (regular) and Chinese checkers. They were well used. A deck of cards was a prize. Mom played a lot of solitaire and sometimes she would let us use her cards.

It was never too cold to go out and if there was no snow, we used the creek, which was frozen over – from the river to the headwaters – with only a ledge or water fall too tall to go over, now and then. Wild Cat Creek only had one between Stringtown and where it went into the river at Tyrone.

Back in the 30's and 40's there was no such thing as boredom because with 10 kids there were plenty of things to do, not matter what kind of weather you had. Wow, how the weather changes us.

HATS

Growing up did not call for wearing a hat very often. Summer time a straw hat for shade and winter time it was a sock cap or anything that could be pulled down over the ears.

Went into the Army and they gave me all kinds of hats. One of them had to be worn anytime you were outside except when doing PT (Physical Training). For dress uniforms we had an overseas cap (little flat one) and the flying saucer (one with a bill and stood up on top). Then, there was the fatigue cap (made like a ball cap) for the work uniform and a steel helmet with the liner (big cap with ear muffs). The styles and colors of these all changed over the years. Where you were, what you were doing and the type of weather you were in – all told you what hat to wear. Was even issued one of the panama hats for desert work.

While in Germany had to get me one of the green hats that the forest misters (one with the broom in the band) wore. If the broom was lying down, this meant you were married. If sticking up, meant you were single and available.

While stationed out West had to have a ten-gallon hat to go with my boots.

For my tours in Korea and Vietnam had to have one of the round pointed hats made out of rice straw or paper. While on these tours the old steel helmet came into use a lot (wearing, cooking, shaving and made a good seat when riding in a helicopter). Also, protection from anyone shooting at you from the ground.

Started collecting hats after retiring from the Army. Mostly baseball type caps, couple of fur hats and a dozen or so sock caps. While working on the road crew went through a lot of hard hats. Lost two of them in the river while working in the I-64 bridges at about the fifty-four mile marker.

Got rid of most of my hats but still have a dozen or so.

It is the season for my Christmas hat right now. Still have to have a hat for all occasions – like fishing, hunting, out to a dance, one for working in the shop and even have what they call "A Big Hat" for the steering wheel of my truck.

My grandson gave me one that I had been trying to find – black beret that the Army wears. He saved me a trip to Fort Knox looking for one.

Also, have an Australian bush hat. If I ever wind up down under, will definitely be ready.

ICE FISHING

I have written a lot of stories about fishing – all true. The one fishing trip that is crystal clear in my mind is the one and only time brother took me ice fishing.

Now, this all came about one Christmas when the wife and I were visiting him in New Hampshire.

I did not know the first thing about ice fishing but will try about anything once. Had no equipment for this, so we went shopping. (If anyone is thinking about taking up ice fishing, check out what you need first).

Must have a pair of boots, heavy socks, long underwear, warm pants and shirt, heavy coveralls, something warm for the head and good gloves.

Bought two of the flip flag poles that sit over the hole in the ice, one short rod and reel and a scoop to keep the ice out of the hole.

Brother had an auger for drilling the holes and a two-hole bob house, which we left at home because the ice was not thick enough to drive the truck on. This was only a one-day trip and the bob house is only used if you plan to fish all winter.

Had to get bait and something to keep the blood warm. (New Hampshire winters are really tough). Put everything on a sled and pulled it out to the middle of the lake, set up, put the lines out and stood around waiting for the fish to bite.

Catching a fish this way is about as exciting as catching a dead fish – no action at all. We did catch a mess of perch and brother got a nice bass (about two pounds).

After about 4 or 5 hours we ran out of bait and went home. We were frozen about as stiff as the fish we had caught and pitched down on the ice.

This was the most unusual Christmas gift that I had ever received and still is. The next time I was offered, I declined and stayed at home.

When we got home I gave the boots away and all the other gear that was bought is still hanging on the wall in my shop.

Still love to fish but one trip out on the ice was enough for a lifetime for me.

CHRISTMAS SHOPPING
(THEN AND NOW)

Well, it is that time of year again – Christmas Shopping – YUCK. In the past, it was not much of a job - then again I am a lousy shopper.

My first Christmas shopping was at a Five & Dime Store in Lawrenceburg. Took a dollar and fifty cents – got everyone something and had fifteen cents left over.

One Christmas I did my shopping at Newberry's 5 & 10 store in Frankfort. Got my girl a diamond bracelet for three dollars but her dad made her give it back.

Bought the wife a new car one year. It made her very happy until January came and the first payment was due – she had to write a check for it.

Got her a bicycle one Christmas. Now, everyone knows the story on this. I did not know she could not ride it.

Another year, I got her an organ. After a short time she could play it pretty good. So, the next year I got her a keyboard and she is still working on it.

Went to Sears and got her one of the fancy sewing machines. She kept it around for a couple of years and then she loaned it to someone. That was about 20 years ago and have not got it back yet and she has not looked for it. That is a good indication that it was another bad move on my part.

I've got this Christmas shopping down to an art now. I go to K-Mart each year and get her a Christmas Bear ($10) and give her what extra money there is in my pocket and tell her to buy what she wants. This also worked good on birthdays and anniversaries.

A few years ago while we were still working we would take our vacation at Christmas and go to Florida for a couple of weeks. This worked great but gets old after a dozen or so trips.

Took her to New Hampshire one Christmas – my big mistake. It gets cold up in the New England woods around this time of year. The ground freezes and the big rocks (size of a VW) come right up through the road. The State keeps them painted red and you have to drive around them until the spring thaw – then they remove them and fix the road.

The wife has already finished our Christmas shopping but I will do my shopping in a few days (30 minutes to an hour).

THANKSGIVING & CHRISTMAS
(PAST & PRESENT)

I took a venture out of the house for a short time on Thursday and the only thing this kind of weather is good for is rabbit and squirrel hunting. It made me think of Thanksgivings past. All I can remember about Thanksgiving days when I was a kid growing up was we all got up early and went hunting. Whatever we killed was what we had for Thanksgiving dinner.

The first turkey dinner that comes to mind was at Ft. Knox about 4 months into my first tour of duty in the Army.

I took advantage of Thanksgiving this year and had three big dinners last week. One of these dinners was in the Bald Knob area, one in Tick Town (Jeffersonville) up in Montgomery County (really up on Willoughby Mountain) and one in the Bridgeport area. All three of these locations have really outstanding cooks. The dinners were complete with turkey, country ham, gravy, mashed potatoes, fruit salad, dumplings, noodles, green beans (cooked with fat bacon), dressing (home-made and stovetop), fried apple pies, assorted pies, corn fritters, cottage cheese with pineapple, broccoli casserole, bar-b-que sausage balls, hot dinner rolls, baked cushaw, banana pudding and dressed eggs.

I am now getting ready for Christmas. If things work out right, should make around six to ten dinners for this big day. I can remember most of my Christmas dinner from about ten years of age. Some of them were really off the wall places to have Christmas dinner. A lot of them were at home, some in other states, and a lot of them in other countries (Japan, Korea, Germany and Vietnam). Some were in mess halls, tents, and one in a foxhole in sub-zero weather. One was even on a troop ship going from North Korea to South Korea in a LST. Believe the meal that day was a can of C-Rations, ham & lima beans, hard crackers, can of peaches, chocolate bar and a cup of cold instant coffee.

Ate a lot of wild game growing up for Thanksgiving and Christmas and that was normal. Maybe not the best food for the holiday feast, but was better than some. Maybe, just maybe, it was because you could sit down, put your feet under the table and eat it with family and friends. Sometimes it was the second sitting, but I can't remember ever leaving the table hungry. Christmas Dinner went from noon until everything was gone – sometimes it went into the night.

Need to loose a few pounds that were put on this month, so I can put it back on next month.

CUSHAW PIE

I can remember as a child watching cushaws grow all summer. You planted the seed some place along the river bank, in the cornfield, the garden or just out by themselves. Did not have to take care of them because they would come up and grow out on top of the weeds or under them. Pop never allowed us to pick them before the first frost. He said this was when they got ripe and were the best.

I have never made cushaw pie but plan on trying it for the first time in the upcoming days.

There are lots of ways to cook them. The oven is the best. Just season them and put them in the oven and bake until done. You can take the neck, slice it and fry it on top of the stove and it is very good. You can also chop it up into squares, boil it in a pan with the right kind of seasonings and it is good.

As a child we just cut them in half and laid them in the fireplace close to the flames. I don't remember putting anything on them but they were good this way.

Cushaws are very easy to keep. After the first frost, just pick them and store them in the barn covered with a little straw or hay. This way they would keep all winter if they were not picked too early or bruised real bad. Now days, just cube them, cook them for a while and put them in the freezer and this keeps them good all winter. Pop would cut the corn and stack it in shocks, then just store the cushaws and pumpkins under the shock. We would go and get them, as we needed them.

I can remember as a very small child living on the river bank in Tyrone when Pop caught a fellow from the other side of the river picking his cushaws that were hanging out over the water by the willow trees. The fellow tried his best to make Pop believe that they belonged to him because this vine had grown across the river, under the water, up into the trees and produced the cushaws. Just another of the many, many wild stories out of Tyrone in the early 30's.

Talked to my doctor about cushaw pie the other day and he had never heard of a cushaw. I am going to make him a pie and show him what he has been missing out on all his life. I told him it was a member of the gourd family, but it is really a winter squash – sometimes called a Chinese squash.

CHRISTMAS SHOPPING

MY, MY, how times have really changed. Growing up, Christmas shopping was something that was looked forward to all year and took months to find just the right gift for everyone.

Back in the 30's and 40's, there were about fifteen to twenty family members to buy for, best friend at school, school teacher, mailman, one to three girlfriends, the people that always gave you a ride to or from school and sometimes a couple of the neighbors.

Can remember sixty years ago, could go to the dime store in Lawrenceburg with $1.50 and get gifts for ten or fifteen people, and they would all be happy with what they got.

Paid thirty cents for a box of candy one Christmas for the girl that I was dating and got to thinking about all that money and wound up eating the candy before I got around to giving it to her.

Growing up, all cards and most of the gifts were hand-made.

Most of what we got came from the Sears Roebuck catalog. By this time we had a good stock of hides on hand – muskrats, coons, opossums, skunks – and maybe a mink or a fox or two. Mom would wrap them and send them to Sears along with her order (mostly clothes and shoes and maybe a little something for the house). Here the order was filled and the hides were counted. If there was any money left over, it was sent in the package by check.

The mailman brought the box and that was the way most Christmas shopping was done.

The wife and I did our shopping the other day. She picked up gifts for sixteen to eighteen people and then I bought her a treadmill and she bought me a new grill. For myself, I got a new spare tire for my truck.

The box of furs Mom used for shopping has been replaced with a plastic card because there is no profit in trapping furs anymore.

COUPONS

I can remember when coupons, box tops and books of green or TV stamps were around and everyone used them. Some of them could save you a little money or get a nice gift.

My sister does all her shopping with coupons. Sometimes I think the store owes her money when she is done shopping.

Got into coupons myself a few years ago. I was helping tear an old house down in Lexington. The former owners had an antique shop.

Was down in the basement one day and found a big stack of old antique magazines. Threw them on the truck and brought them home with me so I could thumb though them at my leisure.

Found a copy of The Modern Priscilla that was printed in July 1914. Some of the coupons in it were unbelievable and then the lights came on all over my brain. I about went mad trying to figure out what I could do with some of them.

Well now, on the back page was a coupon for Lipton Tea. Checked it out and there was not an expiration date. It stated on the coupon, all I had to do was cut it out, paste a dime to it and mail it to the Lipton Company and they would send me a 6oz tin of tea. All this I did over the wife's objections about wasting a 32-cent stamp plus the dime I was sending them. We both thought they would think me a little off but I thought it would be fun.

Took a while before I heard from them but they did send me a letter of apology, as they could not fill the obligation stated on the coupon. The 6oz tin was no longer in their inventory. They sent me a handful of coupons for their tea bags.

They also stated in the letter that my coupon with the dime stuck to it with scotch tape, would be placed in their archives, as they had no record of a coupon coming to them that was over 86 years of age.

Now there are a lot more coupons in the book (coca-cola, Campbell's soup, brands of cereal) and no expiration dates. Who knows what I may do with the rest of them.

FROG GIGGING AT BEAVER LAKE

The wife and I were invited out the other night for a mess of frog legs and it really brought back a lot of memories of nights spent in the pursuit of this most delightful meal.

Frogs were no problem to find but to catch them and put them in a sack was not the easiest thing to do. They were available most places where there was water of any kind. Best place for them was a farm pond – any size from a small ten-foot pond to the largest ones. Problem here was that you just about had to wade the pond to get them and all farm ponds had a mud bank. The older the pond, the deeper the mud. If there were lots of cattails growing around the pond this multiplied the problems because it was about like hunting in a thicket.

One of the best places that I ever used for gigging frogs was Beaver Lake. All that was needed was a small flat bottom john boat, set of oars and a good gig. Also, needed a good light and someone to row the boat and put you close enough to the frog without making too much noise.

Saturday night at Beaver Lake was when the wife and I always went out for the frogs. We did good most of the time but the fish were a hazard at times, with a lot of catfish and turtles in the lake and it was overstocked with bluegills. The catfish made the bluegills very nervous at night and they would hang out close to the bank. Put the oar down in the water close to them and they would leave the water – sometimes eight or ten of them all at once. Some would hit the bank, land in the boat, so over the boat and land in the lake on the opposite side. They also scared a lot of frogs.

Got back to the campsite one night and there were forty-three bluegills in the boat (some good eating size). A lot of times the bluegills would hit you but did not hurt except for scaring the daylights out of us – especially if one got caught in your clothing.

One of the fellows that worked for Fish and Wildlife said that this was impossible. Never could convince him that it did happen, so told him to just ask the wife. She definitely knows from experience that the bluegills will jump in the boat and get caught in clothing.

The river is a good place for frogs but they are not as concentrated as in the lake plus it takes longer to find them. Most creeks were good spots but called for a lot of walking.

I am sure the ones we will be enjoying for our invitation came from the store.

TELEPHONE INSULATORS

Back about 1970 the big thing in collectible items was the glass insulator on the phone poles along the railroads and most of the highways. This was about the time they closed a lot of the railroads.

Donna, one of my nieces, spent a lot of weekends with me and the wife. The wife spent a lot of weekends working on income tax with her mother and great uncle, so Donna and I spent a lot of Saturdays walking the railroads gathering the insulators.

When the railroad from Lawrenceburg to Versailles closed a crew went along and cut the poles down and let them fall over the hill. This is the one we spent most of out time walking. Approximately every 200 yards or so there was the pole, cross bars and insulators still on. Most of what we found were the white ones. The blue, green or lavender ones were the good ones.

These things were heavy, therefore a small sack full of them got real heavy on a two-mile walk back to the car. Gather them, stash them and pick them up on the way back was the best way to work it. We must have gathered over 200 of them before finding out there was no market for them at all.

Had to invent ways to make them sell. Could put them in the oven and heat them, then run cold water over them and make them crack all over – looked good. Could set them upside down on a block of wood and put a candle in the insulator – looked good. This did not make them sell any better.

Gave a lot of them away, but as for selling them – not a one. Still have a few in the attic over the shop and maybe someday they will be worth something.

DIGGING THE DUMPS FOR GLASS

Back in the late 60's when I retired for the first time, I took a three-month break from work and went scouting for antique glass (mostly bottles and jars). This is a phase that everyone needs to experience.

My adventure started in Anderson County where I was raised. The City Dump for Lawrenceburg was on Cedar Brook Road and that is where my work began. At first there was great digging but not too many treasures. Found several milk of magnesium bottles that had glass tops that were used for cups (pretty blue color) and some castor oil bottles.

I knew all the farms on the Lock #5 Road and each one had a sinkhole that was used for a dump. Since there were a lot of caves in the area it meant a lot of sinkholes were available.

This made for hard digging but some great finds. A couple of old single edge razors made of brass and some coffee cups (chipped or the handle missing). Once I found the handle and glued it back and now it is being used for a shaving mug.

Wildcat Road had lots of dumps but all I found were a few old Coca-Cola bottles.

While living at Sinai I covered Baxter Bride Road, Mays Road, Bear Creek Road, Duncan Road, Mills Road, and Lick Skilled Road. The finds were not real good but did find a few patent medicine bottles.

Made a couple of nice finds on Lillard Road – couple of old 5-gallon oilcans that were used for kerosene. They were in good shape from the oily substance hauled in them. (Most metal and wood cans had rusted or rotted away in all the dumps).

Did a lot of digging on the Peaks Mill Road, Glenns Creek Road and Hanley Lane. There were no big finds but did get some fruit jars with tops, and whiskey bottles (none made prior to 1900).

After three months of digging I had the basement full of bottles, jars and a lot of other junk (nothing rare). Over the past 30 years I have given most of them away. The old brown coke bottle was one of the most valuable.

Have a pewter jewelry box (string of glass beads in it) that I dug up on Fort Hill. Also, some wine bottles that were blown prior to 1900 and a few soft drink bottles made in Frankfort.

I did not make any money at this but had a great time doing it, until it came time to clean them. That was a big job.

SCHOOL BACKPACKS

A few years ago going to school with a backpack to put things in to carry would have been very odd.

Books, pencil box and paper were carried in your arms. Have been known to put a belt around the books and carry them that way. Packs, if you had one, were for carrying wild game – trapped or shot on the way to or from school. If you took a gun to school, it was a shotgun or rifle. This was put away while you were at school, then used again on the way home. A squirrel, rabbit or groundhog made a good supplement to supper or a little something to snack on the next morning before school.

If we had backpacks, would not have been able to carry the girls' books for them. That was a big thing if one of the girls let you carry her books for her.

Have not seen a boy carry a girl's backpack for her because it would be hard to put on two backpacks.

Helped Denver clean his backpack out once last year. It had gotten too heavy for him to pack. Contained in the backpack were: couple of workbooks, lots of paper, some toys, and about 15 magazines on hunting and fishing.

I never had a lot of homework when I was in school because most of the work was done at school (most times with help from one of the older students). The teacher had all 8 grades, so she had to spend some time with each grade.

Study books, such as spelling, reading, math, geography and history, were furnished by the school and used for years for each grade as you moved up. The books that I studied in the 8th grade had been used for 8 or 10 years and a couple of them did not have a back on them. All were well worn but they got the job done.

Did not take many books home when I was in school because if you lost one you had to pay for it. It was real easy to put one down while trying to dig out a rabbit or groundhog, then go off and leave it.

Had to buy your own paper, pencils and crayons if you were lucky enough to have them. Sometimes you could borrow them for a while.

I was about 8 when I started to read but now days they are reading at 4 or 5. Things are working but there is still an awful lot of homework for them.

PAINT BALL GUNS

I went to Bald Knob area a short time ago and was asked to participate in a war game with paint ball guns. Should have stayed at home. Having a war with a bunch of kids is not for me because my legs will not let me run fast enough plus my gun only holds ten paint balls. The ones they had would hold one hundred – not good odds for an old man.

In my time it was snowballs, mud balls or just a good old rock fight. Green plums in a sling shot, arrows made from weeds that were straight, shot with an elm limb and a string. A hand full of pea gravel, or wet sand, and eggs were good weapons. The eggs were really good if they were rotten from under a sitting hen that did not hatch.

Got into balloons full of water a few times – but they cost money. Each child getting a bundle of buck bushes was a good fight until someone got mad and forgot the rules.

Food fights were good when there was lots of it around. Cherries and grapes were fun but green apples or pears hurt. Green walnuts were okay but messy.

When I was growing up, paint ball guns would not have worked. The gun, pain balls and the equipment you have to have costs entirely too much.

FRIDAY NIGHT POKER

The late 40's and early 50's – Friday was always payday. Lots of things to do but most of them cost money. After the bills were paid, food laid in for the coming week, money put away for car gas, school lunches and whatever, not much was left.

About $2 worth or pennies was all that was needed for the Friday night poker game and the location where it was going to be held. This was called penny ante poker. Most of the time it was at my brothers house on the river.

Five of the brothers were married by now and the wives liked to play poker as well as we did. Sometimes someone had to wait until one was broke so they could get into the game.

Most of the time the game went on all night. Kids would all run down and go to sleep and sooner or later someone would wind up with all the pennies. This person had to keep them and be the banker the next Friday night.

With as many as 20 or 12 people around all night a lot of coffee was consumed.

The game was always in the kitchen. Every one who was not playing would sit in the front room by the fireplace and talk or play some other type of game.

Some of the rules were: you had to have 200 pennies to get into the game; could not take any more money out of your pocket; ante was one penny; could not bet over five pennies at one time or you were thrown out of the game; not allowed to get mad; cheating was only allowed if you did not get caught; only allowed to smoke cigarettes (no cigars); and once you lost your 200 pennies you could not borrow more and get back in the game later.

There were only two or three people outside the family that were allowed to get in the game.

No one has time for this anymore. To me this was quality time spent with the family. Maybe not the best way to spend a Friday night but here I am 50 plus years later and I still miss them.

Games played were: 5 card draw; 7 card stud; and 5 card stud. When the women started playing, we played deuces wild, one-eyed jacks and one called spit in the ocean. I never did master the last one.

PEN AND PENCIL

Checked a school backpack the other day and did not find a lead pencil in it. There were mechanical pencils, ballpoint pens and magic markers (all colors).

When growing up, school supplies were bought before school started. Everyone a got a wooden lead pencil, tablet with lines, pencil sharpener and box of color crayons (which were shared). If someone was into art, it was possible they got a box of watercolors. Sometime a one-foot ruler was shared for drawing straight lines but most times the ruler was borrowed from a schoolmate.

Seating was a bench with writing table and two people sat on each one. It had a groove on top of it for the pencil or pen and a hole that was for the bottle of ink. An opening under the top held the books. Books consisted of Reader, Spelling, English, History, Geography and Arithmetic (for higher grades). First grade was only a reader. That was all that was allowed in this space.

In the back was a rack for coats, overshoes, hats and gloves and a shelf for lunches.

Your special girl at school was the one who had a pencil box full of all kinds of good things. In order to be really popular, she also had to have a loose-leaf binder with a good supply of paper. It also helped if she was smart.

This is where the note passing came in – no cell phones – just notes and hand signals (when the teacher was not looking).

Work that had to be done in ink was done with a fountain pen. It had its own supply of ink and when it ran out you just stuck it in the ink bottle and pumped it full again (all desks had ink stains from this and so did most of the kids). The pens had a point that lasted for years.

Now the wood pencil was different. This would have to be sharpened when the lead wore down and they soon got too short to use.

This is where the girl with the pencil box came in – all kinds of pencils. Some had the mechanical pencil with a box of replacement lead and her ink well had ink in it most of the time.

Saw a list of school supplies the other day – man, I could not believe it. Enough on the list to start a small business and even the kind of clothes they could wear. If this had applied in the 30' and 40's, we would have had to have a job. Work one day and go to school one day or just stay at home and not go to school!

THE SHOE STRING

The wife and I kept the great grandson a couple of days this week. He was out of school for some reason. He is only four and a half years of age but he teaches me new things every time he comes by. Today, it was a new word – a double knot. I was helping him with his shoes and socks before he left to go home. Got them tied and was informed that they had to be tied in a double knot. All new to me but got it done.

No one thinks much of the shoe string anymore because very few shoes have strings. First there were buttons, then strings and straps with buckles – now we have Velcro, zippers and just slip on with elastic.

When growing up – tying your shoes was one of the first things we had to learn. About all shoes had strings. A few exceptions were penny loafers (had to fit when you got them or you could not keep them on) and straps/buckles (mostly the ladies shoes).

First shoes that were put into my wardrobe with buckles were the boots they issued me when I went into the Army. They had strings on the bottom and two straps with buckles on the top. Thirty plus years ago, when my retirement came up, they had gone to strings that laced all the way to the top.

As a kid, the shoe string was a must when you wore shoes. The first thing on the shoes to wear out was the string. The first time you had to run, without string, you would run right out of them. You would hunt at night and walk upon some cattle in a field – they would start chasing you (no matter what kind they were) – lose your shoes. I only had to retrieve my shoes once because after that they were always kept tied.

The tray of my foot locker (for the twenty years I was in the Army) had a pair of new strings for my boots, along with a pair of socks, bar of soap, razor/blades, toothbrush, toothpaste, powder, handkerchief, pack of cigarettes (whether you smoked or not), wash cloth or towel. The above items plus others had to be in the tray for each inspection with no excuses.

The story they gave us was – the war could be lost because a horse lost his shoe from having a loose nail and the messenger did not get through. They said we could lose a war if the messenger did not get through because his shoe string broke and he did not have a spare set.

Great story if you believe it.

CHRISTMAS TREES OVER THE YEARS

The wife was at a Church Bazaar a couple of years ago and bought a small Christmas tree, about two feet tall. The latest thing in Christmas trees – a piece of wood, dowel pin, some nails, a little garland, small string of lights and a lot of fishing line. The line must be fluorescent and no bigger than 12-pound test.

For the last seventy years, Christmas trees have had a lot of changes.

The first one that I remember was a cedar cut and put on a stand – decorated with chain made of colored paper, popcorn strung on a thread, a few store bought bulbs, a box of icicles, maybe a few sycamore balls wrapped in foil or seed pods from a gum tree. Everything was taken off the tree around New Years Day and put away for next Christmas.

Then came the artificial trees. They have gone through all sizes, colors and shapes. Also, lot of different kinds of pines – some with a dirt ball on them that could be planted in the yard after Christmas. Lots of the trees have been moved outside. I still have a string of lights in a pine tree, about fifty feet tall, that have been there for about ten years now – they are now part of the tree. Have not tried the new fiber optic trees. Have seen them but do not own one, yet.

All Christmas trees are pretty – some prettier than others. I was going to use a cactus one in Arizona but was told it was against the law to cut one. Wound up using the limb of an old ironwood tree. Not many trees in Arizona. You want a pine; you buy one and have it shipped in.

Now, back to this tree made from fishing line. One of my favorite people came by a couple of months ago and saw the one I have. Looked at it, asked a few questions, went home and made me one and trimmed it with fishing tackle (corks and such). She also made the wife and I a five foot one. This one is kept up year round because it is beautiful. It has Santa Claus and is a Christmas theme all the way. Today you can make a Christmas tree out of anything – from a pine tree to a piece of driftwood.

Since the movie came out about the Clark Griswald Family Christmas, the country has gone crazy with lights. I believe everyone is trying to out do everyone else. Some places it is hard to locate the Christmas tree. One good example of this can be observed if you drive through the Bridgeport area after dark. A lot of hard work had to go into this one and it is beautiful.

PANTS WITH POCKETS

The wife came in from shopping at Wal-Mart a few days ago and brought me a pair of shorts. She called them military style, I think. Just short pants with seven pockets.

I can remember back in 1947, the Army issued me work uniforms with the same type of pockets on them – only they were long pants.

Just a square pocket on the legs – on the outside between the knee and thigh. It was about six by eight or ten inches and you could put about anything in them.

Problem with them was they had a flap on top and a button to hold it down. This button had to be buttoned at all times – like the buttons on the uniform. If it was washed, folded and put away, the button had to be buttoned.

During the inspections, if a button was not buttoned on anything, it was one demerit. A number of demerits and you got to go to the mess hall and wash dishes for a Saturday or Sunday.

My big goof was on a road march, on the range or someplace. If the Sergeant caught you with the button not buttoned, he would fill that big pocket full of rocks – about ten or twelve pounds of them. You packed them around all day. Try walking ten miles with them bouncing on your leg – made it seem more like thirty miles.

We also had a one gallon can about half full of sand. If you got caught throwing a cigarette butt down, without field stripping it, you got to wear that can around your neck on a string until the next guy got caught. The bucket of sand and a pocket of rocks made for a very long day.

All this seemed kind of silly back then but was all part of the training. Just one hour of physical training with a pocket full of rocks taught you to keep the pocket buttoned.

Guess the big pockets are back to stay – only now they have zippers and Velcro on them.

OLD RIVERFRONT STADIUM

Sat in front of the television the other day and watched them blow up Cinergy Field (Old Riverfront Stadium). The stadium brought back a lot of good memories and some of the trips that were made over there.

Had just retired and gotten married and there was not better way to spend a weekend than at the ball field (unless the opportunity came up for a fishing trip). The weekend would consist of driving over and watching a game on Saturday, getting a room to spend the night and watching a game on Sunday before coming home. (Night life in Cincinnati was not all that bad).

Had to order tickets early to get good seats and it took a lot of planning for each game. Started out getting tickets for Sunday games but was told by our Preacher to get our tickets for Saturday, so we could make Church on Sunday.

The wife and I would leave home early, drive to Ft. Mitchell, have lunch, then catch the bus to the stadium. After watching the game, we would catch the bus back to Ft. Mitchell, then drive home. Each time we would stop at McDonald's in Dry Ridge for coffee and to stretch our legs. Later we got into playing the Ohio Lottery (before Kentucky Lottery). We would leave early, take I-275 around Cincinnati, pick up lottery tickets, have lunch, then drive to Covington. Get a good parking place (usually), walk across the bridge, watch the game and then come home. Our limit was 5 or 6 games a year - enjoyed all of them even if the Reds lost. This continued until the year they had the strike. We did get our money back for the two remaining games.

At this time, I was smoking the big cigars. It got bad trying to find a place to smoke where no one told you it was bothering them. I was seated next to a fellow one time who said he had something wrong with him and the smoke was choking him up. Being the gentleman that I was, I walked up to the mezzanine to smoke but he followed me. He got right beside me and asked me to put it out. Went back to my seat and smoked the rest of the game. I told him he could stand up and watch the rest of the game or choke, whichever way he wanted it.

Then they made the stadium smoke free, so just did not order any more tickets. Stay home and watch the games on television – not as much fun. Now, I can smoke when I want to and no one is standing up in front of me or spilling beer/chili on me. The seating is better – not as much noise – and no waves to stand up for. Just have to watch a lot of commercials.

ARMY SCHOOLS

The Army has a school for everything. Going over my records I cannot believe how many schools they sent me to. Basic training is just the beginning of it.

My most unusual school assignment was after the Korean War. They assigned me to Ft. Sam Huston, TX, to train to become a male nurse. Now this was a job that I wanted no part of. It took me about a week to convince them that I was not cut out for this type of work. They shipped me to Ft. Hood, TX, and made me a tank operator – more my speed.

First 10 years in the Army, they had me in the Inf. Signal Corp Missile in VA and MP in New Mexico. I blew the job of MP when they put me on a motorcycle.

Spent almost two years in training of some kind when they assigned me to Research and Development (R&D). They had me assigned me to other test projects at the same time. I was testing the new green uniform, walked a few miles around the track each day with test boots on and ate one meal a day testing new types of food and rations. Also worked on the machine that took flour, water, etc. and put out hot rolls by the hundreds. Also, worked on a few of the vehicles they were testing.

It is hard to believe the hours of schooling we had on safety and first-aid.

Was assigned as a Maintenance Sgt. a number of times. Had about 30 men in the maintenance shop. This was our job but we still had so many hours of training each day. Physical training was a daily thing to keep the body in shape. I was sent to NCO Academy twice. Everything new that came out, they had a school for it. Another one that I did not like was CBR Training – about an average of 4 to 6 hours a month. (Chemical Biological and Radiology).

Training on new weapons and trips to the firing range were lots of fun. Somewhere along the line they trained me on weapons from a 22 caliber to a 16-inch weapon the Navy used on battle ships (took place in Arizona when we were testing new types of ammo).

Got into a little training on the helicopter and how to fly an unmanned drone jet plane.

Had to know how to drive every vehicle in the Army from a jeep to a 20-ton crane.

A months training one time on an in-line pump for a 20-inch oil pipeline.

Retired now and don't have to remember most of this except sometimes in my dreams.

YOUNT'S MILL

The wife and I were coming back from the Bald Knob Eagle Ruritan Club meeting the other night and drove down Taylor Avenue. Took notice of the empty space next to Devils Hollow Road (had a house boat parked in it) and could picture in my mind the mill that was there until a few years ago.

Yount's Mill was a landmark in Frankfort. I don't know how long it had been at the location on Taylor Avenue but it was old when it was wrecked.

Growing up there was not a reason for going to Yount's Mill often because we had no farm and did not have any cattle to feed. When we did have dogs, they got by on table scraps most of the time.

Yount's Mill was the place to go when you needed one bale or ten bales of straw to mulch the rose bushes or to put on the lawn when new seed was sown.

Did most of my business with them after 1970, when we started to grow our own fish bait. Take a dry wall bucket; cut a few newspapers to fit into it, a bag of mill or feed, two or three boxes of mill worms from the bait shop. Place them all in the bucket in the right order, add a few apple or potato peelings now and then and bingo, you were ready. You did not have to buy any worms. Need bait, just get it out of the bucket. Will last for years if you do not use all the worms before they turn to bugs and reproduce.

Believe they moved the mill to the country when they tore the old building down. Do not trade with them now. When something is needed, I go to the feed store on Route 60. Picked up a fifty-pound bag of catfish pellets last summer. I was going to use them to bait me a couple of places on the lake but it did not work because they float. The ducks ate them as fast as they were put out.

Have often wondered what they did with all their cats when they moved. There were cats – all kinds – everywhere. They had no mice or rats – not for long anyway. Kind of like Tom and Jerry, only their cats meant it when one showed up at the mill.

Have not read in the paper about Taylor Avenue homes being invaded by cats – guess they have been moved with the mill.

THE GRILL

Looking around the neighborhood the other day, I suddenly realized that almost everyone has a grill on the porch or deck.

I can remember when no one had a grill because only hot dogs were cooked outside and you roasted them on a stick, over an open fire, along with the marshmallows.

As kids we would stack a few rocks together and call it a grill. Could build a wood fire in it and cook on it with a can to boil eggs, ears of corn, a rabbit or squirrel skewered on a stick.

Some of the well to do people who had camp houses on the river, built rock pits with a metal grill and cooked on this. Some people still have this type of grill.

Back in the 40's, anyone who had a grill in the back yard, built out of brick or rock, was living the good life. This is where everyone gathered if there was a cook-out or a big get together of the family.

Building one of these was a major project. They had to have a footer of concrete to hold them up. The brick or rock had to be laid just right and put together with mortar – built to draw just like a fire place.

Fuel for these could be wood or charcoal. Good example of this type of cooking can still be observed at the Game Farm Shelters.

Went from this to the charcoal grill for BBQ, steaks, hot dogs, chicken, pork chops or about anything that you wanted to cook, but still had to start a fire.

Then came the gas grill – just a few rocks in it, turn it on, light it and you are ready to cook. This is the type that sits on my back deck.

They also have them for deep-frying about anything you want fried including a turkey. Some of them today are mounted on trailers and you can cook for a couple of hundred at a time.

The one on my deck just sits there these days with a cover on it. I went and got the wife a Big George Foreman and she does almost all the grilling inside. Not as good as it was when we skewered it on a stick but now I don't have to cook it.

HOT WATER

Well, a new experience today. Found the laundry room with a lot of standing water on the floor. Moved the dryer out, checked the washing machine. Could not find any water running, so had to be coming from the hot water heater.

Heater was still working, plenty of hot water but the bottom had rusted out and it was leaking.

Now the only solution here is to replace the heater. In all my years, and the hundreds of places that I have called home, this was a first for me. First water heater that I have ever bought and put in.

Always took it for granted that all it took for hot water was to turn the spigot on and if someone had not used it all up, there was hot water.

Put a call into brother and he was here in a flash. Took a couple of wrenches, a hack saw and in short order the old heater was sitting on the back porch.

Now, a trip to Lowe's for a new heater, few fitting and a little copper tubing. Should have hot water again by tomorrow night.

Remember when hot water was not so easy to come by. First the wood had to be cut, fire built in the stove, water carried, then wait till it was the right temperature. Put into the tub and hope you were the second or third to get a bath before the water got cold again.

That is how it was early in life. Same with laundry – water was heated on the stove or an open fire in the summer. Hot water for the dishes was taken from the tank on the end of the cooking stove. Guess that was the first hot water heater – not like today but they worked. Just had to keep the water in them. Take a bucket full out and you had to put a bucket full back in.

Was the same with the oven on top of the kitchen stove. Left over food was put there to keep it warm for latecomers or for snacks later. Kept biscuits real good.

NICKEL AND DIME

The dime is the smallest of our coins in size and there is not much you can buy with a dime these days.

I can go back to when a dime was big money. At Thompson's Store in Tyrone, a dime would buy ten all-day suckers, a bag full of jawbreakers or hard candy of any kind. Could get a large Baby Ruth candy bar and a coke for ten cents.

First going to the movies – could get a ticket to a good Roy Rogers or Gene Autry movie (I believe it was called the Lyrics Movie House) in Lawrenceburg, popcorn and something to drink was extra.

Cannot remember ever making a phone call for a nickel but do remember that you could make two phone calls for a dime, if you could find a phone to make the call. I did not like phones when growing up because they were kind of scary. It was not natural for me because if there was something that needed to be said to someone, I would go see them and talk face to face.

The dime was small and could be lost because it only took a very small hole in the pocket. For some things you had to have a dime because it was the only coin that would work in most vending machines – not two nickels – just the dime. Also, drink and snack machines.

The parking meter would take a penny, nickel or dime. Don' remember how much time you got for a penny but think the nickel gave you one hour and the dime gave you two hours.

All the Five and Ten Cent Stores have been phased out. There are not many things you can buy for that amount anymore. Today they call them Dollar Stores.

The one thing that took a dime to operate was the pay toilet. Back a few years, when a lot of people traveled by bus and trains, the depots and stations had pay toilets. You had to have a dime just to get inside. Ran into a lot of these while in the military. Most of the time my pockets were empty, so would have to wait around until someone came out and catch the door before it closed or have been known to crawl under of climb over the top of the stall door.

TAKE WITH A GRAIN OF SALT

I can remember growing up that it was a no-no to run out of salt in the kitchen. Just running low could mean a five-mile walk to the store in Tyrone to get another pound. This could happen in a foot or two of snow, a frog drowning down pour, or a 99-degree temperature in the hot sun. If the kitchen ran out of salt, Mom was unhappy and that meant everyone was unhappy. She could not cook without salt.

Salt was a part of our lives. It was used for preserving almost everything. It was bought in twenty-five pound cloth bags in the fall. Hog killing time called for a lot of salt to cure the meat. Seems that all canning of vegetables called for salt.

Cooking anything called for salt. A table without a salt shaker was not completely set. The old pickle barrel in one of my other stories called for a lot of salt.

During the first ten years of my Army career, salt tablets were used. It the weather was hot, you had to take a salt tablet, especially if you were going to eat in the mess hall. You had to take a salt tablet each day – a tablet about the size of an aspirin. It made you drink a lot of water and prevented heat stroke.

About twenty years ago, when my heart problem put in its appearance, the doctor took me off salt. Well, they told me to take the salt out of my diet. I did try, but you cannot eat these days without getting some salt. I don't use the salt shaker anymore. Started to eat my watermelon with sugar and no salt. This put my blood sugar out of whack, so I just stopped eating watermelon.

Know a fellow that I worked with who would take two slices of bread and a salt shaker, and make him a salt sandwich. He is still around and may still be eating a salt sandwich now and then.

Will not say anything about the rock salt they use on the roads. Only time that was used growing up was for making ice cream.

Don't have this low salt diet down pat yet, but am working on it. All the substitutes on the market are good but would like to know what they are made from. They must be made of salt as nothing tastes like salt except salt.

I was not around but read in a book, someplace, where the Native Americans (Indians) and the Pioneers used salt as a form of currency when trading.

THE DOCTOR

Just returned home from seeing the doctor. This was one of the four that get a visit from me on a regular basis.

I can remember when, very young, the doctor came to the house when someone was sick. With ten kids, someone could come down with something and within three or four days, most of us had it, so the doctor was called in for treatment. Mom already knew what the problem was and she could handle most things except for measles, whooping cough, chicken pox etc. With all the kids down at one time, the doctor had to help a little.

The first doctor's office visit for me was in Lawrenceburg in 1936 or 1937 (the two years I attended school in Tyrone). One of the teachers took a carload of us for a school check-up. Don't know who the doctor was but his office was above the theater on Main Street and we got to it by going up a set of steps next to the theater. I was scared out of my wits – as much from the car ride to Lawrenceburg and back, as from seeing the doctor.

The next trip to a doctor's office for me was about 1945. I was living in Millville and came down with a bad cold, or the flu. Mom was not feeling well enough to go to town with me, Pop was working and all the other kids were in school or working. Being in the dead of winter, Mom had me dress in all my warm clothes (with scarf, sock cap and gloves). She put two one-dollar bills in my pocket and sent me off on my own.

The doctor's office was on Main Street in Frankfort (Dr. L.L. Cull). I walked the seven miles to town, saw the doctor, and gave him the two dollars. Got really lucky and caught a ride home. I don't remember what treatment he gave me but think it was a sheet of paper with instructions for the use of Vick's Vapor Rub for the chest (overnight).

Whatever he did must have worked, as I did survive. It could have been the seven mile walk that cured me.

Went into the Army shortly after my 17th birthday. For the next twenty plus years, there was a doctor, dentist and lots of nurses on hand at all times. The shots and physicals came on a little too often for me. They loved to give shots – 6 or 7 at a time. Shot records had to be kept up to date because this was called preventative maintenance.

"HONEY, HAVE YOU SEEN MY KEYS?"

Have a wire hanging in the shop with approximately 500 keys on it, which range from the old skeleton key of the early 1900's to the modern car keys with the chip to open the car door. A number of locks are also on the wire but without a key that will fit.

I can remember as a kid that we had no use for a key. The homes were never locked and if you had a car, the key was left in the ignition (where it belonged) therefore you could not lose it.

First lock/key I owned was when my Army career started. They issued me a lock and two keys. These were to be on my footlocker at all times and locked except for inspections. This is where my trouble with keys really started. A thing as small as a key is hard to keep up with. Twice during my thirteen weeks basic training I had to break my lock off, take it to the supply room, turn it in, and draw a new one. The new one had to be signed for and the price of it was deducted from my next pay.

Over the next sixty-six years it has at times gotten out of hand in a big way. Bought a rack to hang in the kitchen for keys. Also, got several key rings. All the keys were put on their own key ring and hung on the rack. The following keys were hung: extra set for house (front & back doors); set for shop (front & back doors); freezer; safe; gun rack; boat; storage shed; yard gate; boat ramp; tool box on truck; truck & shop on one key ring; car & house on one key ring; power tools in the shop; concession stand keys; and plenty of others. Had it all worked out hanging on the rack in the kitchen but the wife said it was not very neat and there were entirely too many key rings. She took one of my old dog tag chains and took all the keys off the rings, put them on the chain and then pointed out how much neater it was. Problem is now that it takes me from ten minutes to one hour to get a lock open because most of the keys look alike.

About thirty years ago we got a lock box at the bank to keep some papers in. We were presented with two keys. I put one on my ring with the car keys. The wife took the second key and put it in a place we would always know where it was. Guess what – the key has never been found and since that time we moved and are still looking for the extra lock box key.

Some locks around are now opened with combinations (brief cases, safes etc.). Wrote the safe combination down because I have a hard time remembering numbers. Now, I cannot find the paper with the number. I believe the one for the safe was hidden in the safe – not sure. Have not been able to get into the safe for years.

HIGH WATER

The wife and I drove down to the river the other day to check out the high water. Drove over to Tyrone to Bill Fint's Boat Ramp because this is the place to check out high water. Could not believe the amount of trash there was going down the river.

Looking at all the styrofoam and plastic made me wonder what it would look like when it got to where it was going after it joined what was coming down the Ohio, the Mississippi and the Missouri. Must be a sight to gaze upon when it all gets together somewhere around New Orleans, Louisiana.

Growing up on the river there was always a lot of drift that went down the river during high water – all the brush and logs out of the small and large creeks and anything that would float. There were a few bottles and jars. While we picked up the firewood, we also picked up anything made out of glass because it could be used for something.

All the house boats and boat docks that floated had barge or oil drums under them. They were a prize catch if they broke loose. Now days, they are all on blocks of Styrofoam because it won't sink, is white and is good for nothing when it breaks up. Don't know where all the sheets of plastic strung through the trees along the river comes from.

Pop always had one trotline up the middle of the river for buffalo and carp. Most of the time the buoy was a glass jug. They worked fine if one of the oil barges that plied the river did not hit and break them. This was not a problem because you just got the old drag hook out and dragged it up. Sometime he would come up with a chunk of cork, which you could not sink with a rifle – but cork was hard to come by.

Remember one time in the 40's that Pop was picking up firewood and a board came by – he picked it up and there was a 25 lb. bag (made of cloth) of flour hooked on by a nail. That was the year they had a cloud burst in Morehead and a store got washed away. He brought the bag of flour in with him just to prove he caught it. Don't remember if the chickens or the hogs got it.

Until someone came up with plastic and styrofoam, everything that went down the river during high water was biodegradable. Now, everything stays around forever.

Don't get me wrong; they make life a lot easier and better. We just need a better way to dispose of it because it does not look good floating down the river.

THE TIME PIECE

Here I sit, watching television, and can count twelve time pieces without moving – three clocks hanging on the wall, four sitting on a shelf, one on the television, one on the microwave, one on the coffee pot, and three watches on the table. Know there are two in the living room, one in the bedroom, one in the bathroom, one in the music room, three in the shop, one in the car, cigar box in the truck with thirty-two watches and one pocket watch, box on the shelf with new pocket watch and believe there are two Barbie watches with my dolls. The wife has ten watches somewhere in the house. Also, have a clock on the oven. That is a total of seventy-three time pieces between the wife and I (time piece poor). Now, about all of these clocks and watches have a story back of them.

Will start with the pocket watch that I got at about age twenty (1950) – a nice Hamilton Pocket Watch, a lot of them were gifts from family and friends. Know one of the watches was bought at the airport in Tokyo, Japan. One was bought in Germany. One of the clocks was a gift, was made in Florida, from another brother, Donnie.

One of the clocks in the shop I got from the Pro Shop when the golf course was moved to Two Creeks – an Old Oertels 92 Beer Clock (still works).

A couple of the watches belonged to Howard Black and a couple of the wife's watches belonged to her mother. One of her watches belonged to Howard's wife, Grace Black.

One of the clocks in the living room was a gift to Ruth Powell from Saylor's Restaurant and one is a grandfather clock 3-D puzzle that we put together.

One clock from the Ruritan National, one from the Bluegrass District, one from Donnie & Barbara Fint, one from Paul and Melissa Rice and one from David Marraccini.

We are known to never be late for anything – how could we possibly bet late? One time we were late for a Ruritan meeting in Stamping Ground – we got as far as the Post Office on Wilkinson Boulevard and the car started running rough – had to come back to the house and get the truck – showed up thirty minutes late that night.

INTERSTATE

There was a time before interstate roads when travel was fun. No matter where you went, you had to drive through each and every little town or village where you started and where you were going – from point "A" to point "B". Point "A" being Frankfort, KY, and point "B" could be Dallas, Texas.

Back before interstate roads, I was stationed in Texas and it was a full two days trip if you drove straight though – stopping for gas, food and necessary pit stops.

Made the trip a number of times – was stationed at Ft. Hood, Texas, a couple of times – and could see all the country. Then came the interstate. Everyone got in a big hurry and took all the fun out of cross country trips. Here in Kentucky, the trees have grown up and are tall enough to where you can only see a road or a rock ledge.

Have made a number of trips to Dublin, Virginia (National Headquarters for Ruritan) within the last few years. All trips were for training or a National Board of Directors meeting. We were always in a hurry to get there, so it was a fast trip up I-64, I-77 and I-80. After a couple of days training, it called for a leisurely trip back down Rt. 460. Picked it up about 20 miles out of Dublin and traveled it all the way to Frankfort. It was more miles and took a little longer but that is some kind of drive in Virginia, West Virginia and Kentucky. The miles and time it took did not matter.

A road that was meant to be is Rt. 460. Starts at Spaghetti Junction in East Frankfort and ends at Virginia Beach, Virginia. To me this is one of the most scenic roads in the States. A lot of farm land and the mountains are the most. It is long, curvy and lots of ups and downs but not much traffic.

Was stationed at Ft. Lee, Virginia, Ft. Eustis, Virginia and Ft. Belvoir, Virginia. Used Rt. 460 a number of times until they built I-64. By using I-64, I could spend a lot more time at home, when on leave.

Sure wish I was in a situation where all the interstate roads could be set aside for trucks and all the cars could drive the back roads. Maybe set aside the interstate four days a week for trucks and three days a week for cars only.

This is not going to come about, so will just have to leave early, take the back roads and arrive at my destination a little late maybe.

BROWN AND WHITE BEANS

Put on a big pot of brown beans the other night in the crock-pot. Just finished a couple of bowls with some cornbread and onions. (Really paid for adding the onions).

Going back a few years, I can remember when brown beans were the main dish on special occasions. Rest of the time it was white soup beans or navy beans. Don't remember if the brown beans cost more if it they were just harder to get.

During the winter, beans were what we ate most of the time – but still like them. Mom cooked the beans a number of ways. The one way that I did not like was when she put dumplings in them. Did not like the dumplings but definitely did not fuss about them. Just had to eat around them and then sneak the dumplings out to the dogs.

Beans are best when they are heated and served the second time. Not many were left when growing up with ten kids. It took a large pot of beans to feed them just once.

These could be cooked on top of the drum stove; kitchen stove, or stove in the stripping room. The teacher at Lock Road School cooked them a few times, and then took them home for her family. All you needed was a chunk of bacon fat, salt and water. Had to keep an eye on them and make sure they did not burn.

The beans could be used in lunches if there were any leftovers. You could mix a little flour in them, drop them by the spoonful into a skillet with a little bacon grease and bingo you had bean cakes that could be packed in your lunch.

Always cook more than we can eat, so the next day we can have bean cakes with whatever we fix for supper.

Growing up, we ate beans because that was about all we could afford most of the time.

Don't ever remember going to bed hungry. May not have been the best of food but we always had enough to eat with fish all summer, wild game all winter, and a little canning during the summer. There was plenty to go with the beans – be they brown, white, navy or black-eyed peas.

Still eat them and like them all. It is hard to cook anything that goes any better than a bowl of beans and a wedge of cornbread baked in my big iron skillet.

THINGS MISSED

I can remember growing up that we had our own milk cow. Milk was used for a lot of things but the two things I remember were the buttermilk that was left over after the churning and the butter was removed. A glass of buttermilk and a wedge of cornbread was a meal in itself. The one that was best was the clabber milk but don't remember how we got this. I think you just left the milk out and it set up, kind of like jell-o, and then you could eat it with a spoon but you had to avoid the water like stuff that settled to the bottom. You can buy buttermilk but it is not as good as what we made back in the 30's and 40's.

Cracklings at hog killing time were some good eating. Only got them once a year and guess that is what made them so good. The bacon rinds that you can buy today are close but not the same.

I have only had one groundhog, in the last forty years, baked in the oven with potatoes, carrots and onions. Could have this on a regular basis if I was not too lazy to go out and shoot me one, now and then. Muskrat and opossum are other ones that were a main course at home back in the 30's and you could sell the hides for a few coins. We also had raccoon, now and then, when we could trap or catch one. Have just about forgotten what a rabbit tastes like cooked over an open fire with only a little salt for seasoning.

Honey can be bought about any place but not the same as cutting it out of a sugar maple tree and eating it right out of the honey cone. This always called for a few bee stings but was worth it.

Snow cream was made from freshly fallen snow with just a little sugar and fresh milk. Today the snow is polluted and fresh milk is unheard of. Last glass of fresh milk that I drank was in Germany about thirty-five years ago.

Mom could take a half-gallon of canned blackberries, add what was needed, and boil it down to make two quarts of blackberry jam. This was put on biscuits for school lunches and you could trade it for just about anything that the other kids had. Did not do this most of the time because it was too good. There was nothing better than a hot biscuit with a little fresh butter and jam on it.

Mom could fry up a few squirrels and then re-cook then in a skillet of gravy. It has never been duplicated and I have tried but so far it has not been the same – still trying. Mom could take a couple of boxes of jell-o, mix it up, sit it out on the porch roof for a while, bring it in, cut a couple of bananas up in it and back on the roof to chill – nothing better and we would fight over it. A little whipping cream could be added but there was not any on hand most of the time. I can almost do this myself and the wife does a pretty good job – not quite the same. Mom also made a rice pudding with canned pineapple in it. The wife and I are still working on this and maybe someday we will get it just right.

SWITCHES

I was at the doctor's office the other day and was asked to write a story on a bundle of switches and a lump of coal at Christmas for kids. Did not hear about this until I was about thirty years old and stationed in Germany when someone brought it up.

Growing up, switches were a year round threat. One sat in the corner most of the time and when it dried out, and there was a danger of it breaking, it was used for kindling to start a fire in the stove and a new one was cut.

If we had gotten lumps of coal for Christmas, it would have been a great gift. This would have been used to keep the fire going for a while and we would have had to cut less wood.

There were a number of other things you could lose if you were not good all year. In the summer, they could make you say at the house when the other kids were out on the river (fishing, swimming, using the mud slide) or just running the country side checking all the fruit trees, gardens, melon patches or visiting with the other kids you went to school with. Not being good could make you miss a night of hunting.

If it was winter and you had been bad, there was no sleigh riding, skating, night hunting, rabbit hunting and you could also get extra chores to do (chopping wood, packing water, helping with the washing, etc).

May sound like we were good all year, but we were far from it. Always into something but were just good at not getting caught at it.

It was not just us but all the kids in the school were about the same. Nothing really bad – just little things. I was always taught that I should treat other people the way that I wanted to be treated and most of my life it has worked for me.

As for the switches – if my grandkids got a bundle of switches from me, they would most likely use them on me.

Don't know of anyone who ever got a bundle of switches and a lump of coal for Christmas, but the wife was threatened a few times. Did get a box of coal and box of matches one time for a housewarming but could not use them because we had gas for heating and cooking.

THE UMBRELLA

When growing up the word umbrella was not in my vocabulary. If you were outside and it rained, you got wet. The only way to stay dry was to get under something that would keep the rain off you – which could be most anything. We did not have plastic but a piece of cardboard would work for a short time.

Never owned a raincoat until the Army issued me one. While in the Army we were not allowed to have an umbrella. You had a raincoat and a helmet that was with you at all times when on duty. If something was on schedule, it took place in any kind of weather.

We were told to never get under a tree during a thunderstorm but we did have a couple of hollow trees that we would use for shelter during bad weather. There were a lot of barns around that we could hang out it and was known to use a porch if one was handy. Could even get a handout if anyone was at home (cookie or a leftover biscuit). This all depended in whose house the porch was on.

Most of the river cliffs had rock ledges that you could get under and some of the creeks had ledges that you could get under. One good one was on Wildcat Creek. This one was used a lot when we were hunting at night. Always had lots of wood handy for a fire.

It would take most of the day to dry you out if had to walk to school in the rain. Going home was not so bad because you could change clothes when you got there.

When we were on the river (which was a lot) we just got wet. There is no place to get on a john boat to stay dry. Sometimes there was a tree branch that hung over the water that would keep you dry for a while.

Made me a cape out of tarpaulin one time but never had it with me when it was needed. It just caught the rain and let it soak in at a slower pace.

About the same today. The wife and I own a number of raincoats, ponchos and umbrellas but we never have one around when needed, except on the boat. Still get wet most times when it rains and we are outside some place.

KITES

Well, kite flying weather is here but you don't see many people flying them, Flying a kite has changed a lot over the years. Today, you just go out and buy a ready made kite, ball of string, wait for a wind, go out and fly it.

When we were kids, it took all day just to get ready to fly a kite. First, it had to be made – go to the woods and cut two saplings, trim them down to the right size, borrow Mom's ball of string to tie them together, locate something to cover it with (most times it was a newspaper or brown grocery bag), and a hand full of flour (from the kitchen) to make the paste out of. Paste the paper over the wooden frame and let it dry out for a couple of hours.

While it was drying, you looked up something to make the tail piece out of (piece of old sheet or a feed sack). Had to have this for balance. Sometimes it took a number of tries to get this right – add a little or take some off.

Then the string had to be located. Mom's thread was not strong enough and the twine that Pop made the hoop nets out of was too heavy. The ball of fishing line was about right and it could be used for the kite and then used for the fishing pole later. Thing was, this was not always around so we used whatever we could come up with.

This was not always a pretty kite but sometimes they would fly – not for long and not very high.

Japan was the place to get into flying kites. They had them made to look like everything. All sizes from a few inches to ten foot square with lots of color.

Still like to fly them but now there are a lot of them in the market. The box kite is still the best and have a couple of them around someplace. The great grandson just turned six, so it is time to teach him the art of kite flying. Will do it the modern way and not the way I was taught.

Have them so big now days that people jump off a cliff with them and fly around for hours and some even have engines on them.

THE PARKING LOT

Picture this – schools, churches, businesses, etc., with no parking lots.

Back in the 30's, the two schools that I attended had no parking lots. No one had a car, so a lot was not needed. The school at Tyrone was a two-room school with two teachers. They both came to school in the same car and I believe they lived in Lawrenceburg.

Went to school at Tyrone in 1936 and 1937. There were not over 10 or 12 cars in the whole village of Tyrone. Most were only used on Saturday or Sunday. There were a few trucks around for hauling.

I was out in the area of West Hills High School the other day and there were more cars and trucks in the parking lot than there were in all of Anderson County in 1937.

I remember one car that had a radio in the dash – no CD player, TV ore telephone – on the days that Cincinnati was broadcasting a ball game, he would park it close to the Post Office and everyone that wanted to hear the game would gather around the car. The younger kids were not allowed to stay because they made too much noise.

Tyrone had three churches and none of them had a parking lot. Everyone walked to church and Sunday school. Had two stores and only a gravel space across the road for delivery trucks and a car now and then. Most would just pull off to the side of the road.

Moved down the river and started my third year of schooling at Lock Road School. They put me in the fourth grade (skipping the third) to balance the numbers out because there were too many students in the second and third grades. That is the way they did it at Lock Road School.

This teacher was an older lady that lived on a farm on Lillard Road. If she came to school by the road it was about seven miles but she came across country (or the way the crow flies) and it was only one mile. Trouble was there was a 4-foot woven wire fence with a strand of barb wife on top that she had to climb. Had to get to school early to see this. She was a farmer and always made it without any problem. There was a place, just off the road, that was big enough for one car if the teacher drove.

When Pop went to Lawrenceburg, he parked on the street close to the Kroger store. All parking in Lawrenceburg was on the street because there was not a parking lot anywhere. At the Fair Grounds they all just parked in the field on the grass.

THE NICKNAME

Almost everyone has a nickname and it is very obvious as to how some of them came about. Shorty is for short people; slim is for tall, skinny people. And chubby can be confirmed with a glance.

My nickname has changed over the years. At age seven, everyone started calling me June bug because one of my favorite things was to tie a thread to the leg of a June bug and let him fly around in circles. This did not hurt him and to me it was very entertaining. I just turned him loose when it became boring. Also spent a lot of time watching ants, spiders and tumble bugs. About the age of ten, there was a boy in the colored school (right across the road) from where we went to school and he was also called June bug, so we got together. Dropped the June from mine and just got called Bug. That way we knew who was being called.

When the wife and I got married, everyone called her Lizard, which was supposedly short for Elizabeth. She got hers changed when we got into C.B. radio. A nephew hung her with the nickname and handle of Big E.

The baby brother of mine is called Duck. Believe he got it from the fact that he stayed in the river or creek all summer. Now his wife is called Cricket by her family. Don't know why but I think it is from her movement on the dance floor.

Oldest brother was called Preacher for the obvious reason – he was a Baptist Preacher. My one and only sister is called Cathy, which is short for Catherine. Knew one fellow who was called Tiny. Never did get this one because he weighed three hundred plus pounds. My mother-in-law was called "Ruth in the Booth". She was cashier at Saylor's Restaurant for a number of years and worked in the cashier's booth. She even had a name plate that was placed on the counter when she was working.

The nicknames are not limited to people. Most cities, towns and villages have nicknames. Some pets are also nicknames even if they have a registered name. Cars, boats and such have to have a name. No one says this is my Chevy or Ford and no one definitely calls their boat a boat.

I would never call this house my house because it is my homestead. My street (Poa Drive) is called the speedway.

SPORT IN SCHOOL

Well, March Madness is finally here. It is the only thing on television that is not a rerun except for the news (sometimes that is a rerun). Had no basketball when going to school in the 30's and 40's. Guess that the games were played someplace – just not at the school we went to. We played a little baseball and ran a lot of races.

Got into a little shooting hoops while in the Army and tried a little football. Did not like them, so went into softball. Got to be a pretty good pitcher but gave it up when I joined a bowling league. Do not go to the gym for basketball anymore. Made the game every year at Franklin County High School Gym when the Fireman and Policemen played each year – now that was a game to watch.

Had to become a Tennessee fan a few years ago because the wife was a die-hard Louisville fan and the mother-in-law a die-hard Kentucky fan. Could not agree with one and not the other, so to keep from starting a fight (and losing it), I just became a Tennessee fan. Basketball is the big thing in my neighborhood. Leave the house and there are approximately 10 of the portable hoops set up on the street before we get to Collins Lane. Have to drive really slow as some of the kids do not like to have their game stopped for traffic. Back into softball again for 15 years with the Church League at Bridgeport Ballfield (sponsored by Bridgeport Ruritan Club). I do not play, coach or umpire but sometimes operate the scoreboard, work the concession stand but mostly just watch and enjoy.

What this story is all about is the sports in school today – basketball, baseball, softball, soccer, football, tennis, track, wrestling etc. – what amount of budget goes for all of them? Most of them also have a cheerleading squad. The news is full of cut backs on teachers pay plus a reduction of teachers and all personnel that keep the system working. Have never heard a word on cutting the funding back on any of the sports activities. The colleges, universities, high schools, even grade schools, have to be putting half their budgets into sports. Never heard one of my teachers say anything about not making enough money or going on strike to get more. The only sports we had we came up with on our own. Most of the time we had one ball and one bat (that was furnished by one of the kids).

How much does it cost to add a gym onto a school? Got all my disciplinary training outside some place. Had no track to run on – we used the road or an open field some place. Uniforms were what we had on. Love to watch the sports on television but just wonder how much it does for education that can only be taught in the classroom.

KIDS WITH NOTHING TO DO

Hear it a lot these days – one of the kids is bored – not my kids but someone's kids. Picture this – he is sitting in his room – has television with over sixty channels, hooked to it is a VCR with a cabinet full of movies – a computer with unlimited access to the Internet – video games – boom box with x number of CD's that he can play anytime he wishes. Next door is his toy/play room with about any toy he has every wanted – bookcase full of his favorite books – more pencils, pens, crayons and paper in stacks. Outside they have a bicycle, riding toys with motors, trampoline and some have swimming pools. Also, have a couple of inside pets (hamster or bird) and an outside dog. Big yard with a volleyball net, tennis court plus rackets and balls, basketball hoop plus basketball or two, football, badminton set with net, soccer balls, table and equipment for playing ping-pong, one or two sets of roller-blades or roller skates, bow and arrow plus target, and paint ball gun with lots of targets. They also have drums, guitars, keyboards, horns, flutes and such depending on the type of music they are into.

Growing up we never had any of this stuff. Our swing set was a grapevine in a tree some place. Our ball was played with something sewn inside a sock with a bat made out of a tree limb of some kind we had cut. Our swimming pool was the river, farm pond or a hole of water in a creek some place. The only thing we had to ride was a wagon we had built or a sled. Sometimes we got to ride on the plow horse or mule (when we had one), or maybe the john boat if it was not being used. Only toys we had were something we had made out of wood, rock or mud. Music was a Victrola – if we had one – with records we had borrowed and maybe the radio on Saturday night. Our cartoons were the comic strips and if you were lucky you got to see one at the movie on Saturday.

Guns were a piece of wood. Bow and arrows were an elm limb with a piece of string and a straight weed for arrows. To fly a kite it took most of the day to make one and biggest part of the time it would not fly.

If any of us were ever bored, no one ever said so. With ten of us, someone would always come up with something for us to do, day or night, winter or summer, rain or shine.

The chores we had to do took up a lot of our time, such as – chopping wood, carrying water, cleaning up the nesses we made, working in the garden, fishing, hunting, feeding the stock (horse, cow, lots of chickens and sometimes a couple of hogs and always a few dogs and sometimes a cat or two).

School may have been a little boring at times but just sitting and thinking of what we were going to do when school let out usually took care of things. Too many other kids around to get bored for very long.

THE GRAND

I can remember my first movie at the Grand Theater in the early 40's. I was living on the river in Anderson County just above Lock #5.

Out of ten children Mom and Pop picked me to come to Frankfort to see a movie. Don't know why I was the one kid that got to make the trip but it could have been for any of the following reasons: it was one of my better weeks; got into less trouble than the other kids; or it could have been that I was the one that had a little money left from working one of the farms.

It was quite a trip for a kid who had only been to Lawrenceburg a few times. Left the house and walked about a mile to the top of the hill where the car was parked. Drove to Lawrenceburg and took the road to Frankfort. This was my first trip to Frankfort. I had heard about the hill that you had to go down to get into town from the older brothers that had made the trip. Pop stopped at the top of the hill – put the car in low gear to drive down the hill. The car did not have good brakes (was a Model A Ford – about 1929 model).

Got into town after the scary ride down the hill, parked on Broadway and walked up to the theater. We were early for the next show, so Mom took me to the Drug Store across the street on the corner of Main and Sr. Clair Streets for a fountain soda of some kind. Most likely it was a coke. Pop went down the street for a beer at one of the pool halls. Got a candy bar at the Drug Store before we left.

Met with Pop and got in line to get tickets. This was a grand place with the lobby and the seating was great. The movie was Abbott and Costello in "Flying High". They were in the Army Air Corp and there were lots of airplanes in the show. Cannot remember what the cartoon was – think it was Tom and Jerry. There was also a Flash Gordon serial.

This was my first time at the Grand Theater and my first time to see this team in a movie. This was also my first time in Frankfort with all the lights and more people than I had seen anywhere.

Had the best time of my life up to this point. This was the perfect day for a ten or eleven year old.

Do not remember the trip back home, as I was asleep in the back seat before we got out of town. I was awakened when the car was parked and time for the walk back down the hill. They put me to bed where everyone was asleep by now,

Talked about this experience for weeks afterwards.

THINGS LOST AND FOUND

While growing up, we kids found a lot of things and brought them home. Pop decided whether they were lost or not and most of the time we were made to return them to where we found them. Some things were tools, set of boat oars, fish box, someone's sled, or could have been a bicycle someone rode home on Saturday night.

While working for the state they assigned me to the sweeper and gave me four counties to keep clean. This consisted of cleaning the bridges, curbs and emergency lanes on all four-lane roads that had one. Covered Franklin, Henry, Trimble and Oldham counties with a few trips to Louisville to help out when they got behind.

You would not believe some of the things that people lose or just throw out. I could write a book on this alone. I was cleaning the overlook on Louisville Hill one time and found a fifty-pound bale of marijuana lying behind the rock wall. Stopped a City Policeman and asked him what I should do with it and was told to put it in the dumpster with the rest of the trash – so I did.

Was sweeping in Oldham County on I-71 and found a box with fifty dozen long stem red roses in it. There were no markings on the box, so I could not get them back to the owners. Went back to the shop at LaGrange and gave each of the guys working a dozen each to take home to their wives or girlfriends, or their mothers if that was what they wanted to do with them. Did the same at the Franklin County shop. Gave some of them to the family. When the wife got home from work, she found a dozen in each room of the house. Did not have to get her flowers for quite a spell.

Lost count of the billfolds and purses that someone had lost – got most of them back to the owners. Mailed a few that were never heard from – assume they got them. Found one billfold that belonged to someone that hauled horses across country. It had no cash but there were, I believe, eighteen credit cards. They sent me a reward check for twenty-five dollars.

Still using a twenty-foot ladder that someone lost on I-64. Have a number of rings and watches found while sweeping. Found a roll of money one day. Stopped to pick up case of beer cans that someone had thrown out, which had a wad of money in it amounting to over $500. A safe one time out on Route 60 that someone had stolen – emptied and thrown out. It had some medical supplies in it but no money. This was turned into the Police Station. Don't know what they did with it.

Don't run the roads any more. Guess someone else is finding all these good things now.

THE SWEET POTATO

I was sitting here thinking of all the things that a sweet potato has been used for over the years by me.

Pop did not grow a lot of sweet potatoes; so growing up they would come out of a root cellar of one of the other kids that we hunted with at night.

Would take and build a fire while the dogs were running. Put the potatoes under the ashes and someone would keep the fire going while the others checked out the tree that the dogs made. By the time they got back, the potatoes were done. Also, did this with a regular potato but I liked the sweet potato best.

They make a great pie and can also be baked with marshmallows and a little brown sugar. Both are much better than a pumpkin pie.

One thing that we have used them for is growing vines. Stick one in a glass of water (keeping about half of it covered with water) and it just keeps on growing. Have grown them up to 20 feet long. Makes a very pretty vine when hanging up with the vines growing over the side and hanging down.

The vine does not bloom and putting one out and starting vines off it is the only way I know of to grow them. It is just like an Irish potato – will be a vine coming out from each of the eyes of the potato.

The sweet potato keeps good in the root cellar. If you don't have a root cellar, just bury them deep enough that they don't freeze. Just like turnips they will keep most of the winter. Just dig them up, as you need them.

No Thanksgiving or Christmas dinner is complete unless it has some candied yams on the table – goes really good with ham or turkey.

THE APRON

The apron is still around but is used more in the work place or shop than in the kitchen.

There are all kinds from the small white one that the upstairs maid wears to the heavy leather one that the blacksmith wore when making horseshoes and putting them on the horses.

Mom always wore one when she was at home cooking, cleaning the house, doing the washing and ironing, working on the lawn, gardening, flowers, feeding the chickens or milking the cow. She always wore her apron.

First thing in the morning, after she was dressed, she put the apron on and it was not taken off until time for bed. At this time, it was hung on a nail driven into the door or wall, ready for the next day.

Did not know the purpose of the apron for a while. When I started cooking, after having to change clothes after every meal, I finally went out and invested in a couple of aprons.

Not many people use them these days and when they do, it is only for looks.

Have a number of aprons that are used in the kitchen, shop and when cooking fish for a fish fry.

In the good old days, the apron was like the sun bonnet (that women wore when they were outside) or the hair nets (that they wore when cooking) are all a thing of the past. The hair net was replaced with hair spray. The bonnet just went away. The wife would rather wear the flour or powdered sugar than to put on an apron.

The wife also wears a lot of cake batter, sauces, grease or corn meal. About anything that is mixed in the blender or mixer, and they all look good on her.

COLLECTABLE NAILS
(DATED)

My workshop consists of hundreds of kinds of nails. There are all types and sizes for putting different things together. They run in size from about one-quarter inch to an eight-inch for mounting gutters on the house and shop. These are made out of everything from plastic to a material that can be driven into concrete. Bigger ones for putting down bridge timber and such.

When younger, the only time new nails were bought was when a new building was going up or a john boat was being put together – size and type were limited.

Mostly used the square cut nail a lot when the houses and barns were put together with wooden pegs. Have a nightstand – don't know how old it is – with the only metal in it being the knobs on the drawers. They key holes and everything is made out of wood.

Have a half-gallon jar full of nails that have been gathered off the railroads. They were driven into the cross ties when they were laid down under the rails. These have the dates on them. They are made out of steel, copper and brass. Read in a book that there are over thirty-five hundred kinds of these. Some of the dates go back over one hundred years. They were also used on bridge timbers, utility poles and some of the timbers used in mines.

Plan to make some plaques out of these to hang on the wall. These are just like the ones that were made out of the different types of barbwire.

Most of my railroad nails were gathered from the track between Lawrenceburg and Versailles. Also between Frankfort and the Old Taylor Distillery in Woodford County. A few of them are from out west and other roadbeds in Kentucky. Some came from used ties that were used to build a retaining wall.

Nails we used as kids were pulled and hammered straight and saved. Some of them were used a number of times. If the nails were in a piece of wood that was burnt by the stove, they were no good. It made them soft and you could not drive them.

Every barn, smokehouse, garage or chicken house in Anderson County had a bucket or box that was kept full of used nails. It was okay to borrow a few of these if you needed them for a project, but never use all of them. It was nice if you put some back when you could. If these nails were new you left them alone because they were there for a purpose.

THE CAN OPENER

There has always been a can opener in the kitchen. Mom always had one and sometimes more than one. They all had to be poked in the top of the can and work around the rim – not an easy job most of the time. Some were set on the rim of the can, squeeze the two handles – pushing the blade through the top of the can – then a butterfly type handle was turned. The teeth on the two rollers sent it around the can – a little easier, but not much.

If one of the kids came up with a can of peaches or something – just take the knife, cut two ways across the top, fold the four corners up and eat. Most of the time you would get a finger cut if you did it this way. The can had to be thrown away because it could not be used for anything.

Opener that I remember best was the one the Army gave me in Korea – the P-38 opener. There was one in each case of C-Rations. When you went through the chow line, you got three cans. One had the main course, one had crackers, pack of coffee, can about one-half inch high that had jelly or jam of some kind. Also, had sugar, salt and pepper. Fourth can was about half the size of the other two and it had some kind of fruit in it. All four cans had to be cut open with the P-38. There should have been one on your key chain but I did not have a key chain, so I kept mine on my dog tag chain most of the time. Stationed in Korea for sixteen months and without the P-38 I could have gone hungry a lot. Still have the one that I packed all during the war. By the time of the Vietnam War, rations were packed in a box and the packages just had to be heated and then they were ready to eat.

The opener in the kitchen is now electric which cost about thirty dollars. Over the years, we have bought about eight or ten of them. They work good sometimes. Just stick in the can, push the handle down and can is opened most of the time. Some are really hard to work. Keep a couple of the old type openers on hand just for emergencies.

The old P-38 weighed less than a quarter and mine still works after more than fifty years.

THE LANDFILL

I have read a lot in the papers and seen a lot on the television here of late, about the landfills – which should be outlawed. Everything that is buried in them can be used for something.

Growing up, very little was thrown away. There was never much food left over with ten kids at the table, three times a day. If something spoiled before we ate it, it was put in a bucket along with all the potato peelings, apples cores, melon rinds etc and fed to the hogs, chickens, cats, dogs, goats or put on the garden to feed next year's crop.

If a dish, glass, jar or bottle got broken; it had to be disposed of. Broken window was saved and used to shave a handle down that was being made to fit a hammer, axe, etc. This took the place of a wood rasp.

Anything made out of metal that could no longer be used for anything, was sold as junk.

I have had a woodworking shop for a number of years now (just a hobby shop). Most of the wood that is used in it is scrap that has been picked up at building sites. Hauled a few loads of scrap plywood out of Springfield (from the shop there that builds cabinets).

All sawdust and wood chips that the shop puts out, is used for mulch on my garden and in the flowerbeds. Any small scraps of wood that are too small for anything are used for kindling to start fires in the fireplace or given to the neighbors, Some have been taken camping on weekends, Therefore, I do not have to buy firewood. Very little goes to the landfill from the shop.

Knew a fellow in Millville that built him a rock wall around the corner of his yard – about twelve feet square. Everything that was thrown out was put there – paper, glass, brush, grass clipping, weeds, etc. About once a month he would burn it. When it cooled down he would throw a couple of hand fills of salt on it. Everything that did not burn would rust and go away after a while (except for the glass). This did not hurt the environment. Trees around it did not die. Salt was less than they use on the roads for snow and ice removal. After thirty years there was not enough left to fill up a pick up truck.

This was before the law was passed that all trash had to be picked up and taken to the landfill and before throw away items came out – use it once or a few times, throw it away and buy a new one.

MARCH MADNESS

Well, here I sit watching the last game of March Madness (in April). I don't really like to watch basketball but for weeks now if there was a game on, here I sat watching it. Did not play this game in school because we did not have a basketball or goal to shoot it in.

The only time I can remember playing basketball growing up was with a ball that was half flat and the hoop was a bushel basket with no bottom in it nailed to the barn door. You could not slam dunk the ball without knocking the hoop down and then that called for nailing it back to the door.

Shot a few hoops while in the Army – not many because the game always ended in a big fight. Most of the time it was started by the team that lost. There was not much sportsmanship in these games. There were no rules – just someone to keep score. Therefore, there were no fouls in the games.

After retiring, I would go to one game a year. It was played at Franklin County High School Gym between the Frankfort City Police and the Frankfort Fire Department. Now, they were ballgames. I would never miss one of the. They played because they just like to play. There was no money or scholarships involved – they just liked to play. It really made no difference who won because everyone left the game happy – winners, losers and fans. This was the only way that I could enjoy watching a basketball game.

A lot of people enjoy basketball these days. There are only three streets in my subdivision and there must be twenty basketball goals set up in the driveways and along the streets. The kids and some adults use them – winter and summer – daylight and dark.

The last time I got into shooting hoops, I was at Church. Stepped on the ball, fell on the blacktop parking lot and was laid up for a couple of weeks. Lucky I did not break anything but had a lot of bruises and some missing skin.

I have been thinking about putting a goal up in my driveway for the great grandson because he got into basketball this past winter and seems to like it.

FLOWERING SHRUBS AND TREES

My prettiest flowering shrub is my Crape Myrtle – by far. It does not stay in bloom for very long but if the seedpods are broken off, it will stay in bloom most of the summer.

As a kid, I don't remember the Crape Myrtle. They were probably around but I just don't remember them.

Mom's favorite was the Lilac bush. Any time we moved to another place, her lilac bush went with her – part of it anyway. Another that she a little partial to was the Rose of Sharon. The Japanese Snowball was one of my favorites. Mom did not grow many of them because she said they were hard to grow.

Mom loved the Red Bud and Dogwood but said they were the best when growing wild. Also, the Wild Plum Tree and Black Locust. There were Magnolia trees around but don't think we ever had one.

Mom loved the Hollyhock. Always had a few of them around about six or seven feet tall and a number of colors. This is one of the few flowers that we could catch a bumble bee in. Just had to be fast when you let him out.

Mom always had roses around – not many. She liked the running roses most. Think it was called Blaze but not sure.

Mom raised a lot of flowers. Mostly the kind that would re-seed themselves year after year (cockscomb, four o'clock, zinnias, marigolds and such). Some seeds had to be gathered and dried for the following year.

All were raised outside. May have been a few house plants around but not many. There was no room to move them inside in bad weather.

She loved all the fruit trees that Pop put out. It was Pop's job to take care of them. Mom would not touch them. Pop or one of the kids had to trim them, take care of them and pick the fruit. Mom's job was to put the fruit in jars.

COPY MACHINE

Well, here we go again, another one of those must have gadgets went out today. A small spring flew off and we have yet to find it. I was told that I could send it back to the factory and get it fixed for around one hundred dollars. The wife went out and got a new one for less than one hundred and sixty dollars and it had a new cartridge in it that sells for around ninety dollars.

I can remember the copy machine that we used back in the 40's and 50's. It was operated by hand and was a mess to make copies with.

In order to make a copy, the following had to be done: (a) you had to type your letter on a stencil (which had a thin film on it); (b) then you had to brush the ink on a big roller on the machine; (c) hook the holes in the stencil over the pegs on the roller; (d) press it down on the roller embedding the stencil in the ink; (e) then the thick sheet was pulled off; (f) put the paper in the slot; (g) then crank it with a handle. You got one copy for each completed turn of the handle.

This machine only made a few copies before it used up the ink on the roller. The stencil had to be taken off, drum brushed with ink again and stencil put back on. This was done for every ten or fifteen copies. This was a big job if you needed a hundred or more copies.

The stencil had to be taken off, rolled just right and put away. The big mess came when you had to go through the stack and find the one you needed to run again.

I used this machine a lot in the first few years in the Army. They had gloves and an apron to wear but there was no way to run a few copies without getting ink on you and your clothes. It was hard to wash out of the clothes and a job to get it off your skin.

I don't really know how this new machine works – but do know that when a sheet comes out that is not quite dark enough, the wife takes the cartridge and shakes it a little, puts it back in, and prints more pages.

There have been a lot of changes in copy machines in the last fifty years. We have owned about six or seven. I think they have gone from ink to something else these days. Now a days you just put the ink cartridge and paper in the machine, turn it on, press a button and make the number of copies you need with no mess at all – just a paper hang-up now and then.

ED AND FRED

Just returned from a trip to Tennessee where the wife attended a Cabinet Meeting of the Ruritan National Smoky Mountain District. This was definitely a trip for the books and one to be remembered.

Things started to go wrong about fifty miles from home. Just out of Danville, Kentucky, my mind snapped and told me I was on the wrong road. Actually I was on the right road but I back tracked to Danville and took the wrong road for about ten miles. Stopped and got someone to tell me how to get back on track and things went well all the way to Oak Ridge, Tennessee.

Had put down Route 170 to Farragut when it should have been Route 162. After about thirty minutes of being lost, we came up on I-75 and got on for about a mile, then off at the Farragut Exit, down Route 11 to Concord, down to Northshore Drive on to Choto. This is where I lost it for about the third time.

Was in about every driveway on the side of the lake before finding the right one. Finally wound up at Ed and Margie's place around three o'clock Saturday afternoon.

This is where things got really good and Ed and Fred got into the picture. They were rigging the sail boat so we could all go for a ride on Fort Loundon Lake.

I was never on a sail boat but did watch the operation of getting one ready for a ride. Now, Ed and Fred are both experts at this sport and before long everything was ready. Well, almost – they had put one of the sails on upside down. This was changed, but by now the wind had about stopped blowing. Ed got a tank of gas for the motor. Hooked it up so we could get back if the wind really stopped blowing.

By this time, I had found a nice chair in under the air conditioning and settled in for a while.

Ed came in to set up the meeting. Fred took a ride on a jet ski with his granddaughter. Found out later that it was his first ride on one. When he came back, he was driving.

Spent a while just talking and watching the traffic on the lake. All kinds of boats – fishing, pontoon, hundreds of jet skis, ski boats pulling skiers, houseboats and a few yachts (up to about thirty feet or bigger) and even some guy in a canoe with his girl (just out for a ride).

By now, the other cabinet members had arrived and it was time to eat. Now I like to eat and potluck meals are the best. Everyone cooks what they cook the best. Not being a big eater, I may not eat much, but like to take a little of everything. Ate some carrot casserole and I still cannot believe that it was carrots. Also, a peach cobbler that was fixed differently. Loved it all.

Sat on the deck and talked to Mel during the meeting. After the meeting, back to Farragut. Followed Don and Irma out and still made a wrong turn but Mary caught it and made me turn around.

Spent the night at Nation's Best Motel. Was a nice old motel but Mary lost it when she had to pay fifty cents for a bucket of ice and fifty cents for a phone we did not use.

Up early on Sunday. Had breakfast at McDonald's and took up I-40 to Oak ridge. Made a wrong turn but was only lost for about thirty minutes. Missed a turn at Oneida but only went about a block. Stopped at Wal-Mart. All went well to Stanford, Kentucky, where I drove through downtown when I missed the bypass.

Arrived at home at 3:00 p.m. and all in all it was another great trip.

Still believe someone put a dam across the southern border of Tennessee and every hollow in the state filled up with water.

NEGATIVE THOUGHTS
MOTHER NATURE – SAFE PLACE TO LIVE

NEVER build within fifty feet of running water, creek or river, sink holes or low valleys – sooner or later high water will get to you.

NEVER build on top of a hill or mountain – a tornado or straight wind will blow everything away some day or night.

NEVER live in a cave or hole cut in the rock or built underground – earthquake will shake it down on top of you.

NEVER build on open plains or rolling brush land – prairie fires are fast and sometimes final for everything in its path.

NEVER plan to live in a recreation vehicle (RV) – if a tractor/trailer doesn't get you, some redneck in a pickup will.

NEVER build in a rain forest – jungle rot or mildew will put you down in time.

CANNOT survive in the Antarctic for long – unless you can live on fish, in a house built of ice, and can stand a lot of cold weather.

CANNOT build in the desert – nothing to build out of except sand and not much water around.

NO PLACE is safe from lightning – it strikes about everywhere.

IF YOU BUILD on the ocean floor – you will have a shortage of air and a lot of other things could happen to you (earthquakes, ocean surges, or something large that lives down there that we don't know about yet).

BUILD A SHIP – most likely it will sink.

BUILD A SPACE SHIP – try it out in space-a meteor is likely to get you with a direct hit.

LARGE CITIES are not a good choice. All kinds of bad things can happen to you (too many of them to try to list).

SOME JUNGLES are not too bad but they do have a lot of wild animals and some are rather mean. Plus a lot of insects are not very friendly.

WARS cause a lot of damage and can occur about any place.

RIOTS are devastating.

VOLCANOES take a big toll but are visible most times and can be avoided.

ISLANDS – some are like paradise but have been known to be washed away by tidal waves, hurricanes or destroyed by volcanoes.

NEVER BUILD close to a nuclear plant – it only takes a small leak to do you in.

NEVER BUILD on a mountain side – mud slide will put you in the valley real quick.

ALL KINDS of things take place along the coastline, hurricanes, mud slides, tidal waves, high winds, brush fires, invasions by a foreign country.

LARGE MOUNTAIN RANGES – have slides in wet weather and in winter a lot of avalanches. Dry weather has forest fires etc.

TRIED A TREE HOUSE ONCE BUT THE TREE BLEW DOWN

The house at Gardners Landing. Winter of 1946.
River was frozen enough for skating

Present day home. Picture taken July 10, 2006.

Kirby Fint, Jr.

Born January 12, 1930 in Woodford County, Kentucky. Moved to Anderson County at age four. First eight grades of school were at the two-room school at Tyrone and the one-room school on the Lock Road that went to Lock #5 on the Kentucky River.

Spent one summer working as the assistant lock tender at Lock #5. I was thirteen years old at the time.

Moved to Franklin County around 1943. Worked the farms, some construction and joined the Army on August 2, 1947. Retired October 1, 1969. Spent four tours in Korea, three tours in Germany, one tour in Vietnam. Spent some time at Ft. Knox, Kentucky – Ft. Sam Huston, Texas – Ft. Hood, Texas twice – Ft. Belvoir, Virginia twice – Ft. Eustis, Virginia – Ft. Lee, Virginia – Sandia Base in New Mexico – Yuma Proving Grounds in Arizona – Japan – Camp Stolman, California – Ft. Lewis, Washington and Ft. George Mead in New Jersey.

After retirement, worked as day manager of a liquor store for ten months. I did not like working inside, so went to work for the Transportation Cabinet as a truck driver in highway maintenance. I was on this job for 19½ years when I got sick and had to retire.

Started writing short stories in February 1997 as a hobby. This book is a collection of these stories written over the last few years. They are all true and there is no fiction.

My real passion these days is raising a garden and lots of time on the lakes fishing for catfish.

ISBN 1425101704